AF560032

Textbook of
FORENSIC PHARMACY

Textbook of
FORENSIC PHARMACY

Prof. C.V. Narayan

ANMOL PUBLICATIONS PVT. LTD.
NEW DELHI-110 002 (INDIA)

ANMOL PUBLICATIONS PVT. LTD.
Regd. Office: 4360/4, Ansari Road, Daryaganj,
New Delhi-110002 (India)
Tel.: 23278000, 23261597, 23286875, 23255577
Fax: 91-11-23280289
Email: anmolpub@gmail.com
Visit us at: www.anmolpublications.com

Branch Office: No. 1015, Ist Main Road, BSK IIIrd Stage
IIIrd Phase, IIIrd Block, Bangalore-560 085 (India)
Tel.: 080-41723429 • Fax: 080-26723604
Email: anmolpublicationsbangalore@gmail.com

Textbook of Forensic Pharmacy

© Reserved

First Edition, 2010

ISBN 978-81-261-4476-1

PRINTED IN INDIA

Printed at Mehra Offset Press, Delhi.

Contents

Preface

Forensic pharmacy overlaps with the criminal justice system and other branches of forensics. Forensic pharmacists play an integral role in legal cases relating to malpractice, drunk and drugged driving and adverse side effects of certain drugs. Forensic Pharmacy is the foundation of the structure on which the sacred profession of pharmacy has been built up in our Country.

It provides much needed legal support, professional backing and ethical strength for the systematic growth of the profession. The textbook is suitable for all graduates and postgraduates students and other readers who intend to study the book in terms of knowledge and examination.

Author

Chapter 1

Introduction

DRUG LEGISLATION

HISTORICAL PERSPECTIVE

In the beginning of the current century Drug Industry was practically non-existent in India and pharmaceuticals were being important from abroad. The first world war changed the situation and not only were finished and cheap drugs imported in increasing volume, the demand for indigenous products also was voiced from all sides.

With the clamour for swadeshi goods manufacturing concerns, both Indian and Foreign, sprang up to produce pharmaceuticals at cheaper rates to compete with imported products. Naturally some of these were of inferior quality and harmful for public health. The Government was, therefore, called upon to take notice of the situation and consider the matter of introducing legislation to control the manufacture, distribution and sale of drugs and medicines.

TYPES OF LAWS

There are two laws:

- The Poisons Act
- The Dangerous Drugs Act

The Opium Act was quite old having being adopted as early as 1878. But to have a comprehensive legislation, which the rapid expansion of the pharmaceutical production and drug market required by the end of the second decade for its control, the Indian Government appointed, in 1931, a Drugs

Enquiry Committee under the Chairmanship Lt. Col. R. N. Chopra which was asked to make sifting enquiries into the whole matter of drug production, distribution and sale by inviting opinions and meeting concerned people.

The Committee was asked to make recommendations about the ways and means of controlling the production and sale of drugs and pharmaceuticals in the interest of public health. The Chopra Committee toured all over the country and after carefully examining the data placed before it, submitted a voluminous report to government suggesting creation of drug control machinery at the centre with branches in all provinces.

For an efficient and speedy working of the controlling department the committee also recommended the establishment of a well-equipped Central Drugs Laboratory with competent staff and experts in various branches for data standardization work. Under the guidance of the Central Laboratory, it was suggested, small laboratories would work, in the provinces. For the training of young men and women, the Committee recommended the permission of Central Pharmacy Council, and the Provincial Pharmacy Councils, with registrars who would maintain the lists containing names and addresses of the licensed pharmacists. The outbreak of the second world war in 1939 delayed the introduction of legislation on the lines suggested by the Chopra Committee which the Indian government contemplated and considered as urgent.

However, the Drugs Act was passed in 1940 partly implementing the Chopra recommendations. With the achievement of independence in 1947 the rest of the required laws were put on the Statute Book. In 1985, the Narcotic Drugs and Psychotropic Substances Act was enacted repealing the Dangerous Drugs Act 1930 and the Opium Act of 1878.

At present the following Acts and Rules made there under that govern the manufacture, sale, import, export and clinical research of drugs and cosmetics in India.

- The Drugs and Cosmetics Act, 1940
- The Pharmacy Act, 1948

- The Drugs and Magic Remedies (Objectionable Advertisement) Act, 1954
- The Narcotic Drugs and Psychotropic Substances Act, 1985
- The Medicinal and Toilet Preparations (Excise Duties) Act, 1956

The Drugs (Prices Control) Order 1995 (under the Essential Commodities Act)

SOME OTHER LAWS

There are some other laws which have a bearing on pharmaceutical manufacture, distribution and sale in India.

The important ones being:

- The Industries (Development and Regulation) Act, 1951
- The Trade and Merchandise Marks Act, 1958
- The Indian Patent and Design Act, 1970

FACTORIES ACT

The Drugs and Cosmetics Act 1940

The object of the Act is to regulate the import, manufacture, distribution and sale of drugs.Under the provisions of this Act, the Central Government appoints the Drugs Technical Advisory Board to advise the Central Government and the State Governments on technical matters arising out of the administration of this Act. The board can constitute subcommittees for the consideration of a particular matter.

The Pharmacy Act 1948

The Pharmacy Act was passed in 1948 and was amended in 1959, 1976 and 1984. The aim of this law is to regulate the profession of Pharmacy in India. Under the provisions of this act the Central Government constitutes a Central Pharmacy Council of India consisting of following members:

- Six members from the Teachers of pharmacy.
- Six members from practicing pharmacists or Pharmaceutical Chemists holding degree of diploma.

- One member elected by the Medical Council of India.
- The Director-General of Health Services.
- The Director of the Central Drugs Laboratory.
- The Chief Chemist, Central Revenues.
- One member to represent each state elected by members of State Councils who shall be a registered pharmacist.h) One member to represent each State Government who shall be either registered medical practitioner or a registered pharmacist.

The President and Vice-President of the Central Council of Pharmacy are elected by the members of the Council among themselves, hold office for five years and are eligible for re-election. The conducting of courses of study for pharmacists, and the examinations in Pharmacy in the states are subject to the approval of the Central Council. Besides the Council has the responsibility to supervise the Education of Pharmacy in the States. Where it is found that the course of study is not in conformity with the Education Regulations, the Council may withdraw approval accorded to the course or the examination. The Central Council can approve qualifications granted by an outside authority for qualifying for registration under this Act.

STATE PHARMACY COUNCILS

The Act makes it incumbent upon the State Governments to constitute State.

Pharmacy Councils with the following members:

- Six members elected from amongst themselves by registered Pharmacists of the state.
- Five members of whom at least two shall be persons possessing a prescribed degree or diploma in Pharmacy or Pharmaceutical Chemistry or members of the Pharmaceutical profession nominated by the State Government.

REGISTRATION OF PHARMACISTS

The State Government has under the provisions of the Pharmacy Act to get a register of the State Pharmacists prepared and it is the State Pharmacy Council which has to maintain the register. The register shall contain the name and residential address of Pharmacist, the date of his first admission to the register, qualifications for registration, his professional address, the name of his employer and prescribed particulars.

The Drugs and Magic Remedies (Objectionable Advertisements) Act 1954

This Act is meant to control the Advertisements regarding drugs; it prohibits the advertising of remedies alleged to possess magic qualities and to provide for matters connected therewith.

The Drugs and Magic Remedies Act prohibits a person from taking part in publication of any advertisement referring to any drug which suggests use of the drug for:

- The procurement of miscarriage in women or prevention of conception in women; andb) the maintenance or improvement of the capacity of the human being for sexual pleasure;
- The correction of menstrual disorders in women;
- The diagnosis, cure, mitigation, treatment or prevention of any venereal disease. It is prohibited to directly or indirectly give a false impression regarding the true character of a drug or make false claim for it or to convey any false or misleading information in any material particular about it. No person shall import into or export from India any document containing advertisement of this nature. Whoever contravenes the provisions of this Act shall, on conviction, be punishable with imprisonment which may extend to six months, with or without fine. In case of subsequent convictions the imprisonment can be extended to one year. The document, article or thing which contains the offending advertisement can be seized and confiscated.
- If the person contravening any of the provisions of

the Act is a company, every person who at the time the offence was committed was in charge of the business of the company shall be deemed guilty.

The prohibition under this Act does not apply to: a) any signboard or notice displayed by a registered medical practitioner including the treatment for any of the disease, b) any treaties or book dealing with any of the matters from a bonafide scientific standpoint, c) any advertisement related to any drug sent confidentially to any registered medical practitioners or to chemists for distribution among registered medical practitioners or to a hospital or laboratory, and d) Government advertisements.

The Narcotic Drugs and Psychotropic Substances Act, 1985

This is an Act to consolidate and amend the law relating to Narcotic Drugs, to make stringent provisions for the control and regulation of operations relating to Narcotic Drugs and Psychotropic Substances and for matters connected therewith.

DRUG INJURY

In the modern world we are surrounded by millions of chemicals, thousands of which qualify as a drug. What is a drug? There are a multitude of proper, scientific definitions, but one wag defined it as a substance which when injected into a rat, will produce a scientific report. Eric Hodgins (1899-1971), US writer and editor, once defined a miracle drug as any drug that will do what the label says it will do! These "fun" definitions, more than anything else underscore people's unconcerned, rather apathetic attitude towards modern drugs.

A number of reasons could be advanced for this. One of the reasons is that several drugs don't give you the intended relief, and many might actually aggravate disease and even result in death. Several such cases have led to prosecutions of manufactures, retailers, nurses, doctors, pharmacists - in fact anyone connected with the chain of delivering the drug to the patient. One of the most illustrative examples of this phenomenon occurred in Germany in 1958 when the drug thalidomide ($C_{13}H_{10}O_4$) caused a number of serious birth defects in children. The New Drug Application (NDA) is actually the starting point of the whole process, as can be seen from the accompanying diagram on the right.

This is an application which a drug manufacturer gives to the FDA regarding a new drug which he proposes to launch in the market. Center of Drug Evaluation and Research (CDER) classifies these applications into seven categories, starting from the most innovative (type 1) to the least (type 7). Type 1 drug is an entirely new molecular entity. Type 2 drug is not a new molecular entity, but a new salt of a previously approved drug.

Type 3 drug is neither a new molecular entity, nor a new salt; instead it is a new formulation of a previously approved drug. Type 4 drug is a new combination of two or more drugs. Type 5 drug is actually an already marketed drug product. The only novelty is that the manufacturer is new. Type 6 drug is a drug which is already marketed drug, but for which a new indication has been claimed, i.e. the drug is claimed to be beneficial in a different disease, than it has traditionally been used for.

Finally type 7 drug is a drug which is an already marketed drug product. Review priority of the drug is given by letters A and B. A refers to standard reviews for drugs similar to currently available drugs. B refers to priority reviews for drugs that represent significant advances over existing treatments. When such applications are given to FDA, the manufacturers actually submit results of non-clinical (animal) trials, and clinical trials, and a host of other information, and on the basis of that information, the application is processed further. For reader's benefit, the first chapter gives various statutes applicable to drugs and pharmacists in general. Some among them being the Food and Drug Act of 1906, Federal Food, Drug and Cosmetic Act (1938), Durham-Humphrey Amendment (1951), Drug Amendments of 1962 and Orphan Drug Act (1983). Various relevant provisions of these Acts are summarized. Sample this provision of the Orphan Drug Act (1983). To foster orphan drug development, this law allows the drug companies to take tax deductions for about three-quarters of the cost of their clinical studies (for the uninitiated, "orphan drugs" are drugs and other products for treating rare diseases. They have very little market, and thus offer little or almost no profit to the manufacturer)

This is indeed a useful piece of legislation, for if such a law had not been there, no company would really be interested in developing such drugs. It was an FDA medical officer Frances O. Kelsey, M.D. who was instrumental in keeping the drug thalidomide off the US market.

This news aroused public interest in controlling drugs, and Drug Amendments of 1962 were passed as a result in October 1962. These amendments tightened control over the drugs. As a result of these Amendments, drug companies, now not only had to prove effectiveness, but also safety. Moreover these amendments applied retroactively to 1938, when the FDC Act was passed. Pre-1938 drugs were allowed to be sold without restriction as it was widely perceived that they were safe drugs.

The chapter ends in several interesting and informative appendices (as do several chapters in this book). Appendix A tells us how every one of us can locate correspondence related to drug approval over the internet. The author was asked to investigate the antibiotic Trovan (trovafloxacin). Normally it would have taken lot of paper correspondence, but under the new scenario he could easily retrieve the information via the internet.

CODE OF ETHICS FOR PHARMACISTS

Pharmacists are health professionals who assist individuals in making the best use of medications. This Code, prepared and supported by pharmacists, is intended to state publicly the principles that form the fundamental basis of the roles and responsibilities of pharmacists. These principles, based on moral obligations and virtues, are established to guide pharmacists in relationships with patients, health professionals, and society.

RESPECT

A pharmacist respects the covenantal relationship between the patient and pharmacist. Considering the patient-pharmacist relationship as a covenant means that a pharmacist has moral obligations in response to the gift of trust received from society. In return for this gift, a pharmacist promises to help individuals achieve optimum benefit from their medications, to be committed to their welfare, and to maintain their trust.

PROMOTION

A pharmacist promotes the good of every patient in a caring, compassionate, and confidential manner. A pharmacist places concern for the well-being of the patient at the center of professional practice. In doing so, a pharmacist considers needs stated by the patient as well as those defined by health science.

A pharmacist is dedicated to protecting the dignity of the patient. With a caring attitude and a compassionate spirit, a pharmacist focuses on serving the patient in a private and confidential manner.

RESPECT

A pharmacist respects the autonomy and dignity of each patient. A pharmacist promotes the right of self-determination and recognizes individual self-worth by encouraging patients to participate in decisions about their health. A pharmacist communicates with patients in terms that are understandable. In all cases, a pharmacist respects personal and cultural differences among patients.

HONESTY AND INTEGRITY

A pharmacist acts with honesty and integrity in professional relationships. A pharmacist has a duty to tell the truth and to act with conviction of conscience. A pharmacist avoids discriminatory practices, behavior or work conditions that impair professional judgment, and actions that compromise dedication to the best interests of patients.

PROFESSIONAL COMPETENCE

A pharmacist maintains professional competence. A pharmacist has a duty to maintain knowledge and abilities as new medications, devices, and technologies become available and as health information advances.

VALUES AND ABILITY

A pharmacist respects the values and abilities of colleagues and other health professionals. When appropriate, a pharmacist asks for the consultation of colleagues or other health professionals or refers the patient. A pharmacist acknowledges that colleagues and other health professionals may differ in the beliefs and values they apply to the care of the patient.

NEEDS

A pharmacist serves individual, community, and societal needs. The primary obligation of a pharmacist is to individual patients. However, the obligations of a pharmacist may at times extend beyond the individual to the community and society. In these situations, the pharmacist recognizes the responsibilities that accompany these obligations and acts accordingly.

JUSTICE

A pharmacist seeks justice in the distribution of health resources. When health resources are allocated, a pharmacist is fair and equitable, balancing the needs of patients and society.

PHARMACOKINETICS, AND PHARMACODYNAMICS

An inotrope is an agent that affects myocardial contractility. A positive inotrope causes increased contractility, and a negative inotrope causes decreased contractility. A chronotrope is an agent that affects heart rate. Positive chronotropes cause an increase in heart rate. Negative chronotropes cause a decrease in the heart rate. Examples of negative chronotropes are beta-blockers and rate control calcium channel blockers.

A dromotrope affects atrial-ventricular (AV) node conduction. A positive dromotrope increases AV nodal conduction (eg, atropine sulfate), and a negative dromotrope slows AV nodal conduction. A lusitrope is an agent that affects diastolic relaxation. Many positive inotropes affect preload and afterload; therefore, these terms must be defined to facilitate understanding. Preload is defined as the blood volume remaining in the ventricles at the end of diastole or ventricular end diastolic volume (VEDV).

Preload influences the amount of end diastolic stretch on the myocardial muscle fibers. Venous blood return to the heart is influenced not only by actual blood volume in the venous system but also by venous tone or compliance, which is the relaxation and contraction in the smooth muscle walls of the veins. Preload enhancers are vasopressors and volume expanders (eg, normal saline). Preload reducers are vasodilators and diuretics.

TABLE DEFINITION TERMS

- *Preload:* Left or right ventricular end diastolic volume.
- *Afterload:* Resistance that the left or right ventricle must overcome during systolic ejection.
- *Pharmacokinetics:* Factors that determine the blood concentration of medicine,
- *Bioavailability:* Amount of medication reaching the systemic circulation after oral dosing.
- *Half-life:* Amount of time required for the plasma concentration of a medication to be decreased by 50% after discontinuation of the medication.
- *Steady state:* Medication elimination = medication administration; takes four to five half-lives to reach,
- *Agonist:* Substance promoting receptor activity.
- *Antagonist:* Substance inhibiting receptor activity.
- *Exogenous:* Occurring or originating outside the body.
- *Endogenous:* Occurring or originating inside the body.

Afterload is the pressure that the ventricles must pump against to overcome the resistance to systolic ejection. Afterload is determined primarily by the arterial tone or pressure (ie, blood pressure). A simplistic way to think of afterload is blood pressure.

Patients with systemic hypertension have increased left ventricular afterload, and in pulmonary hypertension, the right ventricular afterload is increased. The most influential factors in afterload are systemic vascular resistance (SVR) and pulmonary vascular resistance (PVR). The SVR and PVR are derived parameters that are influenced by many factors. The Ohms formula equation can be used to determine both SVR and PVR.(2)

TABLE OHMS FORMULA

Systemic vascular resistance = Mean arterial pressure-central venous pressure/cardiac output (CO) x 80 Pulmonary vascular resistance = Mean pulmonary arterial pressure-pulmonary capillary wedge pressure/CO x 80. Medications that increase both right ventricular (RV) and left ventricular (LV) afterload are vasopressors (eg, norepinephrine). Medications that decrease RV and LV afterload are arterial vasodilators (eg, hydralazine).

PHARMACOKINETICS

Understanding positive inotropes requires a short review of basic pharmacology. Pharmacokinetics are factors that determine the concentration of medicine in the blood. Factors include how well the medication is absorbed, the onset of action, and half-life, the manner in which the medication is distributed and metabolized in and excreted from the body. Absorption.

Absorption of medications depends on many factors, including the molecular weight of a compound (ie, smaller weight is easier to absorb), solubility as well as patient factors such as food in the gut, pH of the gastrointestinal (GI) tract, and adequate blood flow to the GI tract.(4) A medication that must be absorbed from the GI tract will have a certain per cent of bioavailability. Bioavailability refers to how much of a medication actually reaches the systemic circulation after oral administration, and it varies from 0% to 100%.(5) All IV medications are 100% available to the serum because they are directly injected and do not need to be absorbed. For example, furosemide has a bioavailability of approximately 70% with oral dosing but has 100% with IV dosing.

The percentage of bioavailability helps determine the amount of medication that, under normal circumstances, reaches the bloodstream after absorption from the GI tract. Half-life. The half-life of a medication is symbolized as t1/2 and is the amount of time required for the plasma concentration of a medication to be decreased by 50% after discontinuation of the medication. A steady state plasma concentration of a medication occurs when the medication elimination is equal to the rate of administration. It usually takes four to five half-lives to reach steady state.

The goal of medication administration is to achieve adequate blood levels to maintain a desired effect (ie, equilibrium). For example, the commonly prescribed medication warfarin has a plasma half-life of approximately 40 hours. Warfarin's steady state is not reached for approximately one week (40 x 5 = 200 hours). Loading doses are sometimes required to overcome long half-lives and to prevent delays in reaching steady states. Medications with long half-lives include digoxin, amiodarone, and warfarin. Metabolism. Most medications are biotransformed or metabolized before they are excreted.

When norepinephrine attaches to the receptors, the action is very different from the action of the receptors on the postsynaptic neuron. Activation of the alpha-2 receptor stimulates the central nervous system to inhibit the release of norepinephrine through feedback inhibition, leading to vasodilation. Clonidine, an antihypertensive medication, works by activating alpha-2 receptors and causing peripheral vasodilation. Beta-1 receptors are located in the myocardium. Binding of the adrenergic beta-1 receptor leads to increased cAMP through adenyl cyclase activity at the receptor site.

Increasing the amount of cAMP allows more intracellular calcium to collect, causing stronger myocardial contractions. Stimulation of beta-1 receptors leads to increased myocardial contractility, tachycardia, and release of renin from the juxtaglomerular apparatus in the kidney, causing the release of aldosterone and reabsorption of sodium and water.

A potent beta-1 medication is dobutamine. Beta-2 receptors are located in the bronchial and vascular smooth muscle. Stimulation of beta-2 receptors leads to vasodilation of bronchioles and peripheral vessels and decreased peripheral resistance. The medication isoproterenol has both beta-1 and beta-2 properties.

Agonists and antagonists. An agonist is a substance that enhances receptor activity. Dobutamine is a beta agonist. An antagonist is a substance that blocks the response of the receptor. Metoprolol, a beta-blocker, is a beta antagonist. Receptors can be activated by both exogenous (ie, synthetic medication) or endogenous (ie, naturally occurring substance in the body) stimulation.

Dobutamine is an exogenous catecholamine, and dopamine is an endogenous catecholamine. Positive inotropes reviewed in this article include catecholamines, phosphodiesterase inhibitors, and cardiac glycosides. Although other medications have positive inotropic properties (eg, angiotensin-converting enzyme [ACE] inhibitors), they are not included in this discussion. Medication indications and dosages are referenced in terms of adult populations.

ADVERSE EFFECTS AND DRUG INTERACTIONS

ADVERSE EFFECTS

In medicine, an adverse effect is a harmful and undesired effect resulting from a medication or other intervention such as surgery. An adverse effect may be termed a "side effect", when judged to be secondary to a main or therapeutic effect, and may result from an unsuitable or incorrect dosage or procedure, which could be due to medical error. Adverse effects are sometimes referred to as "iatrogenic" because they are generated by a physician/treatment. Some adverse effects only occur only when starting, increasing or discontinuing a treatment. Using a drug or other medical intervention which is contraindicated may increase the risk of adverse effects. Adverse effects may cause medical complications of a disease or procedure and negatively affect its prognosis. They may also lead to non-compliance with a treatment regimen.

The harmful outcome is usually indicated by some result such as morbidity, mortality, alteration in body weight, levels of enzymes, loss of function, or as a pathological change detected at the microscopic, macroscopic or physiological level. It may also be indicated by symptomsreported by a patient. Adverse effects may cause a reversible or irreversible change, including an increase or decrease in the susceptibility of the individual to other chemicals, foods, or procedures, such as drug interactions.

In clinical trials, a distinction is made between adverse events (AEs) and serious adverse events (SAEs). Generally, any event which causes death, permanent damage, birth defects, or requires hospitalization is considered an SAE. The results of these trials are often included in the labeling of the medication to provide information both for patients and the prescribing physicians.

Adverse Effects of Medical Procedures

Surgery may have a number of undesirable or harmful effects, such as infection, hemorrhage, inflammation, scarring, loss of function, changes in local blood flow, and so on. They can be reversible or irreversible, and a compromise must be found by the physician and the patient between the beneficial or life-saving consequences of surgery versus its adverse effects.

For example, a limb may be lost to amputation in case of untreatable gangrene, but the patient's life is saved. Presently, one of the greatest advantages of minimally invasive surgery, such as laparoscopic surgery is the reduction of adverse effects. Other non-surgical physical procedures such as high-intensity radiation therapy may cause burns and alterations in the skin. In general, these therapies try to avoid damage to healthy tissues while maximizing the therapeutic effect. Vaccination may have adverse effects due to the nature of its biological preparation, sometimes using attenuated pathogens and toxins.

Common adverse effects may be fever, malaise and local reactions in the vaccination site. Very rarely, there is a serious adverse effect, such as eczema vaccinatum, a severe, sometimes fatal complication which may result in persons who have eczema or atopic dermatitis. Diagnostic procedures may also have adverse effects, depending much on whether they are invasive, non-invasive or minimally invasive. For example, allergic reactions to radiocontrast material often occur, and a colonoscopy may cause the perforation of the intestine wall.

Adverse Effects of Drugs

Adverse effects can occur as a collateral or side effect of many interventions, but they are particularly important in pharmacology, due to its wider, and sometimes uncontrollable, use by way of self-medication. Thus, responsible drug use becomes an important issue here. Adverse effects, like therapeutic effects of drugs, are a function of dosage or drug levels at the target organs, so they may be avoided or decreased by means of careful and precise pharmacokinetics, the change of drug levels in the organism in function of time after administration.

Adverse effects may also be caused by drug interaction. This often occurs when patients fail to inform their physician and pharmacist of all the medications they are taking, including herbal and dietary supplements. The new medication may interact agonistically or antagonistically (potentiate or decrease the intended therapeutic effect). Significant morbidity and mortality is caused around the world because of this. Drug-drug and food-drug interactions may occur, and so-called "natural drugs" used in alternative medicine can have dangerous adverse effects. The scientific field of activity associated with drug safety is increasingly government-regulated and is of major concern for the public as well as to drug manufacturers. The distinction between adverse and non-adverse effects is a major undertaking when a new drug is developed and tested before marketing it. This is done in toxicity studies to determine the non-adverse effect level (NOAEL).

These studies are used to define the dosage to be used in human testing (phase I) as well as to calculate the maximum admissible daily intake. Imperfections in clinical trials, such as insufficient number of patients or short duration, sometimes lead to public health disasters such as those of fenfluramine (the so-called fen-phen episode), thalidomide and, more recently, of cerivastatin (Baycol, Lipobay) and rofecoxib (Vioxx), where drastic adverse effects were observed, like teratogenesis, pulmonary hypertension, stroke, heart disease, neuropathy, etc., and a significant number of deaths, causing the forced or voluntary withdrawal of the drug from the market. Most drugs have a large list of non-severe or mild adverse effects which do not rule out the interruption of usage. These effects have widely variable incidence, according to individual sensitivity. They comprise nausea, dizziness, diarrhea, malaise, vomiting, headache, dermatitis, dry mouth, etc.

Controversies

Sometimes, putative medical adverse effects are regarded as controversial and generate heated discussions in society and lawsuits against drug manufacturers. One example is the recent controversy as to whether autism was linked to the MMR vaccine (or by thiomersal, a mercury-based preservative used in some vaccines).

No link has been found in several large studies and no change in the rate of autism has occurred when thimerosal was removed from vaccines a decade ago in Canada and Europe. Another instance is the potential adverse effects of silicone breast implants, which lead to hundreds of thousands of litigations against manufacturers of gel-based implants, due to allegations of damage to the immune system which have not yet been conclusively proven. Due to the exceedingly high impact on public health of widely used medications, such as hormonal contraception and hormone replacement therapy, which may affect millions of users, even marginal probabilities of adverse effects of a severe nature, such as breast cancer, have led to public outcry and changes in medical therapy, although its benefits largely surpassed the statistical risks.

Limitations of Adverse Effects Reporting

In principle, medical professionals are required to report all adverse effects related to a specific form of therapy. In practice, it is at the discretion of the professional to determine whether a medical event is at all related to the therapy. For example, a leg fracture in a skiing accident in a patient who years before took antibiotics for pneumonia is not likely to get reported. As a result, routine adverse effects reporting may often not include long-term and subtle effects that may ultimately be attributed to a therapy.

Part of the difficulty is identifying the source of a complaint. A headache in a patient taking medication for influenza may be the underlying disease and may be an adverse effect. In patients with end-stage cancer, death is a very likely outcome and whether the drug is the cause or a bystander is often difficult to discern.

PROTEASE INHIBITOR DRUG INTERACTIONS

Recent advances in HIV treatment have brought new hope to many people living with HIV. Often, a new treatment advance is accompanied by new challenges that may sometimes seem overwhelming. The protease inhibitor drugs, in particular, exact a price for all the promise that they offer.

While much has been written about the potential side effects of protease inhibitors and the need to adhere to a strict schedule in order for them to work most effectively, less attention has been paid to the potential for interactions between this class of drugs and other drugs, or even between different members of the class. Combining drugs is rarely simple in the age of protease inhibitors. Every change in a regimen must take into account the potential for each new drug to change the behaviour or concentration of a drug already being used. Each new medicine must be carefully evaluated for safety in the presence of other drugs already being taken. Understanding some of the concepts of drug interactions and their potential for adverse effects can help people avoid danger.

Overview of Drug Metabolism

Drugs taken by mouth pass through the stomach to the small intestine, where they are absorbed into the bloodstream and carried to their site of action. Intravenous drugs are placed directly into the bloodstream. Drugs injected into muscle (intramuscular), under the skin (subcutaneous) or allowed to diffuse through the skin (transdermal) make their way to the bloodstream more slowly through the soft tissues of the body.

Once in the body, many drugs are broken down into other compounds in stages before they are excreted. These other compounds are called metabolites. The chemical structure of a drug and its metabolites helps determine how quickly, in what way and by what route the body will get rid of them. Furthermore, people's bodies are unique and clear drugs at different rates and levels of efficiency.

To estimate the concentration of a drug in the bloodstream and the length of time it will be active, it is necessary to consider how much is taken (the dose), how often it is taken (the schedule), and in what way and how quickly a drug will be excreted.

Understanding these factors helps determine how much of a drug is needed and how often it must be taken to maintain a therapeutic level. The liver breaks down most chemicals and natural waste products in the body. These products are then carried by the blood to the kidneys to be washed out. The kidneys may also clear from the bloodstream directly other drugs which do not need to be broken down by the liver. Medicines that affect the function of either the liver or the kidneys may alter their ability to clear drugs and metabolites. If a drug continues to be taken and its removal from the body has been reduced or blocked, drug levels can rise until they reach toxic (poisonous) levels. If drug elimination has been accelerated, drug concentrations can fall below effective levels.

The Cytochrome P450 System

An important part of the body's disposal mechanism is the cytochrome P450 (CP450) system. CP450 is a collection of enzymes that drive chemical reactions or changes. Most of these enzymes are in the liver. Different enzymes or groups of enzymes break down different drugs. Some people's enzymes are extremely efficient, while others' enzymes work less well or more slowly.

Thus, differences in people's abilities to break down or metabolize drugs will directly affect the length of time that a drug remains in the body, as well as its blood level. Broiled foods, cigarettes and certain vegetables also affect metabolism. Some drugs have very potent effects on these enzymes, and may substantially alter drug effects and toxicities.

Types of Drug Interactions

Drugs can affect one another by acting at any step between intake and excretion.

Absorption

If one drug changes the rate at which other drugs move from the stomach to the small intestine, their rate of absorption into the blood will be affected. If one drug changes the level of acidity in the stomach, absorption of other drugs may change. If one drug binds to another, neither may be absorbed at all.

Distribution

A proportion of some drugs binds to blood proteins. If there are too few binding proteins, or if other drugs have already bound to these proteins, there will be more active drug in the body and drug performance will be changed.

Metabolism

Many drugs, including protease inhibitors, are excreted through the CP450 system. Other drugs stimulate or speed up the action of the CP450 system. If the activity of an enzyme is decreased, drugs requiring that enzyme for metabolism will have increased blood concentrations, effects and toxicities. If, instead, enzyme activity is revved up by one drug, other drugs may be broken down faster and levels may drop too low.

Elimination

Some drugs can alter the way the kidneys remove chemicals from the body. They may also affect the efficiency of the kidneys, particularly their ability to control the concentration of drug being eliminated. Other drugs may be directly toxic to the kidneys, reducing their function and resulting in higher levels of drugs.

Other types of Drug Interactions

Drug effects can be additive (effect + effect = double effect); synergistic (effect + effect = more than double effect); or antagonistic (effect vs effect = less than double effect). Interactions may result from the direct action of a drug or an indirect action several steps removed.

Drug interactions may also affect laboratory values used to judge the performance of other drugs. Any of these types of interactions can lead to unplanned and potentially damaging results called adverse drug events.

Protease Inhibitor Drug Interactions

Much is already known about protease inhibitors and the ways they affect and are affected by other drugs. However, much is still unknown. Table *(see note at beginning of article)* provides a summary of currently recognized drug interactions. Within the CP450 system, the enzyme most affected by protease inhibitors is CYP3A. Ritonavir (Norvir) is the most frequent inhibitor of this enzyme, while indinavir (Crixivan) and nelfinavir (Viracept) have fewer effects on CYP34, and saquinavir (Invirase) affects it even less.

The protease inhibitors also use the CP450 system for their own metabolism. Therefore, other drugs can affect the blood concentra-tions of protease inhibitors as well. Animal studies suggest that protease inhibitors currently in development—141W94 (Glaxo Wellcome/Vertex), ABT-378 (Abbott Laboratories) and KNI-272—may cause fewer drug interactions due to CP450 inhibition. However, human studies have not been completed.

Potential protease inhibitor adverse drug events include nausea, vomiting, diarrhea, taste changes, peripheral neuropathy and mild to significant liver damage. These adverse effects may occur more frequently with increased blood concentrations of protease inhibitors. Indinavir, when present in too high a concentration, can crystallize in the kidneys and form kidney stones.

Antialcohol Drugs

Disulfiram (Antabuse) is used to help people stop drinking alcohol. If the drug is taken with alcohol, intense flushing and abdominal pain can result. Metronidazole (Flagyl) may have a similar effect if taken with alcohol. Ritonavir contains alcohol in both liquid and pill formulations, and should not be used with these drugs.

Antianxiety Drugs

The metabolism of most drugs of the benzodiazepine class, including diazepam (Valium), is inhibited by protease inhibitors and especially by ritonavir.

The result may be oversedation and risk of respiratory depression. Use of ritonavir with most benzodiazepines and with zolpidem (Ambien) should be avoided. On the other hand, Lorazepam (Ativan), oxazepam (Serax) and temazepam (Restoril) can be used with ritonavir, although they may require increased dosing.

Antiarrhythmics

Antiarrhythmic drugs are used to stabilize the heart rate. Elimination of many of these drugs, including digoxin, can be reduced when ritonavir is present in the body. Careful monitoring of antiarrhythmic effects and blood levels is essential.

Antiasthmatics

Levels of the antiasthmatic drug theophylline (Theo-Dur, Uniphyl) can be lowered by ritonavir, so blood levels and response to therapy should be monitored.

Antibiotics

The antibiotics erythromycin and clarithromycin (Biaxin) may have increased serum levels when taken with ritonavir, nelfinavir or saquinavir. This is usually not a worrisome interaction, except in people who also have reduced kidney function. In such cases, the dose of clarithro-mycin should be decreased by 50-75%. Azithromycin (Zithromax) is less likely to interact with protease inhibitors. Metronidazole is discussed above.

Anticancer Agents

The blood levels of some anticancer drugs may be increased in people who take ritonavir. Because of the serious and sometimes irreversible toxicities to the blood, gastrointestinal tract and central nervous system caused by most anticancer drugs, it is probably best to avoid ritonavir and use another protease inhibitor instead.

Anticoagulants

Warfarin (Coumadin) levels are unpredictable when used with ritonavir, and side effects or loss of warfarin effect should be closely monitored.

Antidepressants

Tricyclic antidepressants (TCA), such as amitriptyline (Elavil), desipramine (Norpramin) and nortriptyline

(Pamelor), can build up to dangerous levels when used with ritonavir and should be taken at reduced doses. Blood levels of selective serotonin reuptake inhibitors (SSRI), including fluoxetine (Prozac), paroxetine (Paxil) and sertraline (Zoloft), can also increase when taken with with ritonavir.

Since TCA are sometimes used to treat peripheral neuropathy or headaches, and since both TCA and SSRI are sometimes used together to treat depression, close monitoring for side effects is recommended. Bupropion (Wellbutrin) should not be taken with ritonavir at all, since increased concentrations of this drug can lead to seizures. Ritonavir taken with trazodone (Desyrel), venlafaxine (Effexor) or nefazodone (Serzone) can possibly result in dangerous cardiac side effects.

Antidiabetic Drugs

Because ritonavir may block the breakdown of some antidiabetic drugs such as glyburide (Diabeta, Micronase) and glipizide (Glucotrol), the risk of developing seriously low blood sugar is significant. Careful daily testing of fasting blood sugar, together with close medical monitoring and follow-up, are needed. Newer agents such as metformin (Glucophage) and acarbose (Precose) are not broken down in the liver and no drug interactions have been reported to date. Troglitazone (Rizulin) is extensively broken down by the liver. Even though interactions with protease inhibitors have not yet been reported, combined use should probably proceed with caution.

Antidiarrheals

Diphenoxylate (Lomotil) and loperamide (Imodium) may be less effective when taken with ritonavir, causing a worsening of diarrhea symptoms. Increased dosages or the addition of another antidiarrheal medicine may be necessary.

Antifungals

Ketoconazole (Nizoral) and related drugs block the breakdown of saquinavir, indinavir and perhaps other protease inhibitors, with a resulting increase in protease inhibitor levels. Higher saquinavir levels may be more effective, so no dose adjustment is needed. Due to the potential for increased indinavir toxicity, dose reductions are recommended, especially if used with ketoconazole. Fluconazole (Diflucan) may be the best choice for use with protease inhibitors.

Antihistamines

Non-sedating antihistamines such as astemizole (Hismanal), loratadine (Claritin) and terfenadine (Seldane) should not be used with protease inhibitors, as their levels may increase. Sudden death has been reported as a result of high blood levels of these drugs. In addition, these antihistamines may prolong the elimination of protease inhibitors from the body. Treatment with cetirizine (Zyrtec) may be less risky if a non-sedating antihistamine is required. Traditional over-the-counter antihistamines may be used as usual.

Antihypertensives

There are so many drugs used to lower blood pressure that to name them all would take up an entire article. Here they will be discussed by drug class only. People receiving blood pressure medications should discuss drug interactions with their doctor. Calcium channel blocker levels may be increased by any of the protease inhibitors, but ritonavir increases these levels the most. Ritonavir may increase both beta blocker and alpha blocker levels. Losartan (Cozaar) levels may be either increased or decreased by ritonavir. People should watch closely for increased effects such as low blood pressure and other associated signs of toxicity if they are taking any of these drugs.

Antimigraine Drugs

Migraine is a specific type of headache that may be treated by using blood vessel constrictors, or prevented by using beta blockers or tricyclic antidepressants. The ergot preparation dihydroergotamine (DHE-45) is an example of the former. Use of ritonavir should be avoided with these medications. Beta blocker and calcium channel blocker drug interactions are discussed under "Antihypertensives" above. Tricyclic antidepressant drug levels can be increased by ritonavir. Sumatriptin (Imitrex) has no reported interactions.

Antinausea Drugs

Cisapride (Propulsid) metabolism is decreased when taken with any of the protease inhibitors, which may increase the concentration of cisapride to dangerous levels. Sudden death may result from using this drug with protease inhibitors.

Ondansetron (Zofran) levels may be increased when taken with protease inhibitors also, so a lower dose may be required. Prochlorperazine (Compazine) toxicity should be monitored carefully if ritonavir is taken, as ritonavir may block its metabolism.

Antiparasitics

Ritonavir may increase levels of quinine-based drugs. Atovaquone (Mepron) levels may be increased or decreased by ritonavir. Metronidazole should not be taken with ritonavir because of its disulfiram-like effect.

Antiretrovirals

DDI (Videx) can impair indinavir absorption, and the two drugs should be taken 1-2 hours apart. Ritonavir may increase indinavir and nelfinavir levels, and especially saquinavir levels (by up to 20 times). A study has shown that saquinavir at reduced doses (400-600 mg twice a day) plus ritonavir (400-600 mg twice a day) has potent anti-HIV activity.

Nevirapine (Viramune) may reduce concentrations of indinavir, nelfinavir, saquinavir and, to a lesser degree, ritonavir. Delavirdine (Rescriptor) may increase levels of all protease inhibitors. When taken with delavirdine, indinavir levels have been observed to increase by up to 208%. The clinical significance of these interactions with delavirdine is not yet known.

Antiseizure Medications

Drug interactions between protease inhibitors and antiseizure medications can be quite complicated. Ritonavir may increase blood levels of carbamazepine (Tegretol) and ethosuximide (Zarontin). However, ritonavir may decrease blood levels of lamotrigine (Lamictal), divalproex (Depakote) and valproic acid (Depakene). The effect of ritonavir on blood levels of phenytoin (Dilantin) and fosphenytoin (Cerebyx) can be unpredictable, with either higher or lower levels occurring. Indinavir may increase the blood concentrations of phenytoin and phenobarbitol (Luminal). Conversely, carbamazepine and ethosuxamide may increase nelfinavir levels. Phenytoin and phenobarbitol may decrease saquinavir, ritonavir and indinavir levels. The clinical significance of these increases and decreases is unknown. Serum levels of antiseizure medications should be closely monitored when used in combination with protease inhibitors.

Antitubercular Drugs

Rifampin and rifabutin (Mycobutin), drugs used to treat tuberculosis, tend to decrease protease inhibitor levels. Indinavir may be least affected by this interaction. Protease inhibitors may also cause increased levels of rifampin and rifabutin, potentially resulting in toxic side effects.

The Centers for Disease Control and Prevention (CDC) have suggested that either protease inhibitors be stopped for the 2-6 months that rifampin or rifabutin must be used, or that rifabutin (not rifampin) be used with other antitubercular drugs along with indinavir as the only protease inhibitor in this situation. It is important to discuss any proposed changes in therapy with a physician familiar with the treatment of tuberculosis and HIV. Stopping a protease inhibitor may result in the development of drug resistance and may preclude later use of that drug.

Antiulcer Drugs

Cimetidine (Tagamet) may inhibit saquinavir breakdown and increase saquinavir levels. Ritonavir may increase cimetidine levels and increase the risk of developing side effects. Alterations in gastric acidity due to antiulcer medications may affect the amount of protease inhibitor absorbed into the body. Lansoprazole (Prevacid) and omeprazole (Prilosec) levels may be increased or decreased by ritonavir.

Antivirals

Use of indinavir or ritonavir with drugs that impair kidney function requires close monitoring to avoid additive kidney toxicity. These drugs include, but are not limited to, acyclovir (Zovirax), cidofovir (Vistide) and foscarnet (Foscavir).

Cholesterol-Lowering Agents

Drugs that lower cholesterol may reach increased levels in the presence of ritonavir. Reduced dosing of these drugs should be considered when used with ritonavir.

Hormones

Birth control pills containing ethinyl estradiol may not be as effective for contraception when taken with either indinavir or ritonavir. Alternate means of contraception should be used. Medroxyprogesterone (Provera) levels may also be reduced.

Marijuana Derivatives

Dronabinol (Marinol), a marijuana derivative used to relieve nausea or increase appetite, may reach increased levels in the presence of any protease inhibitor. Therefore, dose adjustment of dronabinol may be necessary.

Nonsteroidal Anti-Inflammatory Drugs

The nonsteroidal anti-inflammatory drug (NSAID) group includes over-the-counter medicines like ibuprofen (Advil) as well as prescription drugs. Ritonavir inhibits the breakdown of these medicines, slowing their elimination and leading to a risk of increased drug levels. Symptoms associated with increased

NSAID levels include nausea, abdominal pain and possibly bleeding ulcers. Piroxicam (Feldene) is especially affected, and should not be used with ritonavir.

Opiates

Ritonavir speeds up the breakdown of some opiates, resulting in low drug levels and inadequate pain control. Other opiates may have their levels increased, resulting in potential oversedation, respiratory depression and shock with potential respiratory failure and death. People who take this combination of medicines should be closely monitored. Heroin and opium, in particular, may rise to dangerous levels. Methadone is broken down by an unknown CP450 system enzyme, and there is concern about increased levels when taken with ritonavir.

Ritonavir should not be used with meperidine (Demerol) or propoxyphene (Darvocet or Darvon). Seizures may result with the use of meperidine, and increased incidence of death has been reported when using propoxyphene with ritonavir.

Other Psychiatric Medications

Traditional antipsychotic drugs like haloperidol (Haldol) may require significant dose reduction when taken with ritonavir. Clozapine (Clozaril) blood concentrations are significantly increased by ritonavir, so the drugs should not be taken together. Risperidone (Risperdal), a newer antipsychotic drug, may be used with ritonavir, but may require dose adjustment. Olanzapine (Zyprexa) is metabolized by the enzyme CYP1A2. There have been no reported drug interactions with olanzapine to date. However, since ritonavir has a weak effect on this enzyme, monitoring for adverse drug events is necessary. Indinavir, nelfinavir and saquinavir have not yet been shown to affect these medications. Antiseizure drugs were discussed above.

Steroids

Prednisone and dexamethasone (Decadron) levels may be increased when taken with ritonavir. Patients should be carefully monitored for increased steroid effects.

Stimulants

Elimination of dexfenfluramine (Redux), methamphetamine (Desoxyn) and methylphenidate (Ritalin) may be altered by ritonavir. The resulting stimulant levels may be higher and therefore more dangerous (e.g., dexfenfluramine), they may be lower (e.g, methamphetamine) or they may be variable (e.g., methylphenidate). Ritonavir should not be used with dexfenfluramine. Ritonavir may also decrease caffeine levels. Nicotine may speed up ritonavir elimination, reducing drug levels and increasing the risk of drug resistance.

Avoiding Protease Inhibitor Interactions

The best way to avoid adverse drug effects resulting from drug interactions is to learn as much as possible about drugs being used. Pharmacists, doctors and nurses can be good resources. People with HIV who take the time to learn about this important aspect of their care can also teach their healthcare providers. Patients should carry a list of all their medications—including dosages—and give this to every doctor, dentist, nurse or pharmacist involved in their care. When possible, all medications should be purchased from the same source. When prescriptions come from more than one doctor, at least one primary physician should be kept abreast of the overall treatment regimen and all proposed changes in treatment. Never adjust doses of medicines without first consulting a physician.

Conclusion

Drug information is a powerful tool for maintaining and improving quality of life when multiple medications are required. Management of the drug interactions that accompany the use of protease inhibitor drugs requires great attention to detail. New drugs in development will expand the possibilities for adverse drug events.

A growing consensus on the need for highly aggressive anti-HIV therapy increases the challenge of avoiding adverse drug events. Healthcare providers experienced in HIV care, or willing to research each potential drug interaction, can provide essential information. People living with HIV can educate themselves and thus be active players in their health care.

THE ADVERSE EFFECTS OF ALCOHOL ON REPRODUCTION

For centuries, observations all over the world have shown that maternal drinking during pregnancy can have serious adverse effects on the health of the newborn and knowledge of alcohol-related birth defects dates back to old Biblical times: "Behold, thou shalt conceive and bear a son and now drink no wine or strong drink!".

Furthermore, in ancient Carthage and Sparta there were even laws prohibiting the use of alcohol by newly married couples in order to prevent conception during intoxication. It took well over a hundred years before the House of Commons reacted, and finally came out with a paper entitled "Effects of Drunkenness on the Nation", which also contained a report on the effects of maternal alcohol consumption on the newborn, stating: "They tend to be born starved, shrivelled and imperfect in form".

Fetal Alcohol Syndrome

The most common characteristics of children born with FAS are as follows:

Growth Abnormalities

Prenatal growth deficiency can be significant and includes all three of the following parameters of growth, weight, length and head circumference. Frequently the growth deficiencies are so severe that the newborn has to be hospitalised because of obvious failure to thrive. Postnatal growth and weight retardation is also significant and this continues for life despite the infant being reared in an ideal nutritional and social environment.

Craniofacial Abnormalities

The eyes of the affected children are often small with exaggerated inner epicanthic folds, and squints are common in later years. The nasal bridge is usually poorly formed, giving the nose a small 'retrousse' appearance. The vertical groove running from the nose down to the upper lip tends to be shallow or absent, and the upper lip itself is often narrow. The ears tend to be large and somewhat simple in form. Cleft palate may also be present.

Musculoskeletal Abnormalities

Variable musculoskeletal and limb defects are found in approximately 40% of cases, ranging in severity from minor problems such as contractures of the finger joints to more severe lesions, such as congenital hip dislocations and thoracic cage abnormalities.

Genital abnormalities are also frequent, such as undescended testes and malformations of the lower wall of the urithera in males and hypoplastic labia in females. Minor kidney abnormalities have also been detected.

Cardiac Abnormalities

Congenital heart disease is found in 29-50% of reported cases. They are commonly atrical or ventricular septal defects, but also complex and sometimes lethal cardiac abnormalities can occur.

Nervous System Abnormalities

When first delivered, the affected infants may show clear evidence of alcohol withdrawal, with signs similar to delirium tremens in adults. They are often fretful, tremulous, have a weak grasp, poor eye-hand coordination and frequently a great difficulty with sucking and feeding. Cerebellar damage is also common, resulting later on in excessive clumsiness and even in recurrent seizures.

Neuro-Developmental Delay or Mental Deficiency

The average IQ in children born with FAS is around 65, indicating moderate mental handicap. Mental retardation also occurs frequently in varying degrees. In fact FAS is now recognised as the leading known cause of mental retardation, surpassing Down's syndrome and spina bifida. Around 70% of children with FAS are severely hyperactive, frequently engaging in disturbing self-stimula-ting behaviours such as body rocking, head banging or head rolling.

Without exception all children with FAS suffer from severe developmental disabilities. With the onset of school, these severe IQ and attention deficits, combined with various behavioural problems, emerge as serious intellectual and learning disabilities.

Adolescents/Adults with FAS

The natural history of FAS has now been traced into adulthood. When children with FAS approach adolescence, the specific craniofacial features associated with the syndrome are not as noticeable as in infancy. However, the short stature and microcephaly seem to be permanent.

The average academic functioning of these adolescents and adults does not seem ever seem to develop beyond early school grade level, even though in one sample of 61 studied, 42% had IQ levels above 70 and all had received constant remedial help at school.

A particular deficit was found in arithmetic skills and extreme difficulties with abstractions like time and space, cause and effect, as well generalising from one situation to another. The most noticeable behaviour problems were found to be with comprehension, judgement and attention skills, causing these adults born with FAS to experience major psychosocial and adjustment problems for the rest of their lives.

The Teratogenic Effects Of Alcohol

Alcohol is a teratogen. There has been no teratogenic agent yet studied in man which has shown a clear threshold effect, i.e. where the substance could be considered safe at a particular level, beyond which its teratogenic effect begins to take hold, and alcohol is no exception. That being the case, the teratogenic effects of alcohol can also induce fetal malformations both at the earliest, as well as at the lowest level of intake, its effectiveness spreading differentially over the whole spectrum of reproduction, affecting the developing fetus in varying degrees, in both extent and severity, depending on the dosage and timing.

This explains also why maternal alcohol consumption can affect the offspring through all gradations of teratogenesis, ranging from transient to very mildly affected, and from moderately affected right up to the full blown Fetal Alcohol Syndrome.

During transient teratogenesis the impact of the agent on the fetal tissue may not inflict permanent damage, as the substance can be degraded by the mother and fetal tissue in time, depending on genetic influences, susceptibility and maternal nutritional status.

Alcohol Teratogenesis on Structural Development

Alcohol is a low molecular substance and is therefore quite capable of crossing the placental barrier and entering the fetus, causing the level of alcohol in the fetus to be approximate to that of the mother. In the first 21 days of the fetal development the preliminary cell organisation of the embryo begins to take place.

If an excessive amount of alcohol is consumed before the blastocyst is embedded in the uterus, the impact can be so severe that the fetus is miscarried. By the end of the 36th day, often long before the woman even realises that she is pregnant, the neural tube is clearly present and open, and most of the rudimentary organs have already been formed, such as limbs, heart, brain, eyes, mouth, digestive tract etc.

It is therefore obvious that if a teratogenic substance such as alcohol is consumed during this most critical period of rapid growth of cell development and organ formation, this can result in various forms of malformation in the newborn, such as defective heart, musculoskeletal abnormalities, mental handicap etc., without any specific outward signs of FAS.

Even though it is considered that the first three months of gestation is the most critical period for alcohol-induced malformations to occur, both human and animal experiments have been able to demonstrate that the teratogenic effects of alcohol continues throughout the whole gestational period, affecting at the later stage particularly the brain development and function.

Alcohol Teratogenesis in Brain Development

Alcohol has the most detrimental effect on both brain development and function. The infant is not only born with a brain smaller in size, but the teratogenic effect of alcohol both reduces the number of brain neurons, as well as alters their distributution, resulting in mental deficiency in varying degrees, from milder behavioural problems to obvious mental handicap.

Animal studies have shown that while many areas of the brain are affected by maternal alcohol exposure, its effects seem to be particularly detrimental on the hippocampus , where it produces marked changes in its mossy fibres and 20% reduction in the pyramidal cells in the CA1 region, as well as a sparsity in the number of dendritic spines in the CA1 pyramidal neurons.

It has been therefore speculated that both the intellectual decrements and the behavioural deficits seen in infants born to mothers using alcohol during pregnancy may result directly from these specific hippocampal structural alterations. Hundreds of experiments have been able to confirm that maternal alcohol consumption indeed causes irreversible brain alterations in both human and non-human infants, which also include abnormalities in EEG patterns , abnormal visual evoked responses , and both defective auditory brain stem and spatial learning developments.

Autopsy reports on deceased patients with FAS have shown widespread anomalies, many of which have been associated with disruption in the migration and integration of neural and glial cells during embryogenesis. In addition, other autopsy studies have shown that the nature and degree of brain malformations in children of alcoholic and heavy drinking mothers are extremely variable, suggesting that a wide variety of broad spectrum neurologic, behavioural and intellectual deficits would therefore also be found in survivors. As only about half of the autopsied cases studied had enough physical characteristics to warrant a diagnosis of FAS, it seems now quite obvious that alcohol-related brain damage, as well as learning and behavioural deficits, do occur frequently in the absence of any external signs of FAS.

FETAL ALCOHOL EFFECTS

The teratogenic effects of alcohol spreads differentially over the whole spectrum of reproduction, varying only in the extent and degree. At one end of the spectrum are the children warranting a firm diagnosis of FAS, and at the other end of the spectrum are the children who lack the common physical characteristics of FAS but who, nevertheless, have some subtle or marked physical and/or mental deficiencies by being exposed to varying amounts of alcohol in utero. It is now widely accepted that the classical diagnosis of FAS is totally inadequate as for every child born with FAS there are thousands of others whose lives are partially handicapped, or limited, by being exposed to alcohol during gestational development. These children, without sufficient physical stigmata for firm diagnosis of FAS, are now identified as suffering from Fetal Alcohol Effects (FAE). Over the years a number of epidemiological studies have investigated both the physical and neurobehavioural effects of varying levels of prenatal alcohol exposure on both human and non-human infants.

One of the foremost experts and contemporary researchers in this field is Dr Ann P. Streissguth, of the Department of Psychiatry and Behavioral Sciences at the University of Washington, who has researched, published and lectured widely on the teratogenic effects of maternal alcohol consumption From the year 1974 Dr Streissguth and her team began a seven and half year longitudinal, prospective, population-based study, examining the long term effects of moderate prenatal alcohol exposure on 486 infants born to mothers who had reported no major problems with alcohol but were, nevertheless, social drinkers i.e. reported consuming on average two or more drinks most days during pregnancy, or reported a "binge- pattern" of drinking e.g. consuming five or more drinks per any occasion in the month before pregnancy recognition.

Only six out of the mothers interviewed felt that they might have used alcohol excessively during pregnancy. The mothers were primarily white, married, middle class, and at low risk for adverse pregnancy outcome, and all were receiving prenatal care by the fifth month of pregnancy. This cohort sample of children, which included 261 boys and 225 girls, were first examined and evaluated on the first and second day after birth, and then approximately at eight and eighteen months, at four years, and at seven and at seven and a half years after birth.

FAE in Infants and Preschool Children

Most of these infants were born basically within normal limits as a group. However, the more the mothers had reported consuming alcohol, the poorer the overall performance of the newborns.

Already, on the first day of life, the infants of the mothers who had been drinking more during pregnancy functioned significantly worse. They were usually born with lighter weight and were more jittery and tremulous. They had difficulties with habituation, which is the ability to turn off redundant stimuli, considered as a basic nervous system function of the newborn.

On the second day of life they had a longer latency to begin sucking and had a weaker suck as measured on a pressure transducer with non-nutritive nipple. They also suffered from disrupted sleep patterns , low level of arousal, unusual body orientation, abnormal reflexes, hypotonia and excessive mouthing.

By eight months, and then onwards, these infants seemed to continue suffering from disrupted sleep-wake patterns, poorer balance and motor control, longer latency to respond, poorer attention, visual recognition and memory, decrements in mental development, spoken language and verbal comprehension, including lower IQ scores. As references indicate, these findings have also been confirmed independently by other workers.

FAE in Young School-age Children

After seven years Dr Streissguth and her team re-examined the cohort of 486 children. The results showed that learning problems and classroom behaviour which were most negatively related to moderate alcohol exposure in utero were: co-operation, sustained attention, retention of information, comprehension of words, impulsiveness, tactfulness, word recall and organisational skills, all indicating increased risk of learning disabilities.

In fact, even though these children were within an average range of intelligence, their overall performance on arithmetic and reading tests were negative. It also became apparent that maternal drinking of two or more drinks per day on average, after statistically adjusting for appropriate covariates, was related to a 7-point decrement in IQ in these seven year olds.

Furthermore, that children of women who reported never drinking five or more drinks on any occasion in the month before pregnancy recognition, were on average one to three months behind in reading and arithmetic skills. In addition 24% of these children were participating in special remedial programmes at school, compared to 15% of children of abstainers. This represents 9% excess of learning disabilities for children of mothers who had never been drinking five or more drinks on one occasion prior to pregnancy recognition. These children were also found to have higher learning problem score of 17% compared to children of abstainers which was 7%.

The conclusion of this study was that two maternal alcohol use patterns have now been identified as being particularly detrimental to the offspring i.e. two or more drinks an average per day during pregnancy, and "binge-pattern" of alcohol consumption, e.g. five or more drinks on any occasion, particularly when consumed in the month so before pregnancy recognition, as both can lead to marked behaviour and learning disabilities in school-age children. It was also concluded that these alcohol-related behaviour and attention decrements seem to have been already clearly observable from an early infancy, long before academic learning had even occurred.

Half an year later, Professor Streissguth and her team selected from the cohort study of 482 children, 384 subjects. The reason for the selection was because some tests were either added or modified after the initial testing had begun, therefore not all tests had been administered to all the 482 children. One of the tests added was Children's Memory Test blocks, which had been completed only by these 384 children.

The results showed that low-level prenatal alcohol consumption is most strongly related to attention and memory deficits across both verbal and visual modalities, poor integration and quality responses, as well as to negative behaviour patterns involving distractibility, inflexibility, and poor organisational skills. Also inadequate perceptual motor functioning was apparent.

This wide pattern of performance deficits uniformly occurred despite the presence of average IQ, suggesting that maternal alcohol induced behaviour decrements in the offspring seem to be a more sensitive indicator of central nervous system damage than the IQ scale itself. The study concluded that maternal social drinking seemed to result in the offspring having similar, but less severe consequences than those seen in children born with FAS, indicating in both cases, the clear occurrence of alcohol-induced permanent and irreversible central nervous system damage during critical stages of fetal development.

FAE in adolescents and adults: As with children born with FAS, population based studies carried out on the offspring born to socially drinking mothers have shown that, on maturation, these children can still show subtle and permanent alcohol-related neurobehavioural deficits, IQ and achievement decrements, combined with various attention, memory and learning problems.

Alcohol and Male Reproduction

Alcohol is a direct testicular toxin. It causes atrophy of semeniferous tubules, loss of sperm cells, and an increase in abnormal sperms. Alcohol is also known to be a strong Leydig cell toxin , and it can have an adverse effect on the synthesis and secretion of testosterone.

Alcohol can cause significant deterioration in sperm concentration, sperm output and motility. Semen samples of men consuming excessive amounts of alcohol have shown distinct morphological abnormalities. It has been also established that approximately 80% of chronic alcoholic men are sterile and, furthermore, that alcohol is one of the most common causes of male impotence.

Alcohol and Nutritional Status

Numerous animal studies of experimental alcoholism, where nutritional status has been well controlled, have shown that the damage to the developing fetus, such as low birth weight, central nervous system impairment and congenital abnormalities, are caused as a direct consequence of the teratogenic effects of alcohol.

In addition, some of these studies have also been able to show a clear continuum effect; the higher the blood alcohol of the mother, the greater the damage to the developing fetus. Even though the direct connection between alcohol intake and birth defects is now indisputable, other etiological factors associated with maternal drinking must also be considered as contributing to adverse pregnancy outcome. The most important of these secondary factors is alcohol-induced malnutrition, as nutritional deficiencies occur frequently with alcohol intake, due to reduced appetite.

However, in cases where nutritional food intake is adequate, alcohol still considerably reduces nutritional status by directly interfering with nutrition utilization, digestion and absorption, as well as greatly increasing urinary excretion of both vitamins and minerals. Alcohol-induced zinc depletion is particularly well documented. This could be of a particular importance, as some studies on human pregnancies have shown a positive correlation with reduced zinc status and low birth weight and fetal malformations, suggesting that inadequate zinc nutriture could also act independently as a teratogenic agent. In addition, folic acid deficiency, which results from alcohol-induced urinary excretion, has been linked directly with the occurrence of spina bifida(. Besides direct malnutrition, other secondary metabolic disturbances due to alcohol consumption may also contribute to an adverse pregnancy outcome, such as alcohol-induced hypoglycaemia, ketoacidosis, as well as various alterations in both lipid, and amino acid metabolism.

Chapter 2

Drug Laws and Policies

INTRODUCTION

Modifications in Drug Policy, 1986

- The Drug Policy of 1986, which was titled "Measures for Rationalisation, Quality Control and Growth of Drugs & Pharmaceuticals industry in India" was evolved under the dynamic guidance and leadership of late Shri Rajiv Gandhi. This was done after a detailed examination of the various issues. The main objectives of the Drug Policy, 1986 are as under:
  - Ensuring abundant availability, at reasonable prices of essential and life saving and prophylactic medicines of good quality;
  - Strengthening the system of quality control over drug production and promoting the rational use of drugs in the country;
  - Creating an environment conducive to channelising new investment into the pharmaceutical industry to encouraging cost-effective production witheconomic sizes and to introducing new technologies and new drugs;
  - Strengthening the indigenous capability for production of drugs.
- For meeting the requirements of medicines for health needs at reasonable prices and strengthening the indigenous base, the Government has, over the years been guided by the above Policy. Implementation of the main policy provisions has been through the

I(D&R) Act on Industrial Licensing aspects and through Drugs(Prices Control) Orders under the Essential Commodities Act in regard to the pricing mechanism. The Drug Policy has also given the policy frame work in regard to Quality Control and Rational Use of Drugs. Enforcement of quality and standards in medicines is done through the provisions contained in the Drugs & Cosmetics Act, which is administered by the Ministry of Health and Family Welfare, Government of India.

PRESENT STATUS AND APPROACH ADOPTED IN REVIEW

- Over the last several years, policy inputs have been directed towards promoting the growth of the industry and in helping it to achieve a broad base in terms of the range of products and technologies needed to produce them from as basic a stage as possible. The results have been very encouraging. As on date, there are about 250 large units and about 8,000 small scale units in operation, which form the core of the Industry (including 5 Central Public Sector Units). These units produce the complete range of formulations i.e. medicines ready for consumption by patients, and about 350 bulk drugs, i.e. chemicals having therapeutic value used for production of formulations. It is estimated that 70 per cent of the indigenous demand for bulk drugs and almost the entire demand for formulations are being met through domestic production.
- During the last decade the production of bulk drugs has grown from Rs. 240 crores in 1980-81 to Rs. 1320 crores in 1993-94 and corresponding increase in production of formulations has been from Rs. 1200 crores to Rs. 6900 crores. The export performance of Industry has also been commendable. The trade balance has been positive for the last four consecutive years. During 1992-93 the trade balance was Rs. 560 crores.

- Since 1986, the Drug Industry has grown significantly, as mentioned earlier, in terms of production of bulk drugs and formulations. In many cases manufacture of bulk drugs has also been established from the desired basic stage. It is estimated that in case of bulk drug production the contribution of small scale sector is approximately 30 per cent of the total production in the country. It may also be mentioned that the pharmaceutical sector has been able to carve a special niche for itself in the international market as a dependable exporter of bulk drugs.

INDUSTRIAL LICENSING

- Import and Economic policies have undergone major changes like pruning of the Negative List for imports, doing away with the Actual User condition and full convertibility of Rupee on trade account. In this changed scenario, it is felt that there is no need to be more restrictive than before in granting industrial approvals, provided the two main concerns i.e., achieving basic stage manufacture and discouraging undue imports, are adequately taken care of. Under the circumstances, these objectives can be achieved only through the tariff mechanism and the EXIM policy and as such Industrial Licensing and conditions stipulated therein have lost their relevance.

It is also felt that, like in the other sectors of the economy, production would get the necessary impetus to meet any future demands as well as of ensuring adequate availability of drugs at reasonable prices if a more liberalised regime is operated in granting industrials approvals. Many of the drugs reserved for the Public Sector Undertakings have lost relevance vis-à-vis production programme of these units. Therefore, there is need to prune the list of items reserved for the Public Sector to only a few select items, where capacity in Public Sector is adequate to meet the country's demand and heavy public investment has been made.

- The Drug Industry is a highly R&D oriented sector in which there is a very high rate of obsolescence. This sector has also been identified as one of the thrust areas for exports. There is, therefore, need to ensure that the technologies used in the country are cost effective and efficient.

It is necessary to attract greater investment into this sector in order to update the existing technologies and for bringing into the country technologies which are not currently available. At the same time it has to be noted that the Indian companies have achieved considerable stature in terms of production as well as in marketing ability and indigenous technology has also reached a commendable level in many cases. However, in view of GATT accord and impending changes in Patent Laws, the subject matter of Basic Research in drug sector has assumed greater importance and needs to be attended to on an urgent basis.

- Keeping in view the need to encourage more investment in this important sector to achieve the future demands likely to be placed on it in order to meet the growing needs of the country as well as to promote exports, it is proposed to treat the entire drugs and pharmaceutical sector as a high priority industry for the purposes of permitting foreign investment in terms of Appendix-III of the New Industrial Policy. It is also proposed to treat companies with foreign equity upto 51 per cent on par with wholly Indian companies.

It may also be mentioned that at present companies with foreign equity upto 40 per cent are already enjoying this facility and, in the circumstances mentioned above there is no need to place any fresh curbs on their activities.

Similarly, it is felt that automatic approval for foreign technology agreements can be permitted for all items in the Drugs and Pharmaceuticals sector to encourage the introduction of newer and more efficient technologies, subject to their fulfilling the standard conditions laid down in the Industrial Policy. However, keeping in mind the levels of technology already available in the country, it is necessary to consider proposals involving foreign equity participation above 51 per cent on merits of each case.

- The aberrations which have come to notice, in the listing of drugs and their categorisation for the purpose of price control, need to be eliminated by the use of transparent criteria applied across the board on all the drugs with the minimum use of subjectivity. The high turnover of a drug is an index of its extent of usage and is considered to meet the requirements of objectivity justifiable on economicconsiderations.

However, the monopoly situation in cases of drugs with comparatively lower turnover has also to be kept in view. Also as an experimental measure, drugs having adequate competition may not be kept under price control and if this proves successful it would pave the way for further liberalisation.

In the event, however, of prices of these drugs not remaining within reasonable limits, the Government would reclamp price control.

- The categorisation of drugs into two lists with different Maximum Allowable Post-manufacturing Expenses (MAPE) allows a lower MAPE of 75 per cent for the drugs required for National Health Programmes (Category I drugs) as against 100% for others (Category II drugs).

To encourage the production and availability of these drugs, it is considered necessary to allow a uniform MAPE in all cases of drugs under price control. Further, to achieve uniformity in prices of widely used formulations, it is considered that there should be ceiling prices for commonly marketed standard pack sizes of price controlled formulations and it should be obligatory for all, including small scale units, to follow the prices so fixed.

Also, to give encouragement to manufacture of drugs from basic stage, it is considered necessary to allow higher return in such cases over the existing rates.

- In the light of the apprehensions expressed in the Parliament on the likely spurt in the prices of medicines, it has been felt that it would not be desirable to allow automaticity in the pricing mechanism. The Government would set up an independent body of experts, to be called the National Pharmaceutical Pricing Authority, to do the work of price fixation.

This expert body would also be entrusted with the task of updating the list of drugs under price control each year on the basis of the established criteria/guideline. Time limits would be provided for deciding the applications of price approvals and, to begin with, it is proposed to set a time limit of two months for formulations and four months for bulk drugs. This body would also monitor the prices of decontrolled drugs and formulations and oversee the implementation of the provisions of the Drugs (Prices Control) Order. The Government would have the power of review.

- Government will keep a close watch on the prices of medicines which are taken out of price control. In case, the prices of these medicines rise unreasonably, the Government would take appropriate measures, including reclamping of price control

QUALITY CONTROL AND RATIONAL USE OF DRUGS

- Quality Control and Rational use of Drugs are important aspects of Pharmaceutical Industry. Steps have been taken for strengthening Drug Control Organisation by sanctioning additional posts at various levels and by establishing sub-zonal offices at Hyderabad, Ahmedabad and Patna. The Bio-Laboratory at Madras has been upgraded to the level of National Laboratory.

The Central Drugs Laboratory at Bombay, functioning from 1992 is in the process of being upgraded while Regional Laboratories at Guwahati, Chandigarh and Hyderabad are in the process of being set up.

- To improve the existing State Drugs Testing Laboratories and to set up new ones, wherever not established, funds have been sanctioned under a Centrally Sponsored Scheme, besides providing funds under this scheme for augmenting Drug Inspectorate Staff. For certain categories of drugs, which had caused adverse effects due to the lack of drug control in one or the other State, the Central Government has taken upon itself the responsibility of granting license. These drugs are;
  - Large Volume Parenterals,
  - Sera and Vaccines and
  - Whole Human Blood and Blood Products. Moreover, the Good Manufacturing Practices (GMP) have been made mandatory.
- Screening of irrational or harmful drugs is an ongoing exercise and 44 categories of formulations have been banned so far and the definition of new drugs has been widened and guidelines issued on clinical trials. With a view to ensuring proper dispensing and rational use of drugs, packaging have been standardised. Five leading hospitals at Pondicherry, Chandigarh, New Delhi, Bombay and Lucknow have been identified as Adverse Drug Reaction Monitoring Centres.
- While Ministry of Health and Family Welfare are taking some action on these matters, the general perception unfortunately is that this area is presently being neglected. In the interest of the consumers, there cannot be any compromise on quality aspects of medicines and the problem has assumed greater dimension in view of the large number of small scale drug manufacturing units which are estimated to be over 8000 in number.

• In view of the above it is envisaged that a National Drug Authority may be set up by a separate Act of Parliament to perform the following functions:

- Develop and define basic appropriate standards

relating to the manufacture, import, supply, promotion and use of drugs

- To approve and register pharmaceutical products for use in the country only if:
  - It meets real medical need,
  - It is therapeutically effective, and
  - It is acceptable safe
- To enforce effectively appropriate quality standards of medicines and Good Manufacturing Practices, throughout the country, having full regard to the needs of public health and standardize dosage strengths and pack sizes of formulations with a view to check proliferation.
- To monitor standard practices in drug promotion and use and to clearly identify those which are acceptable and prohibit those which are unethical and against the consumers' interest.
- To monitor the prescribing practices and to evaluate their appropriateness for the purpose of guiding the medical profession and for achieving the aim of rational prescribing.
- To ensure that appropriate information about registered pharmaceuticals is made available for the guidance of consumers having regard to:
  - He adverse consequences of non-compliance by patients particularly in the case of antibiotics, steriods etc.,
  - Dangers of self-medication, and
  - The need to involve consumers as full partners in the health care system
- To prepare and publish a national formulary and formularies relevant to various levels (like district hospital, community centre, primary health centre) for the guidance of consumers as well as doctors.
- The functions mentioned above involve new responsibilities which will include:-Special focus on examining the technology of bulk drugs; capacity validation of machinery; assessing suitability of

manpower for bulk drug production; undertaking scientific scrutiny of master formulae for manufacture of formulations; developing testing labs for cosmetics, diagnostics and devices; laying down standards for veterinary drugs; examination of labels and promotional claims and prescribing procedures for public hearing under the Drugs and Cosmetics Act; monitoring of clinical trials for the protection of human rights; quality control of herbal medicines; updating new drug approval process; weeding out of irrational combination formulations; and formation of expert committees for examination of new drugs.18.

- In addition, screening promotional literature, monitoring ongoing clinical trials through an Institutional Review Board, unearthing sub-standard and spurious drugs with the help of Legal cum Intelligence Cells, centralising all manufacturing licensees for inter-State commerce, updating Good Manufacturing Practices and education to achieve judicious use of drugs, setting up of new analytical testing labs, as well as imparting continuous education and skills for inspection and testing and setting up of Dispute Mechanism Cell are envisaged.19.
- There is an imperative need to undertake upgradation of the drug testing facilities under the Central and State organizations as well as augmentation of the Drug Control and enforcement staff to enable statutory inspections to be undertaken as provided for under the Act. Therefore, there is need for establishing more zonal and sub-zonal offices under the Central Drug Standards Control Organization as well as additional Regional Drug Testing Laboratories.20. The implementation of the above proposals would require additional funds, which are proposed to be mobilized by levying a cess of 1% on production of drugs and pharmace-uticals,

by a special legislation to be piloted by the Ministry of Health and Family Welfare. The funds mobilized through the cess would be utilized also for encouraging Research and Development in the drug sector.

The Government decided to modify the Drug Policy, 1986 as follows:

- Industrial Licensing for all bulk drugs cleared by Drug Controller (India) and all their intermediates will be abolished, except in the cases of:
  - 5 identified bulk drugs which are to continue to be exclusively reserved for the Public Sector as mentioned in Para 22.3 below,
  - Bulk drugs produced by the use of recombinant DNA technology, and
  - Bulk drugs requiring in-vivo use of nucleic acids as the active principles.
- Conditions stipulating mandatory supply of a percentage of bulk drug production to Non-associated Formulators will be abolished.
- Licensing shall be abolished for formulations except in cases of specific cell/tissue targeted formulations.
- Ratio parameters linking bulk drugs and formulations production and limiting the use of imported bulk drugs will stand abolished.
- Broad-banding, locational restrictions and grant of COB licenses will be in accordance with the Industrial Policy.

(The Memorandum of information prescribed by the Department of Industrial Development shall include an Addendum, to meet the additional requirement of the Drugs & Pharmaceuticals industry, as would be devised by the Department of Chemicals and Petrochemicals.)

BASIC STAGE PRODUCTION

For achieving manufacture from the basic stages and arresting the regression towards manufacturing from later stage intermediates/penultimates, the tariff mechanism would be utilized. Imports of critical intermediates/penultimates may also be put in the negative list so as to arrest regression from basic stage manufacturing.

FOREIGN INVESTMENT

- Investment upto 51 per cent will be permitted in the case of all bulk drugs, their intermediates and formulations
- Investment above 51 per cent will be considered on a case by case basis in areas where investment is otherwise not forthcoming, particularly in the manufacture of bulk drugs from basic stages and their intermediates, and bulk drugs produced by the use of recombinant DNA technology as well as the specific cell/tissue targeted formulations.

FOREIGN TECHNOLOGY AGREEMENTS

Automatic approval for foreign technology agreements shall be given in the case of all bulk drugs, their intermediates and formulations except those produced by the use of recombinant DNA technology, for which the existing procedure would continue.

ENCOURAGEMENT TO RESEARCH & DEVELOPMENT (R&D) EFFORTS

- A new drug which has not been produced elsewhere, if developed through indigenous R&D would be put outside price control for a period of 10 years from thedate of commercial production in favor of the Company who undertook the R&D.
- The Department of Chemicals Petrochemicals would set up an Inter-Ministerial group to decide, within a set time frame, on measures to give further impetus to R&D in the Drug Sector.
- The Ministry of Health and Family Welfare would further streamline the required procedures and steps for the quick evaluation and clearance of new drug

applications, specially those developed through indigenous R&D.

SINGLE LIST OF PRICE CONTROLLED DRUGS & "MAPE"

The system of price control may be operated through a Single list of price controlled drugs and formulations based thereon with a MAPE of 100 per cent.

SPAN OF CONTROL

- The criterion of including drugs under price control will be the minimum annual turnover of Rs.400 lakhs.
- Drugs of popular use, in which there is a monopoly situation will be kept under price control. For this purpose if for any bulk drug, having an annual turnover of Rs. 100 lakhs or more there is a single formulator having 90% or more market share in the Retail Trade (as per ORG) a monopoly situation would be considered as existing.
- Drugs in which there is sufficient market competition viz. at least 5 bulk drug producers and at least 10 formulators and none having more than the 40% market share in the Retail Trade (as per ORG) may be kept outside the price control. However, a strict watch would be kept on the movement of prices as it is expected that their prices would be kept in check by the forces of market competition. The Government may determine the ceiling levels beyond which increase in prices would not be permissible.
- Government will kept a close watch on the price of medicines which are taken out of price control. In case, the prices of these medicines rise unreasonably, the Government would take appropriate measures, including reclamping of price control.
- For applying the above criteria, to start with, the basis would be the data upto 31st March, 1990 collected for the exercise of the Review of the Drug Policy. The updating of the data will be done by the National

Pharmaceutical Pricing Authority as detailed in para 22.7.4 (i).

- Genetically engineered drugs produced by recombinant DNA technology and specific cell/tissue targeted drug formulations will not be under price control for 5 years from the date of manufacture in India.

DRUG POLICY

The drug and pharmaceutical industry in the country today faces new challenges on account of liberalization of the Indian economy, the globalization of the world economy and on account of new obligations undertaken by India under the WTO Agreements.

These challenges require a change in emphasis in the current pharmaceutical policy and the need for new initiatives beyond those enumerated in the Drug Policy 1986, as modified in 1994, so that policy inputs are directed more towards promoting accelerated growth of the pharmaceutical industry and towards making it more internationally competitive. The process of liberalization set in motion in 19901, has considerably reduced the scope of industrial licensing and demolished many non-tariff barriers to imports. Some of the steps taken are:

- Strengthening the system of quality control over drug and pharmaceutical production and distribution to make quality an essential attribute of the Indian pharmaceutical industry and promoting rational use of pharmaceuticals.
- Encouraging R&D in the pharmaceutical sector in a manner compatible with the country's needs and with particular focus on diseases endemic or relevant to India by creating an environment conducive to channelising a higher level of investment into R&D in pharmaceuticals in India.
- Creating an incentive framework for the pharmaceutical industry which promotes new investment into pharmaceutical industry and

encourages the introduction of new technologies and new drugs.

In order to strengthen the pharmaceutical industry's research and development capabilities and to identify the support required by Indian pharmaceutical companies to undertake domestic R&D, a Committee was set up in 1999 by this Department by the name of Pharmaceutical Research and Development Committee (PRDC) under the Chairmanship of Director General of CSIR.

The recommendations of the PRDC in so far as they relate to the Pharmaceutical Policy have been taken into account while formulating the proposals on pricing aspects. The Pharmaceutical Research & Development Committee has recommended in its report, submitted inter-alia, the setting up of a Drug Development Promotion Foundation (DDPF) and a Pharmaceutical Research & Development Support Fund (PRDSF).

Necessary action in this regard has been initiated. As far as the question of price control is concerned, the span of control has been gradually reduced since 1979. Presently, under DPCO, 1995 there are 74 bulk drugs and their formulations under price control covering approximately 40% of the total market. The domestic drugs and pharmaceuticals industry needs reorientation in order to meet the challenges and harness opportunities arising out of the liberalisation of the economy and the impending advent of the product patent regime.

However, keeping in view the interest of the weaker sections of the society, it is proposed that the Government will retain the power to intervene comprehensively in cases where prices behave abnormally. In order to review the current drug price control mechanism, with the objective, inter-alia, of reducing the rigours of price control, where they have become counter-productive, a committee, called the Drugs Price Control Review Committee (DPCRC), under the Chairmanship of Secretary, Department of Chemicals & Petrochemicals was set up in 1999. The recommendations of DPCRC have been examined and taken into account while formulating the "Pharmaceutical Policy - 2002". Industrial LicensingIndustrial licensing for all bulk drugs cleared by Drug Controller General (India), all their intermediates and formulations will be abolished, subject to stipulations laid down from time to time in the Industrial Policy, except in the cases of:

- Bulk drugs produced by the use of recombinant DNA technology,
- Bulk drugs requiring in-vivo use of nucleic acids as the active principles, and
- specific cell/tissue targetted formulations.

Foreign Investment: Foreign investment upto 100% will be permitted, subject to stipulations laid down from time to time in the Industrial Policy, through the automatic route in the case of all bulk drugs cleared by Drug Controller General (India), all their intermediates and formulations, except those, referred to in para 12.I above, kept under industrial licensing.

Foreign Technology Agreements: Automatic approval for Foreign Technology Agreements will be available in the case of all bulk drugs cleared by Drug Controller General (India), all their intermediates and formulations, except those, referred to in para 12.I above, kept under industrial licensing for which a special procedure prescribed by the Government would be followed. Imports of drugs and pharmaceuticals will be as per EXIM policy in force.

A centralized system of registration will be introduced under the Drugs and Cosmetics Act and Rules made thereunder. Ministry of Health and Family Welfare will enforce strict regulatory processes for import of bulk drugs and formulations.

ENCOURAGEMENT TO RESEARCH AND DEVELOPMENT (R&D)

- In principle approval to the establishment of the Pharmaceutical Research and Development Support Fund (PRDSF) under the administrative control of the Department of Science and Technology, which will also constitute a Drug Development Promotion

Board (DDPB) on the lines of the Technology Development Board to administer the utilization of the PRDSF.

- With a view to encouraging generation of intellectual property and facilitating indigenous endeavours in pharma R&D, appropriate fiscal incentives would be provided.

PRICING

Span of Price Control: The guiding principle for identification of specific bulk drugs for price regulation should continue, as per DPCRC's recommendation, to be:

- Mass consumption nature of the drug and absence of sufficient competition in such drugs. However, the DPCRC's recommendation regarding the new criteria for ascertaining the mass consumption nature of a bulk drug on the basis of the top selling brand is not acceptable as it gives rise to anomalies. the Department proposes to undertake the exercise of identifying the bulk drugs of mass consumption nature and having absence of sufficient competition according to the following methodology:
  - The 279 items appearing in the alphabetical list of Essential Drugs in the National Essential Drug List (1996) of the Ministry of Health and Family Welfare and the 173 items, which are considered important by that Ministry from the point of view of their use in various Health Programmes, in emergency care etc., with the exclusion., as in the past, therefrom of sera & vaccines, blood products, combinations etc. should form the total basket out of which selection of bulk drugs be made for price regulation.
  - The ORG-MARG data of March 2001 would form the basis for determining the span of price control as suggested by DPCRC.
- The Moving Annual Total (MAT) value for any formulator in respect of any bulk drug will be arrived

at by adding the MAT values of all his single-ingredient formulations of that bulk drug, its salts, esters, stereo-isomers andderivatives, covering all the strengths, dosage forms and pack sizes listed against that formulator in all groups / categories of the ORG-MARG (March 2001).

- The MAT value for all the formulators, as defined in sub-para (iii) above, in respect of a particular bulk drug will be added to arrive at the total MAT value in the retail trade.
- The MAT value for an individual formulator, in respect of any bulk drug, as arrived at in sub-para (iii) above, will be the basis for calculating the percentage share of that formulator in the total MAT value arrived at as in sub-para (iv) above, in respect of that bulk drug.
- Bulk Drugs will be kept under price regulation if:-
  - The total MAT value, arrived at as in sub-para (iv) above, in respect of any particular bulk drug is more than Rs.2500 lakhs (Rs.25 Crore) and the percentage share, as defined in sub-para (v) above, of any of the formulators is 50% or more.
  - The total MAT value, arrived at as in sub-para (iv) above, in respect of any particular bulk drug is less than Rs.2500 lakhs (Rs.25 Crore) but more than Rs.1000 lakhs (Rs.10 Crore) and the percentage share, as defined in sub-para (v) above, of any of the formulators is 90% or more.
  - All formulations containing a bulk drug as identified above, either individually or in combination with other bulk drugs, including those not identified for price control as bulk drug, will be under price control. The Government shall, however, retain the following over-riding power:- In cases of drugs/ formulations listed by the Ministry of Health and Family Welfare, mentioned in sub-para (i) above, and those presently under price control, having

significant MAT value as per ORG-MARG but not covered under the criteria in sub-para (vi) above, as a result of this proposal, the NPPA would specially monitor intensively their price movement and consumption pattern. If any unusual movement of prices is observed or brought to the notice of the NPPA, the Authority would work out the price in accordance with the relevant provisions of the price control order.

Maximum Allowable Post-manufacturing Expenses (MAPE) Maximum Allowable Post-manufacturing Expenses (MAPE) will be 100% for indigenously manufactured formulations. Margin for Imported Formulations For imported formulations, the margin to cover selling and distribution expenses including interest and importer's profit shall not exceed fifty percent of the landed cost. Pricing of Formulations

- For Scheduled formulations, prices shall be determined as per the present practice. The time frame for granting price approvals will be two months from the date of the receipt of the complete prescribed information.
- The present stipulation that a manufacturer, distributor or wholesaler shall sell a formulation to a retailer, unless otherwise permitted under the provisions of Drugs (Prices Control) Order or any other order made thereunder, at a price equal to the retail price, as specified by an order or notified by the Government, (excluding excise duty, if any) minus sixteen percent thereof in case of Scheduled drugs, will continue.
- The present provision of limiting profitability of pharmaceutical companies, as per the Third Schedule of the present Drugs (Prices Control) Order, 1995, would be done away with. However, if necessary so to do in public interest, price of any formulation including a non-Scheduled formulation would be fixed or revised by the Government.

Ceiling Prices: Ceiling prices may be fixed for any formulation, from time to time, and it would be obligatory for all, including small scale units or those marketing under generic name, to follow the price so fixed.

Exemptions

- A manufacturer producing a new drug patented under the Indian Patent Act, 1970, and not produced elsewhere, if developed through indigenous R&D, would be eligible for exemption from price control in respect of that drug for a period of 15 years from the date of the commencement of its commercial production in the country.
- A manufacturer producing a drug in the country by a process developed through indigenous R&D and patented under the Indian Patent Act, 1970, would be eligible for exemption from price control in respect of that drug till the expiry of the patent from the date of the commencement of its commercial production in the country by the new patented process.
- A formulation involving a new delivery system developed through indigenous R&D and patented under the Indian Patent Act, 1970, for process patent for formulation involving new delivery system would be eligible for exemption from price control in favour of the patent holder formulator from the date of the commencement of its commercial production in the country till the expiry of the patent.
  - The DPCRC has suggested that the low cost drugs measured in terms of "cost per day per medicine" may be taken out of price control. Any formulator can represent to NPPA with proof of per day cost to consumer-patient. NPPA will be authorised to exempt such formulation from price control if its cost to consumer-patient does not exceed Rs. 2/- per day, under intimation to the Government.

Pricing of Scheduled Bulk Drugs

- For a Scheduled bulk drug, the rate of return in case of basic manufacture would be higher by 4 per cent over the existing 14 per cent on net worth or 22 per cent on capital employed. The time frame for granting price approvals will be 4 months from the date of the receipt of the complete prescribed information.
- The Government shall, however, retain the overriding power of fixing the maximum sale price of any bulk drug, in public interest.

MONITORING

The DPCRC's recommendations to have effective monitoring and enforcement system and to move away from the "controlled regime" to a "monitoring regime" is in the present context an extremely important recommendation as imports will increasingly compete with local drugs and pharmaceuticals in the domestic market.

A new system based on solely market prices data is required to be evolved and controls applied selectively only to cases where, either profiteering or monopoly profit seeking is noticed. The National Pharmaceutical Pricing Authority, set up in August, 1997, would need to be revamped and reoriented for this purpose.

It will continue to be entrusted with the task of price fixation / price revision and other related matters, and would be empowered to take final decisions. It would also monitor the prices of decontrolled drugs and formulations and oversee the implementation of the drug prices control orders. The Government would have the power of review of the price fixation/and price revision orders/notifications of NPPA. Although the prices of some bulk drugs have been steadily decreasing, yet the same do not get reflected in the retail price of non-Scheduled formulations.

Also, there is need to check high margin/commission offered to the trade by printing high prices on the labels of medicines to the detriment of the consumers. It is, therefore, proposed to strengthen the National Pharmaceutical Pricing Authority by providing appropriate powers under the DPCO which would make it mandatory for the manufacturer to furnish all information as called for by NPPA and also to regulate such prices, wherever, required.

Other recommendations of DPCRC like giving powers to drug control authorities to dispose of small and petty offences etc., will require an amendment to the Essential Commodities Act. This suggestion is considered not practicable. Monitoring price movement of drugs sold in the country as well as that of imported formulations will require developing appropriate mechanism in the NPPA.

Drug Price Equalization Account (DPEA)Provision would be made in the new Drugs (Prices Control) Order (DPCO) to ensure that amounts which have already accrued to the DPEA and those which are likely to accrue as a result of action in the past, are protected and used for the purpose stipulated in the existing DPCO.

PREVENTION OF CRUELTY OF ANIMALS ACT

In August, international retail giants Eddie Bauer, L.L. Bean, Timberland, Liz Claireborne, Casual Corner, Travel 2000 and Bader joined other retail chains to boycott Indian leather and leather products.

Between April 2000 and January 2001, India exported leather and leather products worth $1.3 billion, registering a 6.8 per cent drop over the corresponding period in the previous year. Germany, with a 19 per cent share, is the largest buyer of Indian leather products followed by the United Kingdom (17 per cent) and the United States (16 per cent). These and other major importers - Italy, France, Spain, the Netherlands, Australia, New Zealand, Denmark, Greece, Hong Kong and Canada - are now threatening to ban Indian leather products.

The Indian leather industry handles approximately 230 million metres of hides and skins annually. According to the Food and Agriculture Organisation (FAO), 24,300,000 head of cattle, 46,700,000 goats and 16,000,000 pigs were killed last year in India. These figures pertain to the 3,600 legally operating abattoirs and do not include animals killed in the estimated 32,000 illegal or unlicensed ones.

The leather industry feels that it is being unfairly targeted. Says M.M. Hashim, chairman of the Council for Leather Exports (CLE) and a Chennai-based exporter: "While no doubt there is widespread violation of animal welfare laws during the transportation and slaughtering of animals, targeting the leather industry serves no purpose." According to the CLE, leather is only a by-product, accounting for barely one-tenth of the value of animals.

According to Hashim, although the CLE's initial reaction to the campaign was just to state that the leather industry was not directly involved in the transportation and slaughtering of animals, it soon took a lead role in urging governments to amend the laws to include proper treatment of animals in slaughterhouses and to book violators of the Prevention of Cruelty to Animals Act, 1960.

In mid-2000, the CLE worked out a detailed action plan, covering every aspect of dealing with animals, including amendments to the legislation and action plans for specific places. This was adopted by 10 State governments in September 2000. The CLE has followed it up by urging the governments to implement the action plans. According to the People for the Ethical Treatment of Animals (PETA), the international voluntary organisation that spearheads the campaign in India, all atrocities listed in the Prevention of Cruelty to Animals Act (beating, kicking, overloading and overcrowding animals during transit; depriving animals of food and water during transportation; selling abused or mutilated animals; and killing animals cruelly) are committed in the leather and meat industries.

Animal transport laws specify that only six cows be transported in a lorry. But, according to PETA, four times as many animals are forced into a single vehicle. Since 1998, various national and international voluntary groups working to prevent cruelty against animals have pressured the Indian government to implement animal protection laws. But, according to PETA, the government has failed to take action against any offenders. According to PETA's Indian representative, James Baker, his organisation was invited by the Indian animal protection groups two years ago to draw international attention to the issue. PETA began sending out letters and meeting government officials, urging them to implement the laws.

Since all its attempts turned futile and animals continued to be treated cruelly, it urged international buyers to stop purchasing Indian leather. Says Baker: "Targeting exports, we felt, would have a major impact as leather and leather products are India's major export earners, valued 11 times more than its meat exports."

PETA has videographed animals being transported and slaughtered under appalling conditions in several States. Baker says: "In the last 21 years that we have been fighting animal abuse the world over, we find India's treatment of cows and cattle to be among the cruellest in the world." PETA has been fighting animal abuse in China, another major leather exporter. Several international buyers have since stopped buying leather products from China.

The organisation's other major campaigns are against the killing of dogs in Taiwan and Turkey, bullfighting in Spain, capture of baby elephants in South Africa and breeding of bears for the preparation of exotic medicines in China. PETA also campaigns against McDonalds and Burger King for the cruel way in which they kill animals for meat. Animals slaughtered for their meat and skin are most often transported in abysmal conditions. Most of them get injured, and many are trampled or gored to death as they are thrown about in the lorries that drive at breakneck speed. Also, animals are tied together with ropes running through their pierced noses and forced into "death marches" for hundreds of kilometres, illegally crossing State borders as several States have banned cow slaughter.

The handlers force the pace of the animals by snapping their tails at each joint and rubbing tobacco, chilly powder or salt into their eyes. Thus, by the time the animals arrive at the slaughterhouses, many of them would be so sick that they have to be dragged inside. As for the method of slaughtering, fortunate are those whose throats are slit. Others have their legs hacked off or are skinned alive.

The animals suffer from factory over-crowding, unanaesthetised castration, branding, tail-docking and dehorning. Since it is illegal to kill healthy young cattle, they are often maimed: their legs are broken or they are poisoned so that they can be declared fit for slaughter.

"Exotic" animals such as alligators are also factory farmed for their skins. According to PETA, ranched alligators, of over 600, are kept in small enclosures that reek of rancid meat, alligator waste and stagnant water. Although alligators may naturally live up to 60 years, on farms they are usually butchered before they are four years old. Snakes and lizards are often skinned alive because of the widespread belief that live flaying enhances the suppleness of the finished leather. Kids are boiled alive to make kid gloves, and the skin of aborted calves and lambs are used as they are considered especially "luxurious".

In May 2000, PETA put its campaign against Indian leather goods on hold for a year at the request of the industry which promised to urge the governments to implement the Prevention of Cruelty to Animals Act and to convince traders not to buy from abattoirs that transport and slaughter animals cruelly.

PETA's investigation found that even after the moratorium period, things had not changed and the government had done little to improve the treatment of animals. So PETA resumed its campaign by circulating the video footage of cruelty against animals.

According to D.K. Mittal, Joint Secretary in the Ministry of Commerce, the Indian leather industry gets most of its raw materials from cows and buffaloes that have died naturally. According to him, most States, barring West Bengal, Kerala, Karnataka and those in the northeastern region, have banned cow slaughter. There are laws governing the treatment and transportation of animals. The leather industry points out that it is not viable to kill an animal for its hide alone. Says CLE's footwear panel chairman M.R. Ahmed: "If any animal is transported cruelly that will damage its skin and the value of the skin falls drastically." The difference in the value of good and bad skin is about 70 per cent.

Motil Lal Sethi, president of the Indian Leather Garments Association, says: "We built our factories to U.S. standards, we were upgrading our tanneries and putting our house in order, when this jolt came." But Maneka Gandhi, Minister for Social Justice and Empowerment and an animal rights activist, believes the leather industry has got what it deserves. According to her, the leather industry not only causes pollution but is responsible for the cruelty to animals.

While Alan Marks, vice-president, Corporate Communications, Gap Inc., which has stopped buying Indian leather and leather products, is unwilling to pass any judgment on the treatment of animals in India, his company does not plan to change its policy in the immediate future unless slaughterhouses and leather garment factories adhere to certain standards.

While the leather industry is the most affected, the implementation of the laws governing animal treatment is not its responsibility. The government, apart from strengthening the law, must monitor animal transportation and implement the slaughter norms strictly in order to save the labour-intensive industry.

Chapter 3

Pharmacy Acts

INTRODUCTION

Short title, extent and commencement:

- This Act may be called the Pharmacy Act, 1948.
- It extends to the whole of India except the State of Jammu and Kashmir.]
- It shall come into force at once, but Chapters III, IV and V shall take effect in a particular State from such date as the State Government may, by notification in the Official Gazette, appoint in this behalf:
- Provided that where on account of the territorial changes brought about by the reorganisation of States on the 1st day of November, 1956, Chapters III, IV and V have effect only in a part of a State, the said Chapters shall take effect in the remaining part of that State from such date as the State Government may in like manner appoint.]
- *Interpretation:* — In this Act, unless there is anything repugnant in the subject or context:
- "agreement" means an agreement entered into under section 20;
- "approved" means approved by the Central Council under section 12 or section 14;
- [(c) "Central Council" means the Pharmacy Council of India constituted under section 3;
- "Central Register" means the register of pharmacists maintained by the Central Council under section 15A;
- (da) "Executive Committee" means the Executive

Committee of the Central Council or of the State Council, as the context may require;

- "Indian University" means a University within the meaning of section 3 of the University Grants Commission Act, 1956, (3 of 1956) and includes such other institutions, being institutions established by or under a Central Act, as the Central Government may, by notification in the Official Gazette, specify in this behalf;]
- *[(f) "medical practitioner" means a person*:
  - Holding a qualification granted by an authority specified or notified under section 3 of the Indian Medical Degrees Act, 1916 (7 of 1916), or specified in the Schedules to the Indian Medical Council Act, 1956 (102 of 1956); or
  - Registered or eligible for registration in a medical register of a State meant for the registration of persons practising the modern scientific system of medicine; or
  - Registered in a medical register of a State, who, although not falling within sub-clause(i) or sub-clause (ii) is declared by a general or special order made by the State Government in this behalf as a person practising the modern scientific system of medicine for the purposes of this Act; or
  - Registered or eligible for registration in the register of dentists for a State under the Dentists Act, 1948 (16 of 1948); or
  - Who is engaged in the practise of veterinary medicine and who possesses qualifications approved by the State Government;]
  - "Prescribed" means in Chapter II prescribed by regulations made under section 18, and elsewhere prescribed by rules made under section 46; [(h) "register" means a register of pharma-cists prepared and maintained under Chapter.

- "Registered pharmacist" means a person whose name is for the time being entered in the register of the State in which he is for the time being residing or carrying on his profession or business of pharmacy;
- "State Council" means a State Council of Pharmacy constituted under section 19, and includes a Joint State Council of Pharmacy constituted in accordance with an agreement under section 20;
- "University Grants Commission" means the University Grants Commission established under section 4 of the University Grants Commission Act, 1956 (3 of 1956).]

1. For Statement of Objects and Reasons, see Gazette of India, 1947, pt. V, p. 469; and for Report of select committee, see Gazette of India, 1948, pt. V, p. 6 The Act has been extended to Dadra and Nagar Haveli by Reg. 6 of 1963, sec. 2 and Sch.1; to Pondicherry by Reg. 7 of 1963, sec. 3 and Sch I; to Goa, Daman and Diu by Reg. 11 of 1963, sec. 3 and Sch.

And to Lakshadweep by Reg. 8 of 1965, sec. 3 and Sch. The Act has been modified in its application to the States of Maharashtra, Gujarat, Mysore and Rajasthan by S.O. 2814, dated 14th August, 1964, Gazette of India, 1964 Extra., Pt. II Sec. 3(ii), p. 717.

The Act has been modified in its application to the State of Tamil Nadu by the Madras adaptation of Laws (Central Acts) Order, 1957 and the Madras Adaptation of Laws (Central Acts) Order, 1961. 2. Subs. by Act 24 of 1959, sec. 2, for sub-section (2) (w.e.f. 1-5-1960)3.

The words "not later than three years from the commencement of this Act, omitted by Act 24 of 1959" sec. 2, (w.e.f. 1-5-1960). 4. Ins. by Act of 24 of 1959 sec. 2 (w.e.f. 1-5-1960).5. Subs. by Act 70 of 1976, sec. 2, for clauses (c), (d) and (e) (w.e.f.1-9-1976).6. Subs. by Act 24 of 1959, sec. 3, for clause (f) (w.e.f. 1-5-1960). 7. Subs. by Act 70 of 1976, sec. 2, for clauses (h), (i) and (j) (w.e.f. 1-5-1976). 8. Clause (k), ins by the A.O. 1950 was omitted by Act 24 of 1959, sec. 3 (w.e.f. 1-5-1960).

CONSTITUTION AND COMPOSITION OF CENTRAL COUNCIL

Constitution and Composition of Central Council. The Central Government shall, as soon as may be, constitute a Central Council consisting of the following members, namely:

- Six members, among whom there shall be at least one teacher of each of the subjects, pharmaceutical chemistry, pharmacy, pharmacology and pharmacognosy elected by the [University Grants Commission] from among persons on the teaching staff of an Indian University or a college affiliated thereto which grants a degree or diploma in pharmacy;
- Six members, of whom at least [four] shall be persons possessing a degree or diploma in, and practising pharmacy or pharmaceutical chemistry, nominated by the Central Government;
- One member elected from amongst themselves by the members of the Medical Council of India;
- The Director General, Health Services, ex officio or if he is unable to attend any meeting, a person authorized by him in writing to do so;
- [(dd) the Drugs Controller, India, ex officio or if he is unable to attend any meeting, a person authorised by him in writing to do so;]
- The Director of the Central Drugs Laboratory, ex officio;
- [(f) a representative of the University Grants Commission and a representative of the All India Council for Technical Education;]
- One member to represent each State elected [from amongst themselves] by the members of each State Council, who shall be a registered pharmacist;
- One member to represent each State nominated by [the] State Government, who shall be a registered pharmacist.
- Provided that for five years from the date on which the Pharmacy (Amendment) Act, 1976, comes into

force the Government of each Union territory shall, instead of electing a member under clause (g) nominate one member, being a person eligible for registration under section 31, to represent that territory.]

- *Incorporation of Central Council*: The Council constituted under section 3 shall be a body corporate by the name of the Pharmacy Council of India, having perpetual succession and a common seal, with power to acquire and hold property both movable and immovable, and shall by the said name sue and be sued.
- President and Vice-President of Central Council. The President and Vice-President of the Central Council shall be elected by the members of the said Council from among themselves.
- [The President] or Vice-President shall hold office as such for a term not exceeding five years and not extending beyond the expiry of his term as member of the Central Council, but subject to his being a member of the Central Council, he shall be eligible for re-election:
- [Provided that if his term of office as a member of the Central Council expires before the expiry of the full term for which he is elected as President or Vice-President, he shall, if he is re-elected or re-nominated as a member of the Central Council, continue to holdoffice as President or Vice-President for the full term for which he is elected to such office.]
- *Mode of elections*: Elections under this Chapter shall be conducted in the prescribed manner, and where any dispute arises regarding any such election it shall be referred to the Central Government whose decision shall be final.
- *Term of office and casual vacancies*: Subject to the provisions of this section, a nominated or elected member shall hold office for a term of five years from the date of his nomination or election or until

his successor has been duly nominated or elected, whichever is longer.

- A nominated or elected member may at any time resign his membership by writing under his hand addressed to the President, and the seat of such member shall thereupon become vacant.
- A nominated or elected member shall be deemed to have vacated his seat if he is absent without excuse, sufficient in the opinion of the Central Council, from three consecutive meetings of the Central Council or if he is elected under clause (a), (c) or (g) of section 3, if he ceases to be a member of the teaching staff, Medical Council of India or a registered pharmacist, as the case may be.
- A casual vacancy in the Central Council shall be filled by fresh nomination or election, as the case may be, and the person nominated or elected to fill the vacancy shall hold office only for the remainder of the term for which the member whose place he takes was nominated or elected.
- No act done by the Central Council shall be called in question on the ground merely of the existence of any vacancy in, or any defect in the constitution of the Central Council.
- Members of the Central Council shall be eligible for re-nomination or re-election.
- *[8. Staff remuneration and allowances.*The Central Council shall-Appoint a Registrar who shall act as the Secretary to that Council and who may also, if deemed expedient by that Council, act as the Treasurer thereof;
- Appoint such other officers and servants as that Council deems necessary to enable it to carry out its functions under this Act;
- Require and take from the Registrar, or any other officer or servant, such security for the due performance of his duties as that Council may consider necessary,

- With the previous sanction of the Central Government, fix:
  - The remuneration and allowances to be paid to the President, Vice-President, and other members of that Council,
  - The pay and allowances and other conditions of service of officers and servants of that Council.]

THE EXECUTIVE COMMITTEE

- The Central Council shall, as soon as may be, constitute an Executive Committee consisting of the President (who shall be Chairman of the Executive Committee) and Vice-President, ex officio, and five other members elected by the Central Council from amongst its members.
- A member of the Executive Committee shall hold office as such until the expiry of his term of office as member of the Central Council, but, subject to his being a member of the Central Council, he shall be eligible for re-election.
- In addition to the powers and duties conferred and imposed upon it by this Act the Executive Committee shall exercise and discharge such powers and duties as may be prescribed.
- *[9A. Other Committees:*—(1) The Central Council may constitute from among its members other committees for such general or special purposes as that Council may deem necessary and for such periods not exceeding five years as it may specify, and may co-opt for a like period persons, who are not members of the Central Council, as members of such committees.
- The remuneration and allowances to be paid to the members of such committees shall be fixed by the Central Council with the previous sanction of the Central Government.
- The business before such committees shall be conducted in accordance with such regulations as may be made under this Act.]

- Subs. by Act 70 of 1976, sec. 3, for "authority known as the Inter-University Board" (w.e.f. 1-9-1976).
- Subs. by Act 70 of 1976, sec. 3, for "three" (w.e.f. 1-9-1976).
- Ins.by Act 24 of 1959, sec.4 (w.e.f. 1-5-1960).
- Subs. by Act 70 of 1976, sec. 3, for clause (f) (w.e.f. 1-9-1976).
- The word and letter "Part A" ommited by the Adaptation of Laws (No.3) Order, 1956.
- Ins. by Act 70 of 1976, sec. 3 (w.e.f. 1-9-1976).
- Subs. by the Adaptation of Laws (No. 3) Order, 1956, for "each such".
- The words "either a registered medical practitioner or" omitted by Act 70 of 1976, sec.3 (w.e.f. 1-9-1976).
- Subs. by Act. 70 of 1976, sec. 3, for the former proviso (w.e.f. 1-9-1976).
- Explanation omitted by Act 70 of 1976, sec.3 (w.e.f. 1-9-1976).
- Proviso omitted by Act 24 of 1959, sec. 5 (w.e.f. 1-5-1960).
- Subs. by Act 70 of 1976, sec. 4, for "An elected President" (w.e.f. 1-9-1976).
- Added by Act 70 of 1976, sec. 4. (w.e.f.1-9-1976).
- The words, "other than a nominated President" omitted by Act 70 of 1976, sec. 5 (w.e.f. 1-9-1976).
- Subs. by Act 70 of 1976, sec. 6, for sec.8 (w.e.f. 1-9-1976).
- Ins. by Act 70 of 1976, sec. 7 (w.e.f. 1-9-1976).

EDUCATION REGULATIONS

- Subject to the provisions of this section, the Central Council may, subject to the approval of the Central Government, make regulations, to be called the Education Regulations, prescribing the minimum standard of education required for qualification as a pharmacist.
- In particular and without prejudice to the generality

of the foregoing power, the Education Regulations may prescribe.

- The nature and period of study and of practical training to be undertaken before admission to an examination;
- The equipment and facilities to be provided for students undergoing approved courses of study;
- The subjects of examination and the standards therein to be attained;
- Any other conditions of admission to examinations.
- Copies of the draft of the Education Regulations and of all subsequent, amendments thereof shall be furnished by the Central Council to all State Governments, and the Central Council shall before submitting the Education Regulations or any amendment thereof, as the case may be, to the Central Government for approval under sub-section (1) take into consideration the comments of any State Government received within three months from the furnishing of the copies as aforesaid.
- The Education Regulations shall be published in the Official Gazette and in such other manner as the Central Council may direct.
- The Executive Committee shall from time to time report to the Central Council on the efficacy of the Education Regulations and may recommend to the Central Council such amendments thereof as it may think fit.
- Application of Education Regulations to States. At any time after the constitution of the State Council and after consultation with the State Council, the State Government may, by notification in the Official Gazette, declare that the Education Regulations shall take effect in the State: Provided that where no such declaration has been made, the Education Regulations shall take effect in the State on the expiry of three years from the date of the constitution of the State Council.
- Approved courses of study and examinations. (1)

Any authority in a State] which conducts a course of study for pharmacists may apply to the Central Council for approval of the course, and the Central Council, if satisfied, after such enquiry as it thinks fit to make, that the said course of study is in conformity with the Education Regulations, shall declare the said course of study to be an approved course of study for the purpose of admission to an approved examination for pharmacists.

- Any authority in a State which holds an examination in pharmacy may apply to the Central Council for approval of the examination, and the Central Council, if satisfied, after such enquiry as it thinks fit to make, that the said examination is in conformity with the Education Regulations, shall declare the said examination to be an approved examination for the purpose of qualifying for registration as a pharmacist under this Act.
- Every authority in the State which conducts an approved course of study or holds an approved examination shall furnish such information as the Central Council may, from time to time, require as to the courses of study and training and examination to be undergone, as to the ages at which such courses of study and examination are required to be undergone and generally as to the requisites for such courses of study and examination.
- Withdrawal of approval. (1) Where the Executive Committee reports to the Central Council that an approved course of study or an approved examination does not continue to be in conformity with the Education Regulations, the Central Council shall give notice to the authority concerned of its intention to take into consideration the question of withdrawing the declaration of approval accorded to the course of study or examination, as the case may be, and the said authority shall within three months from the receipt of such notice forward to the Central

Council through the State Government such representation in the matter as it may wish to make.

- After considering any representation which may be received from the authority concerned and any observations thereon which the State Government may think fit to make, the council may declare that the course of study or the examination shall be deemed to be approved only when completed or passed, as the case may be, before a specified date.
- Qualifications granted outside the territories to which this Act extends. The Central Council, if it is satisfied that any qualification in pharmacy granted by an authority outside the [territories to which this Act extends] affords a sufficient guarantee of the requisite skill and knowledge, may declare such qualification to be an approved qualification for the purpose of qualifying for registration under this Act, and may for reasons appearing to it sufficient at any time declare that such qualification shall be deemed [subject to such additional conditions, if any ,as may be specified by the Central Council,] to be approved only when granted before or after a specified date:

Provided that no person other than a [citizen of India] possessing such qualification shall be deemed to be qualified for registration unless by the law and practice of the State or Country in which the qualification is granted, persons of Indian origin holding such qualification are permitted to enter and practise the profession of pharmacy.

- *Mode of declarations*: All declarations under section 12, section 13 or section 14 shall be made by resolution passed at a meeting of the Central Council, and shall have effect as soon as they are published in the Official Gazette.
- *[15A. The Central Register*: The Central Council shall cause to be maintained in the prescribed manner a register of pharmacists to be known as the Central Register,which shall contain the names of all persons for the time being entered in the register for a State.

- Each State Council shall supply to the Central Council five copies of the register for the State as soon as may be after the first day of April of each year, and the Registrar, of each State Council, shall inform the Central Council, without delay, all additions to, and other amendments in, the Register for the State made from time to time.
- It shall be the duty of the Registrar of the Central Council to keep the Central Register in accordance with the orders made by the Central Council, and from time to time to revise the Central Register and publish it in the Gazette of India.
- The Central Register shall be deemed to be public document within the meaning of the Indian Evidence Act, 1872 (1 of 1872) and may be proved by the production of a copy of the Register as published in the Gazette of India.
- *Registration in the Central Register*: The Registrar of the Central Council shall, on receipt of the report of registration of a person in the register for a State, enter his name in the Central Register.]
- The words "of India" omitted by the A.O. 1950.
- Subs. by the Adaptation of Laws (No 3) Order, 1956, for "Part A States and Part C States" which had been subs. by the A.O. 1950, for "Provinces of India".
- Ins. by Act 70 of 1976, sec. 8 (w.e.f. 1-9-1976).
- Subs. by the A.O. 1950, for "British subject of Indian domicile".
- Ins. by Act 70 of 1976, sec.9 (w.e.f. 1-9-1976).

INSPECTION

- The Executive Committee may appoint such number of Inspectors as it may deem requisite for the purposes of this Chapter.
- *An Inspector may*:
  - Inspect any institution which provides an approvedcourse of study;
  - Attend at any approved examination;

   – Inspect any institution whose authorities have applied for the approval of its course of study or examination under this Chapter, and attend, as it may deem requisite for the purposes of this Chapter at any examination of such institution.

- An Inspector attending at any examination under sub-section (2) shall not interfere with the conduct of the examination, but he shall report to the Executive Committee on the sufficiency of every examination he attends and on any other matter in regard to which the Executive Committee may require him to report.
- The Executive Committee shall forward a copy of every such report to the authority or institution concerned, and shall also forward a copy together with any comments thereon which the said authority or institution may have made, to the Central Government and to the Government of the State in which the authority or institution is situated.
- *Information to be furnished*:The Central Council shal! furnish copies of its minutes and of the minutes of the Executive Committee and annual report of its activities to the Central Government.
- The Central Government may publish in such manner as it may think fit any report,[or copy], furnished to it under this section or under section 16.
- *[17A Accounts and audit*: The Central Council shall maintain proper accounts and other relevant records and prepare an annual statements of accounts, in accordance with such general directions as may be issued and in such form as may be specified by the Central Government in consultation with the Comptroller and Auditor-General of India.
- The accounts of the Central Council shall be audited annually by the Comptroller and Auditor-General of India or any person authorized by him in this behalf and any expenditure incurred by him or any person

so authorized in connection with such audit shall be payable by the Central Council to the Comptroller and Auditor-General of India.

- The Comptroller and Auditor-General of India and any person authorized by him in connection with the audit of the accounts of the Central Council shall have the same rights and privileges and authority in connection with such audit as the Comptroller and Auditor-General of India has in connection with the audit of Government accounts, and in particular, shall have the right to demand the production of books of accounts, connected vouchers and other documents and papers.
- The accounts of the Central Council as certified by the Comptroller and Auditor-General of India or any person authorized by him in this behalf together with the audit report thereon shall be forwarded annually to the Central Council which shall forward the same with its comments to the Central Government.]
- Power to make regulations.— (1) The Central Council may, with the approval of the Central Government [by notification in the Official Gazette,] make regulations consistent with this Act to carry out the purposes of this Chapter.
- In particular and without prejudice to the generality of the foregoing power, such regulations may provide for-
- [(a) the management of the property of the Central Council;]
- The manner in which elections under this Chapter shall be conducted;
- The summoning and holding of meeting of the Central Council, the times and places at which such meetings shall be held, the conduct of business thereat and the number of members necessary to constitute a quorum;
- The functions of the Executive Committee, the summoning and holding meetings thereof, the times

and places at which such meetings shall be held, and the number of members necessary to constitute a quorum;

- The powers and duties of the President and Vice-President;
- The qualifications, the term of office and the powers and duties of the [Registrar, Secretary], Inspectors and other officers and servants of the Central Council, including the amount and nature of the security to be furnished by the [Registrar or any other officer or servant].
- [(g) the manner in which the Central Register shall be maintained and given publicity;
- Constitution and functions of the committees other than Executive Committee, the summoning and holding of meetings thereof, the time and place at which such meetings shall be held, the number of members necessary to constitute the quorum.]
- Until regulations are made by the Central Council under this section, the President may, with the previous sanction of the Central Government, make such regulations under this section, including those to provide for the manner in which the first elections to the Central Council shall be conducted, as may be necessary for carrying into effect the provisions of this Chapter, and any regulations so made may be altered or rescinded by the Central Council in exercise of its powers under this section.
- Every regulation made under this Act shall be laid, as soon as may be after it is made, before each House of Parliament, while it is in session, for a total period of thirty days which may be comprised in one session or in two or more successive sessions, and if, before the expiry of the session immediately following the session or the successive sessions aforesaid, both Houses agree in making any modification in the regulation or both Houses agree that the regulation should not be made, the regulation shall thereafter

have effect only in such modified form or be of no effect, as the case may be; so, however, that any such modification or annulment shall be without prejudice to the validity of anything previously done under that regulation.]

STATE PHARMACY COUNCILS

Constitution and Composition of State Councils: Except where a Joint State Council is constituted in accordance with an agreement made under section 20, the State Government shall constitute a State Council consisting of the following members, namely:

- Six members, elected from amongst themselves by registered pharmacists of the State;
- Five members, of whom at least [three] shall be persons possessing a prescribed degree or diploma in pharmacy or pharmaceutical chemistry or [registered pharmacists], nominated by the State Government;
- One member elected from amongst themselves by the members of each Medical Council or the Council of Medical Registration of the State, as the case may be;
- The chief administrative medical officer of the State ex officio or if he is unable to attend any meeting, a person authorized by him in writing to do so;
- (dd) the officer-in-charge of drugs control organization of the State under the [Drugs and Cosmetics Act, 1940 (23 of 1940)], ex officio or if he is unable to attend any meeting, a person authorized by him in writing to do so;]
- The Government Analyst under the [Drugs and Cosmetics Act, 1940 (23 of 1940)], ex officio, or where there is more than one, such one as the State Government may appoint in this behalf:

Provided that where an agreement is made under clause (b) of sub-section (1) of section 20, the agreement may provide that the State Council to serve the needs of the other participating States also shall be augmented by not more than two members, of whom at least one shall at all times be a person possessing a prescribed degree or diploma in pharmacy or pharmaceutical chemistry or a [registered pharmacist], nominated by the Government of each of the said other participating States, and where the agreement so provides, the composition of the State Council shall be deemed to be augmented accordingly.

- *Inter-State agreements:* Two or more State Government may enter into an agreement to be in force for such period and to be subject to renewal for such further periods, if any, as may be specified in the agreement, to provide:
  - For the constitution of a Joint State Council for all the participating States,
  - That the State Council of one State shall serve the needs of the other participating States.
  - In addition to such matters as are in this Act specified, an agreement under this section may—
  - Provide for the apportionment between the participating State of the expenditure in connection with the State Council or Joint State Council;
  - Determine which of the participating State Governments shall exercise the several functions of the State Government under this Act, and the references in this Act to the State Government shall be construed accordingly;
  - Provide for consultation between the participat-ing State Governments either generally or with reference to particular matters arising under this Act;
  - Make such incidental and ancillary provisions, not inconsistent with this Act, as may be deemed necessary or expedient for giving effect to the agreement.
- An agreement under this section shall be published in the Official Gazettes of the participating States.
- *Composition of Joint State Councils*: A Joint State Council shall consist of the following members, namely.

- Such number of members, being not less than three and not more than five as the agreement shall provide elected from amongst themselves by the registered pharmacists of each of the participating States;
- Such number of members, being not less than two and not more than four as the agreement shall provide, nominated by each participating State Government;
- One member elected from amongst themselves by the members of each Medical Council or the Council of Medical Registration of each participating State as the case may be;
- The chief administrative medical officer of each participating State, ex officio, or if he is unable to attend any meeting, a person authorized by him in writing to do so;
- [(dd) the officer-in-charge of drugs control organization of each participating State under the [Drugs and Cosmetics Act, 1940], ex officio, or if he is unable to attend any meeting, a person authorized by him in writing to do so;]
- The Government Analyst under the [Drugs and Cosmetics Act, 1940 (23 of 1940)], of each participating State, ex officio, or where there is more than one in any such State, such one as the State Government may appoint in this behalf.
- The agreement may provide that within the limits specified in clauses (a) and (b) of sub-section (1), the number of members to be elected or nominated under those clauses may or may not be the same in respect of each participating State.
- Of the members, nominated by each State Government under clause (b) of sub-section (1), [more than half] shall be persons possessing a prescribed degree or diploma in pharmacy or pharmaceutical chemistry or [registered pharmacists].

- Incorporation of State Councils. — Every State Council shall be a body corporate by such name as may be notified by the State Government in the Official Gazette or, in the case of a Joint State Council, as may be determined in the agreement, having perpetual succession and a common seal, with power to acquire or hold property both movable and immovable and shall by the said name sue and be sued.

- *President and Vice-President of State Council*: The President and Vice-President of the State Council be elected by the members from amongst themselves: Provided that for five years from the first constitution of the State Council the President shall be a person nominated by the State Government who shall hold office at the pleasure of the State Government and where he is not already a member, shall be a member of the State Council in addition to the members referred to in section 19 or section 21, as the case may be.
- The President or Vice-President shall hold office as such for a term not exceeding five years and not extending beyond the expiry of his term as a member of the State Council, but subject to his being a member of the State Council, he shall be eligible for re-election: Provided that if his term of office as a member of the State Council expires before the expiry of the full term for which he is elected as President or Vice-President, he shall, if he is re-elected or re-nominated as a member of the State Council, continue to hold office for the full term for which he is elected as President or Vice-President.

MODE OF ELECTIONS

Mode of elections. —Elections under this Chapter shall be conducted in the prescribed manner, and where any dispute arises regarding any such election, it shall be referred to the State Government whose decision shall be final.

- *Term of office and casual vacancies*: Subject to the provisions of this section, a nominated or elected member, other than nominated President, shall hold office for a term of five years from the date of his nomination or election or until his successor has been duly nominated or elected, whichever is longer.
- A nominated or elected member may at any time resign his membership by writing under his hand addressed to the President, and the seat of such member shall thereupon become vacant.
- A nominated or elected member shall be deemed to have vacated his seat if he is absent without excuse sufficient in theopinion of the State Council from three consecutive meetings of the State Council, or if he is elected under clause (a) or (c) of section 19 or 21, if he ceases to be a registered pharmacist or causes to be a member of the Medical Council or Council of Medical Registration of the State, as the case may be.
- A casual vacancy in the State Council shall be filled by fresh nomination or election, as the case may be, and the person nominated or elected to fill the vacancy shall hold office only for the remainder of the term for which the member whose place he takes was nominated or elected.
- No act done by the State Council shall be called in question on the ground merely of the existence of any vacancy in, or any defect in the constitution of, the State Council.
- Members of the State Council shall be eligible for re-nomination or re-election.
- *Staff, remuneration and allowances*: The State Council may, with the previous sanction of the State Government,
- Appoint a Registrar who shall also act as Secretary and, if so decided by the State Council, Treasurer, of the State Council;
- Appoint such other officers and servants as may be

required to enable the State Council to carry out its functions under this Act;
- Fix the salaries and allowances and other conditions of service of the Secretary and other officers and servants of the State Council;
- Fix the rates of allowances payable to members of the State Council:

Provided that for the first four years from the first constitution of the State Council, the Registrar shall be a person appointed by the State Government, who shall hold office during the pleasure of the State Government.

- *Inspection*: A State Council may, with the previous sanction of the State Government, appoint Inspectors having the prescribed qualifications for the purposes of Chapters of this Act.
- *An Inspector may*: Inspect any premises where drugs are compounded or dispensed and submit a written report to the Registrar;
- Enquire whether a person who is engaged in compounding or dispensing of drugs is a registered pharmacist;
- Investigate any complaint made in writing in respect of any contravention of this Act and report to the Registrar;
- Institute prosecution under the order of the Executive Committee of the State Council;
- Exercise such other powers as may be necessary for carrying out the purposes of Chapters III, IV and V of this Act or any rules made thereunder.
- Any person wilfully obstructing an Inspector in the exercise of the powers conferred on him by or under this Act or any rules made thereunder shall be punishable with imprisonment for a term which may extend to six months, or with fine not exceeding one thousand rupees, or with both.
- Every Inspector shall be deemed to be a public servant within the meaning of section 21 of the Indian Penal Code (45 of 1860).]

- *The Executive Committee*: The State Council shall, as soon as may be, constitute an Executive Committee consisting of the President (who shall be Chairman of the Executive Committee) and Vice-President, ex officio and such number of other members elected by the State Council from amongst themselves as may be prescribed.
- A member of the Executive Committee shall hold office as such until the expiry of his term of office as member of the State Council, but, subject to his being a member of the State Council, he shall be eligible for re-election.
- In addition to the powers and duties conferred and imposed upon it by this Act, the Executive Committee shall exercise and discharge such powers and duties as may be prescribed.
- *Information to be furnished*: The State Council shall furnish such reports, copies of its minutes and of the minutes of the Executive Committee, and abstracts of its accounts to the State Government as the State Government may from time to time require and copies thereof shall be sent to the Central Council.
- The State Government may publish, in such manner as it may think fit, any report, copy, abstract or other information furnished to it under this section.

REGISTRATION OF PHARMACISTS

Preparation and maintenance of register:

- As soon as may be after this chapter has taken effect in any State, the State Government shall cause to be prepared in the manner hereinafter provided a register of pharmacists for the State.
- The State Council shall as soon as possible after it is constituted assume the duty of maintaining the register in accordance with the provisions of this Act.
- *The register shall include the following particulars, namely*:
  - The full name and residential address of the registered person;

- The date of his first admission to the register;
- His qualifications for registration;
- His professional address, and if he is employed by any person, the name of such person;
- Such further particulars as may be prescribed.

Preparation of first register: For the purpose of preparing the first register, the State Government shall by notification in the Official Gazette constitute a Registration Tribunal consisting of three persons, and shall also appoint a Registrar who shall act as Secretary of the Registration Tribunal.

- The State Government shall, by the same or a like notification, appoint a date on or before which applications for registration, which shall be accompanied by the prescribed fee, shall be made to the Registration Tribunal.
- The Registration Tribunal shall examine every application received on or before the appointed date, and if it is satisfied that the applicant is qualified for registration under section 31, shall direct the entry of the name of the applicant on the register.
- The first register so prepared shall thereafter be published in such manner as the State Government may direct, and any person aggrieved by a decision of the Registration Tribunal expressed or implied in the register as so published may, within sixty days from the date of such publication, appeal to an authority appointed by the State Government in this behalf by notification in the Official Gazette.
- The Registrar shall amend the register in accordance with the decisions of the authority appointed under sub-section (4) and shall thereupon issue to every person whose name is entered in the register a certificate of registration in the prescribed form.
- Upon the constitution of the State Council, the register shall be given into its custody, and the State Government may direct that all or any specified part of the application fees for registration in the first register shall be paid to the credit of the State Council.

- Qualifications for entry on first register. 1[A person who has attained the age of eighteen years shall be entitled] on payment of the prescribed fee to have his name entered in the first register if he resides, or carries on the business or profession of pharmacy, in the State and if he:–
- Holds a degree or diploma in pharmacy or pharmaceutical chemistry or a chemist and druggist diploma of an Indian University or a State Government, as the case may be, or a prescribed qualification granted by an authority outside 2 India, or
- Holds a degree of an Indian University other than a degree in pharmacy or pharmaceutical chemistry, and has been engaged in the compounding of drugs in a hospital or dispensary or other place in which drugs are regularly dispensed on prescriptions of medical practitioners for a total period of not less than three years, or
- Has passed an examination recognised as adequate by the State Government for compounders or dispensers, or
- Has been engaged in the compounding of drugs in a hospital or dispensary or other place in which drugs are regularly dispensed on prescriptions of medical practitioners for a total period of not less than five years prior to the date notified under sub-section (2) of section 30.
- *Qualifications for subsequent registration*: (1) After the date appointed under sub-section (2) of section 30 and before the Education Regulations have, by or under section 11, taken effect in the State, 3[a person who has attained the age of eighteen years shall on payment of the prescribed fee] be entitled to have his name entered in the register if he resides or carries on the business or profession of pharmacy in the State and if he satisfies the conditions prescribed with the prior approval of the Central Council, or where no

conditions have been prescribed, the conditions entitling a person to have his name entered on the first register as set out in section 31.

- Is a registered pharmacist in another State,
- Possesses a qualification approved under section 14.
- Provided that no person shall be entitled [under clause (a) of clause (c)] to have his name entered on the register unless he has passed a matriculation examination or an examination prescribed as being equivalent to a matriculation examination.
- After the Education Regulations have by or under section 11 taken effect in the State, a person shall on payment of the prescribed fee be entitled to have his name entered on the register if he has attained the age of [eighteen years], if he resides, or carries on the business or profession of pharmacy, in the State and if he has passed an approved examination or possesses a qualification approved under section 14 [or is a registered pharmacist in another State.]
- Special provisions for registration of certain persons. Notwithstanding anything contained in section 32, a State Council may also permit to be entered on the register.
- The names of displaced persons who have been carrying on the business or profession of pharmacy as their principal means of livelihood from a date prior to the 4th day of March, 1948, and who satisfy the conditions for registration as set out in section 31;
- The names of citizens of India who have been carrying on the business or profession of pharmacy in any country outside India and who satisfy the conditions for registrations as set out in section 31;
- The names of persons who resided in an area which has subsequently become a territory of India and who satisfy the conditions for registration as set out in section 31;
- The names of persons who carry on the business or profession of pharmacy in the State, and (i) would

have satisfied the conditions for registration as set out in section 31, on the date appointed under sub-section.

- Of section 30, had they applied for registration on or before that date; or (ii) have been engaged in the compounding of drugs in a hospital or dispe-nsary or other place in which drugs are regularly dispensed on prescriptions of medical practitioners as defined in sub-clause (iii) of clause (f) of section 2 for a total period of not less then five years prior to the date appointed under sub-section (2) of section 30;
- The names of persons who were qualified to be entered in the register for a State as it existed immediately before the 1st day of November, 1956, but who, by reason of the area in which they resided or carried on their business or profession of pharmacy having become part of a State as formed on that date, are not qualified to be entered having in the register for the latter State only by reason of their not having passed either a matriculation examination or an examination prescribed as being equivalent to a matriculation examination or an approved examination or of their not possessing a qualification approved under section 14; (f) the names of persons.
- Who were included in the register for a State as it existed immediately before the 1st day of November, 1956;
- Who, by reason of the area in which they resided or carried on their business or profession of pharmacy having become part of a State as formed on that date, reside or carry on such business or profession in the latter State;
- The names of persons who reside or carry on their business of profession or pharmacy in an area in which this Chapter takes effect after the commencement of the Pharmacy (Amendment) Act, 1959 (24 of 1959), and who satisfy the conditions for registration as set out in section 31.

- Any person who desires his name to be entered in the register in pursuance of sub-section (1) shall make an application in that behalf to the State Council, and such application shall be accompanied by the prescribed fee.
- The provisions of this section shall remain in operation for a period of two years from the commencement of the Pharmacy (Amendment) Act, 1959.

Provided that the State Government may, by notification in the Official Gazette, extend the period of operation of clause (a), clause (b) or clause (c) of sub-section (1) by such further period or periods, not exceeding two years in the aggregate, as may be specified in the notification.

Explanation 1: For the purpose of clause (a) of sub-section (1), "displaced person" means any person who on account of the setting up of the Dominions of India and Pakistan or on account of civil disturbances or the fear of such disturbances in any area now forming part of Pakistan, has on or after the 1st day of March, 1947, left or been displaced from his place of residence in such area and who has since then been residing in India.

Explanation 2: For the purposes of clauses (b), (c) and (g) of sub-section (1), the period referred to in clause (d) of section 31 shall be computed with reference to the date of application.] Special provisions for registration of displaced persons, repatriates and other persons. (1) Notwithstanding anything contained in section 32 or section 32A, a State Council may permit to be entered on the register

- The names of persons who posses the qualifications specified in clause (a) or clause (c) of section 31 and who were eligible for registration between the closing of the First Register and the date when the Education Regulations came into effect. The names of persons approved as "qualified persons" before the 31st December, 1969 for compounding or dispensing of medicines under the Drugs and Cosmetics Act, 1940 (23 of 1940) and the rules made thereunder;

- The names of displaced person or repatriates who were carrying on business or profession of pharmacy as their principal means of livelihood in any country outside India for a total period of not less than five years from a date prior to the date of application for registration.

Explanation: In this sub-section.

- Displaced persons" means any persons who, on account of civil disturbances or the fear of such disturbances in any area now forming part of Bangla Desh, has, after the 14th day of April , 1957 but before the 25th day of March , 1971 , left , or has been displaced from , his place of residence in such area and who has since then been residing in India repatriate" means any person of Indian origin who on account of civil disturbances or the fear of such disturbances in any area now forming part of Burma Sri Lanka or Uganda, or any other country has after the 14th day of April , 1957 , left or has been displaced from , his place of residence in such area and who has since then been residing in India.
- The provisions of clauses (a) and (b) of sub–section (1) shall remain in operation for a period of two years from the commencement of the Pharmacy (Amendment)Act , 1976.]
- Scrutiny of applications for registration. —(1) After the date appointed under sub-section (2) of section 30 , applications for registration shall be addressed to the Registrar of the State Council and shall be accompanied by the prescribed fee.
- If upon such application the Registrar is of opinion that the applicant is entitled to have his name entered in the register under the provisions of this Act for the time being applicable , he shall enter the name of the applicant in the register:
- Provided that no person whose name has under the provisions of this Act been removed from the register of any State shall be entitled to have his name entered

in the register except with the approval of the State Council recorded at a meeting.

- Any persons, whose application for registration is rejected by the Registrar, may within three months from the date of such rejection appeal to the State Council, and the decision of the State Council thereon shall be final.
- Upon entry in the register of a name under section, the Registrar shall issue a certificate of registration in the prescribed form.

RENEWAL FEES

- The State Government may, by notification in the Official Gazette, direct that for the retention of a name on the register after the 31st day of December of the year following the year in which the name is first entered on the register , there shall be paid annually to the State Council such renewal fee as may be prescribed , and where such direction has been made, such renewal fee shall be due to be paid before the first day of April of the year to which it relates.
- Where a renewal fee is not paid by the due date, the Registrar shall remove the name of the defaulter from the register:
- Provided that a name so removed may be restored to the register on such conditions as may be prescribed.
- On payment of the renewal fee, the Registrar shall[issue a receipt therefor and such receipt shall be proof of renewal of registration.]
- *Entry of additional qualifications*: A registered pharmacist shall on payment of the prescribed fee be entitled to have entered in the register any further degrees or diplomas in pharmacy on pharmaceutical chemistry which he may obtain.
- *Removal from register*: Subject to the provisions of this section, the Executive Committee may order that the name of a registered pharmacist shall be removed

from the register, where it is satisfied, after giving him a reasonable opportunity of being heard and after such further inquiry, if any, as it may think fit to make:

- That his name has been entered into the register by error or on account of misrepresentation or suppression of a material fact, or
- That he has been convicted of any offence or has been guilty of any infamous conduct in any professional respect which in the opinion of the Executive Committee, renders him unfit to be kept in the register, or
- That a person employed by him for the purposes of his business of pharmacy [or employed to work under him in connection with any business of pharmacy] has been convicted of any such offence or has been guilty of any such infamous conduct as would, if such person were a registered pharmacist, render him liable to have his name removed from the register under clause.
- Provided that no such order shall be made under clause (iii) unless the Executive Commi-ttee is satisfied

- That the offence or infamous conduct was instigated or connived at by the registered pharmacist, or
- That the registered pharmacist has at any time during the period or twelve months immediately preceding the date on which the offence or infamous conduct took place committed a similar offence or been guilty of similar infamous conduct,
- That any person employed by the registered pharmacist for the purposes of his business of pharmacy [or employed to work under him in connection with any business of pharmacy] has at any time during the period of twelve months immediately preceding the date on which the offence or infamous conduct took place, committed a similar

offence or been guilty of similar infamous conduct, and that the registered pharmacist had, or reasonably ought to have had, knowledge of such previous offence or infamous conduct ,

- That where the offence or infamous conduct continued over a period, the registered pharmacist had, or reasonably ought to have had, knowledge of the continuing offence or infamous conduct,
- That where the offence is an offence under the [Drugs and Cosmetics Act, 1940, the registered pharmacist has not used due diligence in enforcing compliance with the provisions of that Act in his place of business and by persons employed by him[or by persons under his control].
- An order under sub–section (1) may direct that the person whose name is ordered to be removed from the register shall be ineligible for registration in the State under this Act either permanently or for such period as may be specified.
- An order under sub-section (1) shall be subject to confirmation by the State Council and shall not take effect until the expiry of three month from the date of such confirmation.
- A person aggrieved by an order under sub-section (1) which has been confirmed by the State Council may, within thirty days from the communication to him of such confirmation, appeal to the State Government, and the order of the State Government upon such appeal shall be final.
- A person whose name has been removed from the register under this section or under sub-section (2) of section 34 shall forthwith surrender his certificate or registration to the Registrar, and the name so removed shall be published in the Official Gazette.
- *Restoration to register*: The State Council may at any time for reasons appearing to it sufficient order that upon payment of the prescribed fee the name

of a person removed from the register shall be restored thereto:

- Provided that where an appeal against such removal has been rejected by the State Government, an order under this section shall not take effect until it has been confirmed by the State Government.
- *Bar of other jurisdiction*: No order refusing to enter a name on the register or removing a name from the register shall be called in question in any Court.
- Issue of duplicate certificate of registration. – Where it is shown to the satisfaction of the Registrar that a certificate of registration has been lost or destroyed, the Registrar may, on payment of the prescribed fee, issue a duplicate certificate in the prescribed form.
- *Printing of register and evidentiary value of entries therein*: (1) As soon as may be after the 1st day of April subsequent to the commencement of the Pharmacy (Amendment) Act, 1959, the Registrar shall cause to be printed copies of the register as it stood on the said date.
- The Registrar shall thereafter cause to be printed as soon as may be after the 1st day of April in each year copies of the annual supplement to the register referred to in sub-section (1), showing all additions to and other amendments in, the said register.
- The register shall be brought up-to-date three months before ordinary elections to the State Council are held and copies of this register shall be printed.
- The provisions of sub-section (2) shall apply to the register as so printed as they apply to the register referred to in sub-section (1).
- The copies referred to in sub-section (1) or sub-section (2) or sub-section (3) shall be made be available to persons applying therefor on payment of the prescribed charge and shall be evidence that on the date referred to in the register or annual supplement, as the case may be, the persons whose name are entered therein were registered pharmacists.

PENALTY FOR FALSELY CLAIMING TO BE REGISTERED

If any person whose name is not for the time being entered into the register of the State falsely pretends that it is so entered or uses in connection with his name or title any words or letters reasonably calculated to suggest that his name is so entered, he shall be punishable on first conviction with fine which may extend to five hundred rupees and on any subsequent conviction with imprisonment extending to six months or with fine not exceeding one thousand rupees or with both: Provided that it shall be a defence to show that the name of the accused is entered in the register of another State and that at the time of the alleged offence under this section an application for registration in the State had been made.

- *For the purposes of this section*:
  - It shall be immaterial whether or not any person is deceived by such pretence or use as aforesaid;
  - The use of the description "pharmacist", "chemist", "druggist", "pharmaceutist", "dispenser", "dispensing chemist", or any combination of such words [or of any such word with any other word] shall be deemed to be reasonably calculated to suggest that the person using such description is a person whose name is for the time being entered in the resister of the State;
  - The onus of proving that the name of a person is for the time being entered in the register of a State shall be on him who asserts it.

Cognizance of an offence punishable under this section shall not be taken except upon complaint made by order of the State Government or [any officer authorized in this behalf by the State Government or by order of] the Executive Committee of the State Council.

Dispensing by unregistered persons: On or after such date as the State Government may by notification in the Official Gazette appoint in this behalf, no person other than a registered pharmacist shall compound, prepare, mix, or dispense any medicine on the prescription of a medical practitioner.

Provided that this sub-section shall not apply to dispensing by a medical practitioner of medicine for his own patients, or with the general or special sanction of the State Government, for the patients of another medical practitioner. Whoever contravenes the provisions of sub-section (1) shall be punishable with imprisonment for a term which may extend to six months, or with fine not exceeding one thousand rupees or with both.

Cognizance of an offence punishable under this section shall not be taken except upon complaint made by [order of the State Government or any officer authorized in this behalf by the State Government or by order of the Executive Committee of the State Council]:

Provided further that where no such date is appointed by the Government of a State, this sub-section shall take effect in that State on the expiry of a period of [eight years] from the commencement of the pharmacy (Amendment) Act, 1976.]

Failure to surrender certificate of registration. —(1) If any person whose name has been removed from the register fails without sufficient cause forthwith to surrender his certificate of registration he shall be punishable with fine which may extend to fifty rupees.

Cognizance of an offence punishable under this section shall not be taken except upon complaint made by an order of the Executive Committee. Payment of part of fees to Central Council. The State council shall before the end of June in each year pay to the Central Council a sum equivalent to one-fourth of the total fees realized by the State Council under this Act during the period of twelve months ending on the 31st day of March of that year.

Appointment of Commission of Enquiry. —(1) Whenever it appears to the Central Government that the Central Council is not complying with any of the provisions of this Act, the Central Government may appoint a Commission of Enquiry consisting of there persons, two of whom shall be appointed by the Central Government one being the Judge of a High Court, and one by the Council; and refer to it the matters on which the enquiry is to be made.

The Commission shall proceed to enquire in such manner as it may deem fit and report to the Central Government on the matters referred to it together with such remedies, if any, as the Commission may like to recommend. The Central Government may accept the report or remit the same to the Commission for modification or reconsi-deration.

After the report is finally accepted, the Central Government may order the Central Council to adopt the remedies so recommended within such time as may be specified in the order and if the Council fails to comply within the time so specified, the Central Government may pass such order or take such action as may be necessary to give effect to the recommendations of the Commission.

Whenever it appears to the State Government that the State Council is not complying with any of the provisions of the Act, the State Government may likewise appoint a similar Commission of Enquiry and pass such order or take such action as specified in sub –sections (3) and (4).

- Power to make rules.
  - The State Government may, by notification in the Official Gazette, make rules to carry out the purposes of Chapters III, IV and V.
  - In particular and without prejudice to the generality of the foregoing power such rules may provide for-
  - The management of the property of the State Council, and the maintenance and audit of its accounts;
  - The manner in which elections under Chapter III shall be conducted;
  - The summoning and holding of meetings of the State Council, the times and places at which such meetings shall be held, the conduct of business thereat and the number of members necessary to form a quorum;

  - The powers and duties of the President and Vice-President of the State Council;
  - The constitution and function of the Executive Committee, the summoning and holding of meetings thereof, the times and places at which such meetings shall be held, and number of members necessary to constitute a quorum;
  - The qualifications, the term of office and the powers and duties of the Registrar and other officers and servants of the State Council including the amount and nature of thesecurity to be given by the Treasurer; the qualifications, powers and duties of an Inspector;
- The particulars to be stated, and the proof of qualifica-tions to be given, in application for registration under Chapter;
- The conditions for registration under sub-section (1) of section 32;
- Fees payable under Chapter and the charge for supplying copies of the register;
- The form of certificates of registration.
- The maintenance of a register;
- The conduct of pharmacists and their duties in relation to medical practitioners the public and the profession of pharmacy;]
- Any other matter which is to be or may be prescribed under Chapters III, IV and V except sub-sections (1),(2),(3) and (4) of section 45.
- Every rule made by the State Government under this section shall be laid, as soon as may be after it is made, before the State Legislature.]

Chapter 4

Act and Rules of Drug and Cosmetic

INTRODUCTION

The Central Government shall, by notification in the Official Gazette and with effect from such date as may be specified therein, constitute a Board (to be called the {Ayurvedic, Unani & Siddha Drugs Technical Advisory Board}) to advise the Central Government and the State Governments on technical matters arising out of this chapter and to carry out the other functions assigned to it by this chapter.

- *The Board Shall consist of the following members, namely:*
  - The Director-General of Health Services, ex officio;
  - The Drugs Controller, India, ex officio;
  - The principal officer dealing with Indian system of medicine in the Ministry of Health, ex officio;
  - The Director of the Central Drugs Laboratory, Calcutta, ex officio;
  - One person holding the appointment of Govt. Analyst under section 34-F, to be nominated by the Central Govt.;
  - One Pharmacognocist to be nominated by Central Govt.;
  - One Phyto-chemist to be nominated the Central Govt.
  - Four persons to be nominated by Central Govt.,

two from amongst the members of the Ayurvedic Pharmacopoeia Committee, one from amongst the members of the Unani Pharmacopoeia Committee and one from amongst the members of the Siddha Pharmacopoeia Committee;

- One teacher in Darvyaguna, and Bhaishajya Kalpana, to be nominated by the Central Government;
- One teacher in ILM-UL-ADVIA and TAKLIS-WA DAWASZAI, to be nominated by the Central Government;
- One teacher in Gunapadam to be nominated by Central Government;
- Three persons, one each to represent the Ayurvedic, Siddha & Unani drug industry, to be nominated by the Central Government;
- Three persons, one each from among the practitioners of Ayurvedic, Siddha & Unani Tibb systems of medicine to be nominated by the Central Government;

- The Central Govt. shall appoint a member of the Board as its Chairman.
- The nominated members of the Board shall hold office for three years but shall be eligible for renomination.
- The Board may, subject to the previous approval of Central Govt. make bye-laws fixing a quorum and regulating its own procedure and conduct of all business to be transacted by it.
- The functions of the Board may be exercised not withstanding any vacancy therein.
- The Central Govt. shall appoint a person to be Secretary of the Board and shall provide the Board with such clerical and other staff as the Central Govt. considers necessary.

The Ayurvedic, Siddha & Unani Drugs Consultative Committee. The Central Govt. may constitute an advisory committee to be called the Ayurvedic, Siddha and Unani

Drugs Consultative Committee to advise the Central Govt., the State Govt. and the Ayurvedic, Siddha and Unani Drugs Technical Advisory Board on any matter for the purpose of securing uniformity throughout India in the administration of this Act in so far as it relates to Ayurvedic, Siddha and Unani Drugs. The Ayurvedic, Siddha and Unani Drugs Consultative Committee shall consist of two persons to be nominated by the Central Govt. as representatives of that Govt. and not more than one representative of each State to be nominated by the State Govt. concerned. The Ayurvedic, Siddha and Unani Drugs Consultative Committee shall meet when required to do so by the Central Govt. and shall regulate is own procedure.

Misbranded drugs Ayurvedic, Siddha or Unani drug shall be deemed to be misbranded: If it is so colored, coated, powdered or polished that the damage is concealed or if it is made to appear of better or greater therapeutic value than it really is; or If it is not labelled in the prescribed manner; or If its label or container or anything accompanying the drug bears any statement, design or device which makes any false claim for the drug or which is false or misleading in any particular. Adulterated drugs Ayurvedic, Siddha or Unani drug shall be deemed to be adulterated If it consist, in whole or in part, of any filthy, putrid or decomposed substances; or If it has been prepared, packed or stored under insanitary conditions whereby it may have been contaminated with filthy or whereby it may have been rendered injurious to health; or It its container is decomposed, in whole or in part, of any poisonous or deleterious substances which may render the contents injurious to health; or If it bears or contains, for purpose of colouring only, a colour other than one which is prescribed; or If it contains any harmful or toxic substances which may render it injurious to health; or If any substance has been mixed therewith so as to reduce its quality or strength.

Explanation: For the purpose of clause (a), a drug shall not be deemed to consist, in whole or in part, of any decomposed substance only by reason of the fact that such decomposed substance is the result of any natural decomposition of the drug. Provided that such decomposed is not due to any negligence on the part of the manufacturer of the drug or the dealer thereof and that it does not render the drug injurious to health.

- Spurious Drugs Ayurvedic, Siddha or Unani drug shall be deemed to be spurious:-
  - If it is sold, or offered or exhibited for sale, under the name which belongs to another drug;
  - If it is an imitation of, or is a substitute for, another drug or resembles another drug in a manner likely to deceive, or bears upon it or upon its label or container the name of another drug, unless it is plainly and conspicuously marked as to revealed its true character and its lack of identity with such other drug; or
  - If the label or container bears the name of an individual or company purporting to be the manufacturer of the drug, which individual or company is fictitious or does not exist; or
  - If it has been substituted wholly or in part by any other drug or substance; or
  - If it purports to be the product of manufacturer of whom it is not truly a product.

Regulation of manufacture for sale of Ayurvedic, Siddha and Unani drugs. No person shall manufacture for sale or for distribution any Ayurvedic, Siddha or Unani drug except in accordance with such standards, if any, as may be prescribed in relation to that drug. Prohibition of manufacture and sale of certain Ayurvedic, Siddha and Unani drugs From such date as the State Government may, by notification in the Official Gazette. Specify in this behalf, no person, either by himself or by any other person on his behalf, shall

- *Manufacture for sale or for distribution*:
  - Any misbranded, adulterated or spurious Ayurvedic, Siddha or Unani drug;
  - Any patent or proprietary medicine, unless there is displayed in the prescribed manner on the

label or container thereof the true list of all the ingredients contained in it; and

- Any Ayurvedic, Siddha or Unani drug in contravention of any of the provisions of this chapter or any rule made thereunder;
- Sell, stock or exhibit or offer for sale or distribute any Ayurvedic, Siddha or Unani drug which has been manufactured in contravention cf any of the provisions of this Act, or any rule made thereunder;
- Manufacture for sale or for distribution, any Ayurvedic, Siddha or Unani drug, except under, and in accordance with the conditions of a licence issued for such purpose under this Chapter by the prescribed authority.

Provided that nothing in this section shall apply to Vaidyas and Hakims who manufacture Ayurvedic, Siddha or Unani drug for the use of their own patients. Provided further that nothing in this section shall apply to the manufacture, subject to the prescribed conditions of small quantities of any Ayurvedic, Siddha or Unani drug for the purpose of examination, test or analysis.

Power of Central Government to prohibit manufacture, etc, of Ayurvedic, Siddha or Unani drugs in public interest. Without prejudice to any other provision contained in this Chapter, if the Central Government is satisfied on the basis of any evidence or other material available before it that the use of any Ayurvedic, Siddha or Unani drug is likely to involve any risk to human beings or animals or that any such drug does not have the therapeutic value claimed or purported to be claimed for it and that in the public interest it is necessary or expedient so to do then, that Government may, by notification in the Official Gazette, prohibit the manufacture, sale or distribution of such drug.

Government Analysis

The Central Government may, by notification in the Official Gazette, appoint such persons as it thinks fit, having the prescribed qualifications, to the Government Analysis for such areas as may be assigned to them by the Central Government or the State Government, as the case may be.

Notwithstanding anything contained in the sub-section (1), neither the Central Government nor a State Government shall appoint as a Government Analyst any official not serving under it without the previous consent of the Government under which he is serving. No person who has any financial interest in the manufacture or sale of any rug shall be appointed to a Government Analyst under this section.

Inspectors: The Central Government or a State Government may, by notification in the Official Gazette, appoint such persons as it thinks fit, having the prescribed qualifications, to be Inspectors for such areas as may be assigned to them by the Central Government or the State Government as the case may be.

The powers which may be exercised by an Inspector and the duties which may be performed by him and the conditions, limitations or restrictions subject to which such powers and duties may be exercised or performed shall be such as mat be prescribed.

No person who has any financial interest in the manufacture or sale of any drug shall be appointed to be an Inspected under this section. Every Inspector shall be deemed to be a public servant within the meaning of Section 21 of the Indian Penal Code and shall be officially sub-ordinate to such authority as the Government appointing him may specific in this behalf.

CENTRAL DRUGS LABORATORY

Constitution of references to any law not in force or any functionary not in existence in the State of Jammu and Kashmir. Any reference in this Act to any law which is not in force, or any functionary not in existence, in the State of Jammu and Kashmir, shall, in relation to that State, be construed as a reference to the corresponding law in force, or to the corresponding functionary in existence, in that State. Presumption as to poisonous substances. – Any substance specified as poisonous by rule made under Chapter II or Chapter IV [(Note: Ins. by Act 13 of 1964, sec.3 (w.e.f. 15-9-1964)) or Chapter IVA] shall be deemed to be a poisonous substance for the purpose of Chapter III or Chapter IV [(Note: Ins. by Act 13 of 1964, sec.3 (w.e.f. 15-9-1964)) or Chapter IVA], as the case may be.

The Drugs Technical Advisory Board. – (1) The Central Government shall, as soon as may be, constitute a Board (to be called the Drugs Technical Advisory Board) to advise the Central Government and the State Governments on technical matters arising out of the administration of this Act and to carry out the other functions assigned to it by this Act.

Note: Subs. by Act 13 of 1964, sec.4, for sub-section (2) (w.e.f. 15-9-1964)) The Board shall consist of the following members, namely,

- The Director General of Health Services, ex officio, who shall be Chairman;
- The Drugs Controller, India ex officio;
- The Director of the Central Drugs Laboratory, Calcutta, ex-officio;
- The Director of the Central Research Institute, Kasauli, ex-officio;
- The Director of the Indian Veterinary Research Institute, Izatnagar, ex-officio;
- The President of the Medical Council of India, ex-officio;
- The President of the Pharmacy Council of India, ex-officio;
- The Director of the Central Drug Research Institute, Lucknow, ex-officio;
- Two persons to be nominated by the Central Government from among persons who are in charge of drugs control in the States;
- One person, to be elected by the Executive Committee of the Pharmacy Council of India, from among teachers in pharmacy or pharmaceutical chemistry or pharmacognosy on the staff of an Indian university or a college affiliated thereto;

- One person, to be elected by the Executive Committee of the Medical Council of India, from among teachers in medicine or therapeutics on the staff of an Indian university or a college affiliated thereto;
- One person to be nominated by the Central Government from the pharmaceuticalindustry;
- One pharrmacologist to be elected by the Governing Body of the Indian Council of Medical Research;
- One person to be elected by the Central Council of the Indian Medical Association;
- One person to be elected by the Council of the Indian Pharmaceutical Association;
- Two persons holding the appointment of Government Analyst under this Act, to be nominated by the Central Government.]

The nominated and elected members of the Board shall hold office for three years, but shall be eligible for re-nomination and re-election.

Note: Subs. by Act 13 of 1964, sec.4, for the Proviso (w.e.f. 15-9-1964)). Provided that the person nominated or elected, as the case may be, under clause (ix) or clause (x) or clause (xi) of clause (xvi) of sub-section (2) shall hold office for so long as he holds the appointment of the office by virtue of which he was nominated or elected to the Board.] The Board may, subject to the previous approval of the Central Government, make bye-laws fixing a quorum and regulating its own procedure and the conduct of all businessto be transacted by it.

The Board may constitute sub-committees and may appoint to such sub-committees for such periods, not exceeding three years, as it may decide, or temporarily for the consideration of particular matters, persons who are not members of the Board.

The functions of the Board may be exercised notwithstanding any vacancy therein. The Central Government shall appoint a person to be Secretary of the Board and shall provide the Board with such clerical and other staff as the Central Government considers necessary. The Central Drugs Laboratory. The Central Government shall, as soon as may be, establish a Central Drugs Laboratory under the control of a Director to be appointed by the Central Government, to carry out the functions entrusted to it by this Act or any rules made under this Chapter.

Provided that, if the Central government so prescribes, the functions of the Central Drugs Laboratory in respect of any drug or class of drugs [(Note: Ins. by Act 21 of 1962, sec.5 (w.e.f. 27-7-1964)) or cosmetic or class of cosmetics] or class of cosmetics] shall be carried out at the Central Research Institute, Kasauli, or at any other prescribed Laboratory and the functions of the Director of the Central Drugs Laboratory in respect of such drug or class of drugs [(Note: Ins. by Act 21 of 1962, sec.5 (w.e.f. 27-7-1964)) or such cosmetic or class of cosmetics] shall be exercised by the Director of that Institute or of that other Laboratory, as the case may be.

- The Central Government may, after consultation with the Board, make rules prescribing:–
  - The functions of the Central Drugs Laboratory
  - *Note*: Clause (b) omitted by Act 11 of 1955, sec.4
  - *Note*: Clause (c) omitted by Act 11 of 1955, sec.4

The procedure for the submission of the said Laboratory [(Note: Subs. by Act 13 of 1964, sec.5, for "under Chapter IV" (w.e.f. 15-9-1964)) under Chapter IV or Chapter IVA] of samples of drugs [(Note: Ins. by Act 21 of 1962, sec.5 (w.e.f. 27-7-1964)) or cosmetics] for analysis or test, the forms of the Laboratory's reports thereon and the fees payable in respect of such reports; Such other matters as may be necessary or expedient to enable the said Laboratory to carry out its functions. The matters necessary to be prescribed for the purposes of the proviso to sub-section (1).

THE DRUGS CONSULTATIVE COMMITTEE

The Central Government may constitute an advisory committee to be called "the Drugs Consultative Committee" to advise the Central Government, the State Governments and the Drugs Technical Advisory Board on any matter tending to secure uniformity throughout [(Note: Ins. by Act 3 of 1951, sec.3 and Sch., for "the States") India] in the administration of this Act. The Drugs Consultative Committee shall consist of two representatives of the Central Government to be nominated by that Government and one representative of each State Government to be nominated by the State Government concerned. The Drugs Consultative Committee shall meet when required to do so by the Central Government and shall have power to regulate its own procedure.7A. Section 5 and 7 not to apply to Ayurvedic, Siddha or Unani drugs. – Nothing contained in sections 5 and 7 shall apply to [(Note: Subs. by Act 68 of 1982, sec.2, for certain words (w.e.f. 1-2-1983)). Ayurvedic, Siddha or Unani] drugs.

- *Standards of quality*: [(1)(Note: Subs. Act 21 of 1962, sec.2, for sub-section (1) (w.e.f. 27-7-1964)) For the purposes of this Chapter, the expression "standard quality" means.
  - In relation to a drug, that the drug complies with the standard set out in [(Note: Subs. by Act 13 of 1964, sec.7, for "the Schedule" (w.e.f. 15-9-1964)) the Second Schedule], and
  - In relation to a cosmetic, that the cosmetic complies with such standard as may be prescribed.]

The Central Government, after consultation with the Board and after giving by notification in the Official Gazette not less than three months' notice of its intention so to do, may be a like notification add to or otherwise amend [(Note: Subs. by Act 13 of 1964, sec.7, for "the Schedule" (w.e.f. 15-9-1964)) the Second Schedule], for the purposes of this Chapter, and thereupon [(Note: Subs. by Act 13 of 1964, sec.7, for "the Schedule" (w.e.f. 15-9-1964))the Second Schedule] shall be deemed to be amended accordingly. 9. Misbranded drugs: For the purposes of this Chapter, a drug shall be deemed to be misbranded.

- If it is so coloured, coated, powdered or polished that damage is concealed or if it is made to appear of better or greater therapeutic value than it really is;

- If it is not labeled in the prescribed manner;
- If its label or contained or anything accompanying the drug bears any statement, design or device which is false or misleading in any particular.]9A. Adulterated drugs. For the purposes of this Chapter, a drug shall be deemed to be adulterated,
- If it consists, in whole or in part, of any filthy, putrid or decomposed substance;
- If it has been prepared, packed or stored under insanitary conditions whereby it may have been contaminated with filth or whereby it may have been rendered injurious tohealth;
- If its contained is composed in whole or in part, of any poisonous or deleterious substance which may render the contents injurious to health;
- If it bears or contains, for purposes of colouring only, a colour other than one which is prescribed; or
- If it contains any harmful or toxic substance which may render it injurious to health;
- If any substance has been mixed therewith so as to reduce its quality or strength. 9B. Spurious drugs. For the purposes of this Chapter, a drug shall be deemed to be spurious,
- If it is imported under a name which belongs to another drug;
- If it is an imitation of, or is a substitute for, another drug or resembles another drug in a manner likely to deceive or bears upon it or upon its label or contained the name of another drug unless it is plainly and conspicuously marked so as to reveal its true character and its lack of identity with such other drug;
- If the label or container bears the name of an individual or company purporting to be the manufacturer of the drug, which individual or company is fictitious or does not exist;
- If it has been substituted wholly or in part by another drug or substance;
- If it purports to be the product of a manufacturer of

whom it is only truly a product. 9C. Misbranded Cosmetics. For the purposes of this Chapter, a cosmetic shall be deemed to be misbranded.

- If it contains a colour which is not prescribed;
- If it is not labeled in the prescribed manner;
- If the label or container or anything accompanying the cosmetic bears any statement, which is false or misleading in any particular. 9D. Spurious cosmetics. For the purposes of this Chapter, a cosmetic shall be deemed to be spurious,
- If it is imported under a name which belongs to another cosmetic;
- If it is an imitation of, or is a substitute for, another cosmetic or resembles another cosmetic in a manner likely to deceive or bears upon it or upon its label or container the name of another cosmetic, unless it is plainly and conspicuously marked so as to reveal its true character and its lack of identity with such other cosmetic;
- If the label or container bears the name of an individual or a company purporting to be the manufacturer of the cosmetic which individual or company is fictitious or does not exist;
- If it purports to be the product of a manufacturer of whom it is.]

STANDARDS OF QUALITY

Note: Subs. by Act 21 of 1962, sec.12, for sub-section (w.e.f. 27-7-1964)) For the purposes of this Chapter, the expression "standard quality" means –In relation to a drug, that the drug complies with the standard set out in [the Second Schedule], and (b) In relation to a cosmetic, that the cosmetic complies with such standard as may be prescribed.] The [(Note: Subs. by Act 11 of 1955, sec.8, for "State Government".) Central Government], after consultation with the Board and after giving by notification in the Official Gazette not less than three months' notice of its intention so to do, may by a like notification add to or otherwise amend [(Note: Subs. by Act

13 of 1964, sec.11, for "the Schedule" (w.e.f. 15-9-1964)) the Second Schedule] for the purposes of this Chapter, and thereupon [(Note: Subs. by Act 13 of 1964, sec.11, for "the Schedule" (w.e.f. 15-9-1964)) the Second Schedule] shall be deemed to be amended accordingly.

COMMENTS

The standards of qualities are fixed by the Government after due deliberation and after consulting a committee of competent men, it is for them to give due allowance forprobable errors before fixing a standard. When a standard has been fixed it has to be observed strictly; State of Kerala v.Vasudevan Nair, 1974 KLT 617 (FB): 1975 Cri LJ 97.

Misbranded drugs: For the purposes of this Chapter, a drug shall be deemed to be misbranded.

- If it is so coloured, coated, powdered or polished that damage is concealed or if it is made to appear of better or greater therapeutic value than it really is;
- If it is not labeled in the prescribed manner;
- If its label or container or anything accompanying the drug bears any statement, design or device which makes any false claim for the drug or which is false or misleading in any particular.
- *Adulterated drugs*: For the purposes of this Chapter, a drug shall be deemed to be adulterated,
  - If it consists in whole or in part, of any filthy, putrid or decomposed substance; or
  - If it has been prepared, packed or stored under unsanitary conditions whereby it may have been contaminated with filth or whereby it may have been rendered injurious tohealth;
  - If its container is composed, in whole or in part, of any poisonous or deleterious substance which may render the contents injurious to health;
  - If it bears or contains, for purposes of colouring only, a colour other than one which is prescribed;
  - If it contains any harmful or toxic substance which may render it injurious to health;

  - If any substance has been mixed therewith so as to reduce its quality or strength.
- *Spurious drugs*: For the purposes of this Chapter, a drug shall be deemed to be spurious,
  - If it is manufactured under a name which belongs to another drug;
  - If it is an imitation of, or is a substitute for, another drug or resembles another drug in a manner likely to deceive or bears upon it or upon its label or container the name of another drug unless it is plainly and conspicuously marked so as to reveal its true character and its lack of identity with such other drug;
  - If the label or container bears the name of an individual or company purporting to be the manufacturer of the drug, which individual or company is fictitious or does not exist;
  - If it has been substituted wholly or in part by another drug or substance;
  - If it purports to be the product of a manufacturer of whom it is not truly a product.
- *Misbranded cosmetics*: For the purposes of this Chapter, a cosmetic shall be deemed to be misbranded, If it contains a colour which is not prescribed;
  - If it is not labeled in the prescribed manner;
  - If the label or container or anythig accompanying the cosmetic bears any statement which is false or misleading in any particular.
- *Spurious cosmetics*: For the purposes of this Chapter, a cosmetic shall be deemed to be spurious,
  - If it is manufactured under a name which belongs to another cosmetic;
  - If it is an imitation of, or a substitute for, another cosmetic or resembles another cosmetic in a manner likely to deceive or bears upon it or upon its conspicuously marked so as to reveal its true character and its lack of identity with such other cosmetic;

- If the label or container bears the name of an individual or a company purporting to be the manufacturer of the cosmetic which individual or company is fictitious or does not exist;
- If it purports to be the product of a manufacturer of whom it is not truly a product. Purchaser of drug or cosmetic enabled to obtain

TEST OR ANALYSIS

Any person [(Note: Ins. by Act 71 of 1986, sec.2 (w.e.f. 15-9-1987)) or any recognised consumer association, whether such person is a member of that association or not] shall, on application in the prescribed manner and on payment of the prescribed fee, be entitled to submit for test or analysis to a Government Analyst any drug [(*Note*: Ins. by Act 21 of 1962, sec.15 (w.e.f. 27-7-1964)) or cosmetic] [(Note: Subs. by Act 71 of 1986, sec.2) purchased by him or it] and to receive a report of such test or analysis signed by the Government Analyst.

(*Note*: Added by Act 71 of 1986, sec.2) Explanation. For the purposes of this section and section 32, "recognised consumer association" means a voluntary consumer association registered under the Companies Act, 1956 or any other law for the time being in force.]

Powers of Central Government to prohibit manufacture, etc., of drug and cosmetic in public interest. – Without prejudice to any other provision contained in this Chapter, if the Central Government is satisfied, that the use of any drug or cosmetic is likely to involve any risk to human beings or animals or that any drug does not have the therapeutic value claimed or purported to be claimed for it or contains ingredients and in such quantity for which there is no therapeutic justification and that in the public interest it is necessary or expedient so to do, then, that Government may, by notification in the Official Gazette, prohibit the manufacture, sale or distribution of such drug or cosmetic.]

COMMENT

The State's obligation of enforce production of qualitative

drugs and elimination of the injurious ones from the market must take within its sweep an obligation to make useful drugs available at reasonable price so as to be within the common man's reach; Vincent Panikurlangara v. Union of India; AIR 1987 SC 990.

Penalty for manufacture, sale,of drugs in contravention of this Chapter. Whoever, himself or by any other person on his behalf, manufacturers for sale or for distribution, or sells, or stocks or exhibits or offers for sale or distributes,-any drug deemed to be adulterated under section 17A or spurious under section 17B or which when used by any person for or in the diagnosis, treatment, mitigation, or prevention of any disease or disorder is likely to cause his death or is likely to cause such harm on his body as would amount to grievous hurt within the meaning of section 320 of the Indian Penal Code solely on account of such drug being adulterated or spurious or not of standard quality, as the case may be, shall be punishable with imprisonment for a term which shall not be less than five years but which may extend to a term of life and with fine which shall not be less than ten thousand rupees.

DRUG

Deemed to be adulterated under section 17A, but not being a drug referred to in clause (a), or Without a valid licence as required under clause © of section 18 , shall be punishable with imprisonment for a term which shall not be less than one year but which may extend to three years and with fine which shall not be less than five thousand rupees: Provided that the Court may, for any adequate and special reasons to be recorded in the judgment, impose a sentence of imprisonment for a term of less than one year and of fine of less than five thousand rupees: Any drug deemed to be spurious under section 17B, but not being a drug referred to in clause (a) shall be punishable with imprisonment for a term which shall not be less than three years but which may extend to five years and with fine which shall not be less than five thousand rupees: Provided that the Court may, for any adequate and special reasons, to be recorded in the judgement, impose a sentence of imprisonment for a term of less than three years but not less than one year any drug, other than a drug referred to in clause (a) or clause (b) or clause (c), in contravention of any other provision of this Chapter or any rule made there under, shall be punishable with imprisonment for a term which shall not be less than one year but which may extend to two years and with fine: Provided that the Court may for any adequate and special reasons to be recorded in the judgement impose a sentence of imprisonment for a term of less than one year.

COMMENT

The absence of any comma after the word "stocks" clearly indicates that the clause "stocks or exhibits for sale" is one indivisible whole and it contemplates not merely stocking the drugs but stocking the drugs for the purposes of sale and unless all the ingredients of this category are satisfied, section 27 of the Act would not be attracted; Mohd Shabir v. State of Maharashtra, (1979) 1 SCC 568.

Penalty for manufacture, sale, etc., of cosmetics in contravention of this Chapter. Whoever himself or by any other person on his behalf manufacturers for sale or for distribution, or sells, or stocks or exhibits or offers for sale. Any cosmetic deemed to be spurious under section 17C shall be punishable with imprisonment for a term, which may extend to three years and with fine; Any cosmetic other than a cosmetic referred to in clause (I) above in contravention of any provisions of this Chapter or any rule made there under shall be punishable with imprisonment for a term which may extend to one year or with fine which may extend to one thousand rupees or with both.

Penalty for non-disclosure of the name of the manufacturer,. Whoever contravenes the provisions of section 18A [or section 24] shall be punishable with imprisonment for a term which may extend to one year, or with fine which may extend to [one thousand rupees], or with both. Penalty for not keeping documents., and for non-disclosure of information. Whoever without reasonable cause or excuse, contravenes the provision of section 18B shall be punishable with imprisonment for a term which may extend to one year or with fine which may extend to one thousand rupees or both.

Penalty for use of Government Analyst's report for advertising. Whoever uses any report of a test or analysis made by the Central Drugs Laboratory or by a Government Analyst, or any extract from such report, for the purpose of advertising any drug [(Note: Ins. by Act 21 of 1962, sec.15 (w.e.f. 27-7-1964)) or cosmetic], shall be punishable with fine which may extend to five hundred rupees.

Penalty for subsequent offences. [(1) (Note: Subs. by Act 68 of 1982, sec.25, for sub-section (1) (w.e.f. 1-2-1983)) Whoever having been convicted of an offence, Under clause (b) of section 27 is again convicted of an offence under that clause, shall be punishable with imprisonment for a term which shall not be less than two years but which may extend to six years and with fine which shall not be less than ten thousand rupees:

Provided that the Court may, for any adequate and special reasons to be mentioned in the judgement, impose a sentence of imprisonment for a term of less than two years and of fine of less than ten thousand rupees: Under clause (c) of section 27, is again convicted of an offence under that clause shall be punishable with imprisonment for a term which shall not be less than two years but which may extend to four years or with fine which shall not be less than five thousand rupees, or with both.] Under clause (d) of section 27, is again convicted of an offence under that clause shall be punishable with imprisonment for a term which shall not be less than two years but which may extend to four years or with fine which shall not be less than five thousand rupees, or with both.]

(1A) (Note: Ins. by Act 21 of 1962, sec.20 (w.e.f. 27-7-1964)) Whoever, having been convicted of an offence under section 27A is again convicted under that section, shall be punishable with imprisonment for a term which may extend to two years, or with fine which may extend to [(Note: Subs. by Act 68 of 1982, sec.25, for "one thousand rupees" (w.e.f. 1-2-1983)) two thousand rupees], or with both].

Whoever, having been convicted of an offence under (Note: The words and figures "section 28 or" omitted by Act 13 of 1964, sec.20 (w.e.f. 15-9-1964)) section 29 is again convicted of an offence under the same section, shall be punishable with imprisonment which may extend to [(Note: Subs. by Act 13 of 1964, sec.20, for "two years") ten years], or with fine, or with both.]

CONFISCATION

Note: Re-numbered as sub-section (1) by Act 35 of 1960, sec.9 (w.e.f. 16-3-1961))] Where any person has been convicted under this Chapter for contravening any such provision of this Chapter or any rule made there under as may be specified by rule made in this behalf, the stock of the drug [(Note: Ins. by Act 21 of 1962, sec.21 (w.e.f. 27-7-1964)) or cosmetic] in respect of which the contravention has been made shall be liable to confiscation [(Note: Added by Act 13 of 1964, sec.21 (w.e.f. 15-9-1964)) and if such contravention is in respect of –

Note: Subs. by Act 68 of 1982, sec.26, for clause (i) (w.e.f. 1-2-1983)) Manufacture of any drug deemed to be misbranded under section 17, adulterated under section 17A or spurious under section 17B; or] *Note:* Subs. by Act 68 of 1982, sec.26, for certain words (w.e.f. 1-2-1983)) manufacture for sale, or for distribution, sale, or stocking or exhibiting or offering for sale,] or distribution of any drug without a valid licence as required under clause (c) of section 18,any implements or machinery used in such manufacture, sale or distribution and any receptacles, packages or coverings in which such drug is contained and the animals, vehicles, vessels or other conveyances used in carrying such drug shall also be liable to confiscation].

Note: Sub-section (2) ins. by Act 35 of 1960, sec.9, subs. by Act 21 of 1962, sec.21 (w.e.f. 27-7-1964)) Without prejudice to the provisions contained in sub-section (1), where the Court is satisfied, on the application of an Inspector or otherwise and after such inquiry as may be necessary that the drug or cosmetic is not of standard quality [(Note: Subs. by Act 13 of 1964, sec.21, for "or is a misbranded drug" (w.e.f. 15-9-1964)) or is a [(Note: Subs. by Act 68 of 1982, sec.26, for certain words (w.e.f. 1-2-1983)) misbranded, adulterated or spurious drug or misbranded or spurious cosmetic,] such drug or, as the case may be, such cosmetic shall be liable to confiscation.]

Application of provisions to Government departments. – The provisions of this Chapter except those contained in section 31 shall apply in relation to the manufacture, sale or distribution of drugs by any department of Government as they apply in relation to the manufacture, sale or distribution of drugs by any other person. Cognizance of offences. (1) No prosecution under this Chapter shall be instituted except by an Inspector [(Note: Ins. by Act 71 of 1986, sec.3 (w.e.f. 15-9-1987)) or by the person aggrieved or by a recognised consumer association whether such person is a member of that association or not.]

No court inferior to that of [(Note: Subs. by Act 68 of 1982, sec.27, for "a Presidency Magistrate or of a Magistrate of the first class" (w.e.f. 1-2-1983)) a Metropolitan Magistrate or of a Judicial Magistrate of the first class] shall try an offence punishable under this Chapter.

Nothing contained in this Chapter shall be deemed to prevent any person from being prosecuted under any other law for any act or omission, which constitutes an offence against this Chapter. Power of Court to implead the manufacturer, etc.

Where, at any time during the trial of any offence under this Chapter alleged to have been committed by any person, not being the manufacturer of a drug or cosmetic or his agent for the distribution thereof, the Court is satisfied, on the evidence adduced before it, that such manufacturer or agent is also concerned in that offence, then, the Court may, notwithstanding contained [(Note; Subs. by Act 68 of 1982, sec.28, for "in sub-section (1) of section 351of the Code of Criminal Procedure, 1898" (w.e.f. 1-2-1983)) in sub-sections (1), (2) and (3) of section 319 of the Code of Criminal

Procedure, 1973], proceed against him as though a prosecution had been instituted against him under section 32.]

COMMENT

The object to the section seems to be that such a power enables speedy trial of the really guilty parties; Bhagwandas v. Delhi Admn. (1975) 1 SCC 866; 1975 Cri LJ 1091. Power of Central Government to make rules. – [(Note: Subs. by Act 11 of 1955, sec.15, for sub-section (1)) (1) The Central Government may [(Note: Subs. by Act 68 of 1982, sec.29, for "after consultation with the Board" (w.e.f. 1-2-1983)) after consultation with, or on the recommendation of, the Board] and after previous publication by notification in the Official Gazette, make rules for the purpose of giving effect to the provisions of this Chapter.

Provided that consultation with the Board may be dispensed with if the Central Government is of opinion that circumstances have arisen which render it necessary to make rules without such consultation, but in such a case the Board shall be consulted within six months of the making of the rules and the Central Government shall take into consideration any suggestions which the Board may make in relation to the amendment of the said rules.

- Without prejudice to the generality of the foregoing power, such rules may provide for the establishment of laboratories for testing and analyzing drugs [(Note: Ins. by Act 21 of 1962, sec.22 (w.e.f. 27-7-1964)) or cosmetics]
- Prescribe the qualifications and duties of Government Analysts and the qualifications of Inspectors;
- Prescribe the methods of test or analysis to be employed in determining whether a drug [(Note: Ins. by Act 21 of 1962, sec.22 (w.e.f. 27-7-1964)) or cosmetic] is of standard quality;
- Prescribe, in respect of biological and organ metallic compounds, the units or methods of standardization [(dd) (Note: Ins. by Act 13 of 1964, sec.24 (w.e.f. 15-9-1964)) Prescribe under clause (d) of [(Note: Subs.

by Act 68 of 1982, sec.29, for "section 17B" (w.e.f. 1-2-1983)) section 17A] the colour or colours which a drug may bear or contain for purposes of colouring;]

Prescribe the forms of licences [(Note: Subs. by Act 68 of 1982, sec.29, for "for the manufacture for sale" (w.e.f. 1-2-1983)) for the manufacture for sale or for distribution], for the sale and for the distribution of drugs or any specified drug or class of drugs [(Note: Ins. by Act 21 of1962, sec.22 (w.e.f. 27-7-1964)) or of cosmetic or any specified cosmetic or class of cosmetics], the form of application for such licences, the conditions subject to which such licences may be issued, the authority empowered to issue the same [(Note: Ins. by Act 68 of 1982, sec.29 (w.e.f. 1-2-1983)) the qualifications of such authority] and the fees payable therefore [(Note: Ins. by Act 68 of 1982, sec.29 (w.e.f. 1-2-1983)) and provide for the cancellation or suspension of such licences in any case where any provision of this Chapter or the rules made there under is contravened or any of the conditions subject to which they are issued is not complied with]

- [(Note: Ins. by Act 68 of 1982, sec.29 (w.e.f. 1-2-1983)) Prescribe the records, registers or other documents to be kept and maintained under section 18B;
- (eea) Prescribed the fees for the inspection)for the purposes of grant or renewal of licences) of premises, wherein any drug or cosmetic is being or is proposed to be manufactured;
- (eeb) Prescribe the manner in which copies are to be certified under sub-section (2A) of section 22,]
- Specify the diseases or ailments, which a drug may not purport or claim [(Note: Subs. by Act 11 of 1955, sec.15, for "to cure or mitigate") to prevent, cure or mitigate] and such other effects which a drug may not purport or claim to have;
- Prescribe the conditions subject to which small quantities of drugs may be manufactured for the purpose of examination, test or analysis;

Require the date of manufacture and the date of expiry of potency to be clearly and truly stated on the label or container of any specified drug or class of drugs, and prohibit the sale, stocking or exhibition for sale, or distribution of the said drug or class of drugs after the expiry of a specified period from the date of manufacture or after the expiry of the date of potency;

Prescribe the conditions to be observed in the packing in bottles, packages, and other containers of drugs [(Note: Ins. by Act 21 of 1962, sec.22 (w.e.f. 27-7-1964)) or cosmetics], [(Note: Ins. by Act 68 of 1982, sec.29 (w.e.f. 1-2-1983)) including the use ofpacking material which comes into direct contact with the drugs] and prohibit the sale, stocking or exhibition for sale, or distribution of drugs [(Note: Ins. by Act 21 of 1962, sec.22 (w.e.f. 27-7-1964)) or cosmetics] packed in contravention of such conditions;

Regulate the mode of labeling packed drugs [(Note: Ins. by Act 21 of 1962, sec.22 (w.e.f. 27-7-1964)) or cosmetics], and prescribe the matters, which shall or shall not be included in such labels;

Prescribe the maximum proportion of any poisonous substance which may be added to or contained in any drug, prohibit the manufacture, sale or stocking or exhibition for sale, or distribution of any drug in which that proportion is exceeded, and specify substances which shall be deemed to be poisonous for the purposes of this Chapter and the rules made there under; Require that the accepted scientific name of any specified drug shall be displayed in the prescribed manner on the label or wrapper of any patent or proprietary medicine containing such drug

Note: Clause (m) omitted by Act 13 of 1964, sec.24 (w.e.f. 15-9-1964))

[(Note: Subs. by Act 35 of 1960, sec.10, for clause (n) (w.e.f. 16-3-1961)) Prescribe the powers and duties of Inspectors [(Note: Ins. by Act 68 of 1982, sec.29 (w.e.f. 1-2-1983)) and the qualifications of the authority to which such Inspectors shall be subordinate] and [(Note: Subs. by Act 21 of 1962, sec.22, for "the drugs or class of drugs" w.e.f. 27-7-1964)) specify the drugs or classes of drugs or cosmetics or classes of cosmetics] in relation to which and the conditions, limitations or restrictions subject to which, such powers and duties may be exercised or performed;]

- Prescribe the forms of report to be given by Government Analysts, and the manner of application for test or analysis under section 26 and the fees payable therefore;
- [(Note: Subs. by Act 13 of 1964, sec.24 for clause (p) (w.e.f. 15-9-1964)) specify the offences against this Chapter or any rule made there under in relation to which an order of confiscation may be made under section 31; and]
- Provide for the exemption, conditionally or otherwise, from all or any of the provisions of this Chapter or the rules made there under, of any specified drug or class of drugs [(Note: Ins. by Act 21 of 1962, sec.22 (w.e.f. 27-7-1964)) or cosmetic or class of cosmetics].

GOVERNMENT ANALYSTS

The Central Government or a State Government may, by notification in the Official Gazette, appoint such persons as it thinks fit, having the prescribed qualifications to be Government Analysts for such areas as may be assigned to them by the Central Government or the State Government, as the case may be.

Notwithstanding anything contained in sub-section (1), neither the Central Government nor a State Government shall appoint as a Government Analyst any official not serving under it without the previous consent of the Government under which he is serving.

[(Note: Subs. by Act 68 of 1982, sec.32 (w.e.f. 1-2-1983)) No person who has any financial interest in the manufacture or sale of any drug shall be appointed to be a Government Analyst under this section.]

COMMENT

The opinion of an Analyst, not recognized under section 33F, cannot be relied upon, whatever may be his qualifications; State v. Rajamani, 1982 Cri LJ (NOC) 71. 33G. *Inspectors*: (1) The Central Government or a State Government may, by notification in the Official Gazette, appoint such persons as it thinks fit, having the prescribed qualifications, to be Inspectors for such areas as may be assigned to them by the Central Government or the State Government as the case may be.

The powers which may be exercised by an Inspector and the duties which may be performed by him and the conditions, limitations or restrictions subject to which such powers and duties may be exercised or performed shall be such as may be prescribed.

No person who has any financial interest in the manufacture or sale of any drug shall be appointed to be an Inspector under this section.

Every Inspector shall be deemed to be a public servant within the meaning of section 21 of the Indian Penal Code and shall be officially sub-ordinate to such authority as the Central Government appointing him may specify in this behalf.

Application of provisions of sections 22, 23, 24 and 25. – The provisions of sections 22, 23, 24 and 25 and the rules, if any, made there under shall, so far as may be, apply in relation to an Inspector and a Government Analyst appointed under this Chapter as they apply in relation to an Inspector and a Government Analyst appointed under Chapter IV, subject to the modification that the references to "drug" in the said sections, shall be construed as references to [(Note: Subs. by Act 68 of 1982, sec.2 for certain words (w.e.f. 1-2-1983)) Ayurvedic, Siddha or Unani] drug.

Penalty for manufacture, sale., of Ayurvedic, Siddha or Unani drug in contravention of this Chapter. Whoever himself or by any other person on his behalf—

Manufactures for sale or for distribution:

- Any Ayurvedic, Siddha or Unani drug
- Deemed to be adulterated under section 33EE, or
- Without a valid licence as required under clause (c) of section 33EEC, shall be punishable with imprison-

ment for a term which may extend to one year and with fine which shall not be less than two thousand rupees.

- Any Ayurvedic, Siddha or Unani drug deemed to be spurious under section 33EEA, shall be punishable with imprisonment for a term which shall not be less than one year but which may extend to three years and with fine which shall not be less than five thousand rupees.

Provided that the Court may, for any adequate and special reasons to be mentioned in the judgment, impose a sentence of imprisonment for a term of less than one year and of fine of less than five thousand rupees; or Contravenes any other provisions of this Chapter or of section 24 as applied by section 33H or any rule made under this Chapter, shall be punishable with imprisonment for a term which may extend to three months and with fine which shall not be less than five hundred rupees. 33J Penalty for subsequent offences. – Whoever having been convicted of an offences, Under clause (a) of sub-section (1) of section 33I is again convicted of an offence under that clause, shall be punishable with imprisonment for a term which may extend to two years and with fine which shall not be less than two thousand rupees; Under clause (b) of sub-section (1) of section 33I is again convicted of an offence under that clause, shall be punishable with imprisonment for a term which shall not be less than two years but which may extend to six years and with fine which shall not be less than five thousand rupees: Provided that the Court may, for any adequate and special reasons to be mentioned in the judgment, impose a sentence of imprisonment for a term of less than two years and of fine of less than five thousand rupees; Under sub-section (2) of section 33I is again convicted of an offence under that sub-section, shall be punishable with imprisonment for a term which may extend to six months and with fine which shall not be less than one thousand rupees.

Confiscation: Where any person has been convicted under this Chapter, the stockof the [(Note: Subs. by Act 68 of 1982, sec.2, for certain words (w.e.f. 1-2-1983)) Ayurvedic, Siddha or Unani] drug, in respect of which the contravention has been made, shall be liable to confiscation. Application of provisions to Government departments.

The provisions of this Chapter except those contained in section 33K shall apply in relation to the manufacture for sale, sale or distribution of any [(Note: Subs. by Act 68 of 1982, sec.2, for certain words (w.e.f. 1-2-1983)) Ayurvedic, Siddha or Unani] drug by any department of Government as they apply in relation to the manufacture for sale, sale or distribution of such drug by any other person.

33M. Cognizance of offences. (1) No prosecution under this Chapter shall be instituted except by an Inspector [(Note: Ins. by Act 68 of 1982, sec.34 (w.e.f. 1-2-1983)) with the previous sanction of the authority specified under sub-section (4) of section 33G].

No Court inferior to that [(Note: Subs. by Act 68 of 1982, sec.34, for "of a Presidency Magistrate or of a Magistrate of the first class" (w.e.f. 1-2-1983)) of a Metropolitan Magistrate or of a Judicial Magistrate of the first class] shall try an offence punishable under this Chapter.33N. Power of Central Government to make rules. – (1) The Central Government may, [(Note: Subs. by Act 68 of 1982, sec.35, for "after consultation with the Board" (w.e.f. 1-2-1983)) after consultation with, or on the recommendation of, the Board] and after previous publication by notification in the Official Gazette, make rules for the purpose of giving effect to the provisions of this Chapter: Provided that consultation with the Board may be dispensed with if the Central Government is of opinion that circumstances have arisen which render it necessary to make rules without such consultation, but in such case, the Board shall be consulted within six months of the making of the rules and the Central Government shall take into consideration any suggestions which the Board may make in relation to the amendment of the said rules.

- Without prejudice to the generality of the foregoing power, such rules may.
- Provide for the establishment of laboratories for

testing and analyzing [(Note: Subs. by Act 68 of 1982, sec.2, for certain words (w.e.f. 1-2-1983)) Ayurvedic, Siddha or Unani] drugs;

- Prescribe the qualifications and duties of Government Analysts and the qualifications of Inspectors;
- Prescribe the methods of test or analysis to be employed in determining whether a drug [(Note: Ins. by Act 21 of 1962, sec.22 (w.e.f. 27-7-1964)) or cosmetic] is of standard quality;
- Prescribe, in respect of biological and organ metallic compounds, the units or methods of standardization

[(dd) (Note: Ins. by Act 13 of 1964, sec.24 (w.e.f. 15-9-1964)) Prescribe under clause (d) of [(Note: Subs. by Act 68 of 1982, sec.29, for "section 17B" (w.e.f. 1-2-1983)) section 17A] the colour or colours which a drug may bear or contain for purposes of colouring;] Prescribe the forms of licences [(Note: Subs. by Act 68 of 1982, sec.29, for "for the manufacture for sale" (w.e.f. 1-2-1983)) for the manufacture for sale or for distribution], for the sale and for the distribution of drugs or any specified drug or class of drugs [(Note: Ins. by Act 21 of1962, sec.22 (w.e.f. 27-7-1964)) or of cosmetic or any specified cosmetic or class of cosmetics], the form of application for such licences, the conditions subject to which such licences may be issued, the authority empowered to issue the same [(Note: Ins. by Act 68 of 1982, sec.29 (w.e.f. 1-2-1983)) the qualifications of such authority] and the fees payable therefore [(Note: Ins. by Act 68 of 1982, sec.29 (w.e.f. 1-2-1983)) and provide for the cancellation or suspension of such licences in any case where any provision of this Chapter or the rules made there under is contravened or any of the conditions subject to which they are issued is not complied with]; [(ee) [(Note: Ins. by Act 68 of 1982, sec.29 (w.e.f. 1-2-1983)) Prescribe the records, registers or other documents to be kept and maintained under section 18B; (eea) Prescribed the fees for the inspection)for the purposes of grant or renewal of licences) of premises, wherein any drug or cosmetic is being or is proposed to be manufactured; (eeb) Prescribe the manner in which copies are to be certified under sub-section (2A) of section 22;]. Specify the diseases or ailments, which a drug may not purport or claim [(Note: Subs. by Act 11 of 1955, sec.15, for "to cure or mitigate") to prevent, cure or mitigate] and such other effects which a drug may not purport or claim to have Prescribe the conditions subject to which small quantities of drugs may be manufactured for the purpose of examination, test or analysis; Require the date of manufacture and the date of expiry of potency to be clearly and truly stated on the label or container of any specified drug or class of drugs, and prohibit the sale, stocking or exhibition for sale, or distribution of the said drug or class of drugs after the expiry of a specified period from the date of manufacture or after the expiry of the date of potency; Prescribe the conditions to be observed in the packing in bottles, packages, and other containers of drugs [(Note: Ins. by Act 21 of 1962, sec.22 (w.e.f. 27-7-1964)) or cosmetics], [(Note: Ins. by Act 68 of 1982, sec.29 (w.e.f. 1-2-1983)) including the use ofpacking material which comes into direct contact with the drugs] and prohibit the sale, stocking or exhibition for sale, or distribution of drugs [(Note: Ins. by Act 21 of 1962, sec.22 (w.e.f. 27-7-1964)) or cosmetics] packed in contravention of such conditions.

Regulate the mode of labeling packed drugs [(Note: Ins. by Act 21 of 1962, sec.22 (w.e.f. 27-7-1964)) or cosmetics], and prescribe the matters, which shall or shall not be included in such labels; Prescribe the maximum proportion of any poisonous substance which may be added to or contained in any drug, prohibit the manufacture, sale or stocking or exhibition for sale, or distribution of any drug in which that proportion is exceeded, and specify substances which shall be deemed to be poisonous for the purposes of this Chapter and the rules made there under

Require that the accepted scientific name of any specified drug shall be displayed in the prescribed manner on the label or wrapper of any patent or proprietary medicine containing such drug;(m) (Note: Clause (m) omitted by Act 13 of 1964, sec.24 (w.e.f. 15-9-1964))[(n) [(Note: Subs. by Act 35 of 1960, sec.10, for clause (n) (w.e.f. 16-3-1961)) Prescribe the powers and duties of Inspectors [(Note: Ins. by Act 68 of 1982, sec.29

(w.e.f. 1-2-1983)) and the qualifications of the authority to which such Inspectors shall be subordinate] and [(Note: Subs. by Act 21 of 1962, sec.22, for "the drugs or class of drugs" (w.e.f. 27-7-1964)) specify the drugs or classes of drugs or cosmetics or classes of cosmetics] in relation to which and the conditions, limitations or restrictions subject to which, such powers and duties may be exercised or performed

- Prescribe the forms of report to be given by Government Analysts, and the manner of application for test or analysis under section 26 and the fees payable therefore;
- [(Note: Subs. by Act 13 of 1964, sec.24 for clause (p) (w.e.f. 15-9-1964)) specify the offences against this Chapter or any rule made there under in relation to which an order of confiscation may be made under section 31; and]
- Provide for the exemption, conditionally or otherwise, from all or any of the provisions of this Chapter or the rules made there under, of any specified drug or class of drugs [(Note: Ins. by Act 21 of 1962, sec.22 (w.e.f. 27-7-1964)) or cosmetic or class of cosmetics].

GOVERNMENT ANALYSTS

- The Central Government or a State Government may, by notification in the Official Gazette, appoint such persons as it thinks fit, having the prescribed qualifications to be Government Analysts for such areas as may be assigned to them by the Central Government or the State Government, as the case may be.
- Notwithstanding anything contained in sub-section (1), neither the Central Government nor a State Government shall appoint as a Government Analyst any official not serving under it without the previous consent of the Government under which he is serving.
- [(Note: Subs. by Act 68 of 1982, sec.32 (w.e.f. 1-2-

1983)) No person who has any financial interest in the manufacture or sale of any drug shall be appointed to be a Government Analyst under this section.]

COMMENT

The opinion of an Analyst, not recognized under section 33F, cannot be relied upon, whatever may be his qualifications; State v. Rajamani, 1982 Cri LJ (NOC) 71. 33G. Inspectors. (1) The Central Government or a State Government may, by notification in the Official Gazette, appoint such persons as it thinks fit, having the prescribed qualifications, to be Inspectors for such areas as may be assigned to them by the Central Government or the State Government as the case may be.

- The powers which may be exercised by an Inspector and the duties which may be performed by him and the conditions, limitations or restrictions subject to which such powers and duties may be exercised or performed shall be such as may be prescribed.
- No person who has any financial interest in the manufacture or sale of any drug shall be appointed to be an Inspector under this section.
- Every Inspector shall be deemed to be a public servant within the meaning of section 21 of the Indian Penal Code and shall be officially sub-ordinate to such authority as the Central Government appointing him may specify in this behalf.

33H. Application of provisions of sections 22, 23, 24 and 25. The provisions of sections 22, 23, 24 and 25 and the rules, if any, made there under shall, so far as may be, apply in relation to an Inspector and a Government Analyst appointed under this Chapter as they apply in relation to an Inspector and a Government Analyst appointed under Chapter IV, subject to the modification that the references to "drug" in the said sections, shall be construed as references to [(Note: Subs. by Act 68 of 1982, sec.2 for certain words (w.e.f. 1-2-1983)) Ayurvedic, Siddha or Unani] drug.

33-I. Penalty for manufacture, sale., of Ayurvedic, Siddha or Unani drug in contravention of this Chapter. Whoever himself or by any other person on his behalf.

- *Manufactures for sale or for distribution:*
  - Any Ayurvedic, Siddha or Unani drug
  - Deemed to be adulterated under section 33EE,
  - Without a valid licence as required under clause (c) of section 33EEC, shall be punishable with imprisonment for a term which may extend to one year and with fine which shall not be less than two thousand rupees;

Any Ayurvedic, Siddha or Unani drug deemed to be spurious under section 33EEA, shall be punishable with imprisonment for a term which shall not be less than one year but which may extend to three years and with fine which shall not be less than five thousand rupees: Provided that the Court may, for any adequate and special reasons to be mentioned in the judgment, impose a sentence of imprisonment for a term of less than one year and of fine of less than five thousand rupees;

Contravenes any other provisions of this Chapter or of section 24 as applied by section 33H or any rule made under this Chapter, shall be punishable with imprisonment for a term which may extend to three months and with fine which shall not be less than five hundred rupees.

33J. Penalty for subsequent offences. Whoever having been convicted of an offences. Under clause (a) of sub-section (1) of section 33I is again convicted of an offence under that clause, shall be punishable with imprisonment for a term which may extend to two years and with fine which shall not be less than two thousand rupees;

Under clause (b) of sub-section (1) of section 33I is again convicted of an offence under that clause, shall be punishable with imprisonment for a term which shall not be less than two years but which may extend to six years and with fine which shall not be less than five thousand rupees:

Provided that the Court may, for any adequate and special reasons to be mentioned in the judgment, impose a sentence of imprisonment for a term of less than two years and of fine of less than five thousand rupees;

Under sub-section (2) of section 33I is again convicted of an offence under that sub-section, shall be punishable with imprisonment for a term which may extend to six months and with fine which shall not be less than one thousand rupees.

33K. Confiscation. Where any person has been convicted under this Chapter, the stockof the [(Note: Subs. by Act 68 of 1982, sec.2, for certain words (w.e.f. 1-2-1983)) Ayurvedic, Siddha or Unani] drug, in respect of which the contravention has been made, shall be liable to confiscation. 33L. Application of provisions to Government departments. The provisions of this Chapter except those contained in section 33K shall apply in relation to the manufacture for sale, sale or distribution of any [(Note: Subs. by Act 68 of 1982, sec.2, for certain words (w.e.f. 1-2-1983)) Ayurvedic, Siddha or Unani] drug by any department of Government as they apply in relation to the manufacture for sale, sale or distribution of such drug by any other person.

33M. Cognizance of offences. (1) No prosecution under this Chapter shall be instituted except by an Inspector [(Note: Ins. by Act 68 of 1982, sec.34 (w.e.f. 1-2-1983)) with the previous sanction of the authority specified under sub-section (4) of section 33G]. No Court inferior to that [(Note: Subs. by Act 68 of 1982, sec.34, for "of a Presidency Magistrate or of a Magistrate of the first class" (w.e.f. 1-2-1983)) of a Metropolitan Magistrate or of a Judicial Magistrate of the first class] shall try an offence punishable under this Chapter.

33N. Power of Central Government to make rules. (1) The Central Government may, [(Note: Subs. by Act 68 of 1982, sec.35, for "after consultation with the Board" (w.e.f. 1-2-1983)) after consultation with, or on the recommendation of, the Board] and after previous publication by notification in the Official Gazette, make rules for the purpose of giving effect to the provisions of this Chapter:

Provided that consultation with the Board may be dispensed with if the Central Government is of opinion that circumstances have arisen which render it necessary to make rules without such consultation, but in such case, the Board shall be consulted within six months of the making of the rules and the Central Government shall take into consideration any suggestions which the Board may make in relation to the amendment of the said rules.

- Without prejudice to the generality of the foregoing power, such rules may.
- Provide for the establishment of laboratories for testing and analyzing [(Note: Subs. by Act 68 of 1982, sec.2, for certain words (w.e.f. 1-2-1983)) Ayurvedic, Siddha or Unani] drugs;
- Prescribe the qualifications and duties of Government Analysts and the qualifications of Inspectors;
- Prescribe the methods of test or analysis to be employed in determining whether any [(Note: Subs. by Act 68 of 1982, sec.2, for certain words (w.e.f. 1-2-1983)) Ayurvedic, Siddha or Unani] drug is labeled with the true list of the ingredients which it is purported to contain;
- Specify any substance as a poisonous substance;
- Prescribe the forms of licences for the manufacture for sale of [(Note: Subs. by Act 68 of 1982, sec.2, for certain words (w.e.f. 1-2-1983)) Ayurvedic, Siddha or Unani] drugs, [(Note: Ins. by Act 68 of 1982, sec.35 (w.e.f.1-2-1983)) and for sale of processed Ayurvedic, Siddha or Unani drugs,] the form of application for such licences, the conditions subject to which such licences may be issued, the authority empowered to issue the same and the fees payable therefore, [(Note: Ins. by Act 68 of 1982, sec.35 (w.e.f.1-2-1983)) and provide for the cancellation or suspension of such licences in any case where any provision of this Chapter or rules made there under is contravened or any of the conditions subject to which they are issued is not complied with];
- (Note: Subs. by Act 68 of 1982, sec.35, for "clause (f)" (w.e.f. 1-2-1983)) Prescribe the conditions to be

observed in the packing of Ayurvedic, Siddha and Unani drugs including the use of packing material which comes into direct contact with the drugs, regulate the mode of labeling packed drugs and prescribe the matters which shall or shall not be included in such labels;]

- Prescribe the conditions subject to which small quantities of [(Note: Subs. by Act 68 of 1982, sec.2 for certain words (w.e.f. 1-2-1983)) Ayurvedic, Siddha or Unani] drugs may be manufactured for the purpose of examination, test or analysis; and
- [(gg) (Note: Ins. by Act 68 of 1982, sec.35 (w.e.f. 1-2-1983)) Prescribe under clause (d) of section 33EE the colour or colours which an Ayurvedic, Siddha or Unani drug may bear or contain for purposes of colouring;
- (gga) Prescribe the standards for Ayurvedic, Siddha or Unani drugs under section 33EB;]
- Any other matter which is to be or may be prescribed under this Chapter.

33-O. Power to amend First Schedule. The Central Government, after consultation with the Board and after giving, by notification in the Official Gazette, not less than three months' notice of its intention so to do, may, by a like notification, add to or otherwise amend the First Schedule for the purposes of this Chapter and thereupon the said Schedule shall be deemed to be amended accordingly.

33P. Power to give directions. The Central Government may give such directions to any State Government as may appear to the Central Government to be necessary for carrying into execution in the State any of the provisions of this Act or of any rule or order made there under.

CLAIMS AND CONTRADICTION

The purpose of the study was to prove in cancer cells the activity that was discovered by the JHU Biology Professor, Dr. Ru Chih C. Huang, and her associates in viruses. The objective was to prove in human trials the inhibition of growth in tumour cells that the JHU team had observed in studies conducted in animals. Dennis O'Shea, JHU spokesperson, claimed that the university had never "directly" funded the study. However, his claim was contested by the RCC project leader, Dr. Manoj Pandey. According to Pandey, the RCC had received two cheques, signed by JHU treasurer William E. Snow Jr, worth $19,400 and was awaiting the third. Dr. M. Krishnan Nair, RCC Director, is also reported to have stated in March that the project is funded by the JHU.

He said that the RCC was to receive Rs.25 lakhs and the amount could later be increased to Rs.1.25 crores. Interestingly, Pandey claimed that the JHU received permission from the U.S. government to import the tissue of Indian cancer patients for study. O'Shea told the journal Science: "I am not saying we know where these funds came from. Just because Johns Hopkins cuts a cheque it does not necessarily mean that it approved the project being funded. Making sense of the financial transactions is a task for the new investigative panel."

O'Shea's remark that the study was not directly funded by the JHU assumes significance in the light of Huang's comments to Science. She told Science that the funding for the project came entirely from private sources, including the JHU and a Minnesota-based company, Biocure Medical LLC. The company was set up with the objective of designing and conducting clinical trials of compounds derived from nor-dihydro-guaiaretic acid (NDGA).

According to Huang, the supporters of the project have committed about $2.5 million to conduct pilot trials in four places in Asia. Dr. Krishnan Nair had stated that Phase II trials were also to be carried out at, besides RCC, the K.J. Hospital, Kanpur, and the Banaras Hindu University, Varanasi, under the RCC's supervision.

The catch was that let alone the Food and Drug Administration of the U.S., even the JHU's Institutional Review Board (IRB) had not approved the trial although Huang had submitted the protocol for the clinical trials to the IRB early this year. More pertinently, according to a press release issued by the Press Information Bureau (PIB) on behalf of the Union Health Ministry in the wake of the controversy, the approval by the Drug Controller General of India (DCGI) seems to have been granted only in February this year, months after the experiments were conducted.

The PIB press release said that the RCC was granted permission on February 2, 2001, to import M4N (tetra-O-methyl nor-dihydro-guaiaretic acid) from the JHU to undertake a study to evaluate its efficacy in advanced oral and cervical malignancies on the basis of pre-clinical and other relevant data submitted by the RCC Director.

It is not a retrospective sanction. The proposal came to us only then. We do not know if the trials had been going on earlier," said S. Ramteke, Deputy DCGI. On the other hand, Dr. Krishnan Nair had claimed that the initial application for the trial had been submitted to the DCGI on September 12, 1998, and the Ethics Committee of the RCC had granted its permission for the conduct of the study on November 10, 1999. Meanwhile, according to Dr. Krishnan Nair, discussions were held with the DCGI and, based on his verbal consent, the study was commenced.

The DCGI refused to comment on Dr. Krishnan Nair's claim and said that a central committee had been constituted to investigate the issue. When asked about the granting of sanction after two years of trials, DCGI Ashwini Kumar said: "Clinical trials of new molecules, experimental drugs and so on are new to our country. The systems are still evolving. We shall know whether the trials had been going on since 1999 only after the investigating team submits its report."

Meanwhile, the three-member team constituted by the Union Health Minister to inquire into the controversy was in Thiruvananthapuram waiting for Dr. Pandey to return from the U.S. The committee was expected to submit its report by August 16. The normal procedure for obtaining approval for clinical trials (Phase I, II and III) is to submit the toxicological data collected from animal experiments to the DCGI. The toxicological data are sent by the DCGI to the Indian Council of Medical Research's (ICMR) Toxicology Committee for evaluation and, if found to be safe, the DCGI gives sanction for Phase I trials. However, Ranjit Roy Choudhury, chairman of the ICMR Toxicology Committee, said the committee had not received any proposal from the RCC for trials or any data regarding the proposed trials. He added that of late the DCGI did not refer all cases to the committee. Choudhury said that with many new drugs coming into the market, imported and otherwise, the DCGI had begun to refer the data to its expert committee or a chosen set of experts rather than to the ICMR committee.

Regulations with regard to Good Clinical Practices (GCP), Good Laboratory Practices (GLP) and Standard Operating Procedures (SOP) are still in the draft stage. However, N.K. Ganguly, Director General of the ICMR, said that the basic regulations governing clinical trials were put in place by the Drugs and Cosmetics Act, 1940 and several clinical trials on new drugs and molecules had been carried out in India in conformity with the Act.

Moreover, the ICMR had brought out a base document on Ethical Guidelines for Biomedical Research on Human Subjects in September 2000. The ICMR document makes clear the legal provision for clinical trials: "The proposed trial should be carried out only after the approval of the DCGI as is necessary under Schedule Y of the Drugs and Cosmetics Act. The investigator should also get the approval of the Ethics Committee of the institution before submitting the proposal to the DCGI. All the guiding principles should be followed irrespective of whether the drug has been developed in this country or abroad or whether clinical trials have been carried out outside India or not."

The DCGI is being evasive when he tries to make a distinction between an experimental drug for a research project and a new drug and says that the regulations for experimental studies do not exist. The Drugs and Cosmetics Act is clear on the definition of a new drug as part of the Rules framed under the Act and it includes any new chemical entity (NCE). Schedule Y of the Act states: "For new drug substances discovered in other countries, Phase I trials [the kind being carried out at the RCC] are not usually allowed to be initiated in India unless Phase I data from other countries are available. However, such trials may be permitted in the absence of Phase I data from other countries if the drug is of special relevance to the health problems of India." Since even Phase I data from the U.S. were not available, on what basis did the DCGI give its approval in February 2001?

According to informed sources in the ICMR, the RCC had applied for a financial grant for the study from the ICMR during 1998-99. The ICMR raised some objections about the proposal and rejected the application. The exact grounds on which the proposal was rejected are not known, according to them. Four and a half years ago, the ICMR had rejected an application for financial grant to conduct a study on foetal tissue transplantation in patients of retinitis pigmentosa under an India-U.S. collaborative research programme at the L.V. Prasad Eye Institute, Hyderabad.

The application was rejected on the grounds that undertaking such clinical trials on Indian subjects for an experimental procedure, which were not done on U.S. subjects, was not ethical and hence not acceptable. In a statement issued then, the ICMR said: "The ICMR stands by the decision unless documentary evidence is provided by the principal investigator that the conduct of such experiments in human beings will be done (or has already been done) on subjects of both countries collaborating in the project, the proposal cannot be considered ethical." Hence, the ICMR may have turned down the RCC's request for financial support because in the RCC- JHU drug trial case too no parallel studies on U.S. subjects were proposed to be done.

Chapter 5

Narcotic Drugs and Psychotropic Substances Act

DEFINITIONS

In this Act, unless the context otherwise requires, - [(i) "Addict" means a person who has dependence on any narcotic drug or psychotropic substance](ii) "Board" means the Central Board of Excise and Customs constituted under the Central Boards of Revenue Act, 1963;(iii) "Cannabis (hemp)" means (a) Charas, that is, the separated resin, in whatever form, whether crude or purified, obtained from the cannabis plant and also includes concentrated preparation and resin known as hashish oil or liquid hashish, (b) Ganja, that is, the flowe-ring or fruiting tops of the cannabis plant (excluding the seeds and leaves when not accompanied by the tops), by whatever name they may be known or designated; and (c) Any mixture, with or without any neutral material of any of the above forms of cannabis or any drink prepared therefrom; (iv) "Cannabis plant" means any plant of the genus cannabis; (v) "Coca derivative" means:

- Crude cocaine, that is, any extract of coca leaf, which can be used, directly or indirectly, for the manufacture of cocaine;
- Ecgonine and all the derivatives of ecgonine from which it can be recovered;
- Cocaine, that is, methyl ester or benzoyl-ecgonine and its salts;

- All preparations containing more that 0.1 percent of cocaine;
- Coca leaf " means
- The leaf of coca plant except a leaf from which all ecgonine, cocaine and any other ecgonine alkaloids have been removed;
- Any mixture thereof with or without any neutral material, but does not include any reparation containing not more than 0.1 percent of cocaine;

But does not include any preparation containinh not more than 0.1 per cent of cocaine; (vii) "Coca plant" means the plant of any species of the genus Erythroxylon;[(viia) "Commercial quantity", in relation to narcotic drugs and psychotropic substances, means any quantity greater than the quantity specified by the CentralGovernment by notification in the Official Gazette;(viib) "Controlled delivery" means the technique of allowing illicit or suspect consignments of narcotic drugs.

Psychotropic substances, controlled substances or substances substituted for them to pass out of, or through or into the territory of India with the knowledge and under the supervision of an officer empowered in this behalf or duly authorised under section 50A with a view to identifying the persons involved in the commission of an offence under this Act; (viic) "corresponding law" means any law corresponding to the provisions of this Act;] [(viid) "Controlled substance" means any substance which the Central Government may, having regard to the available information as to its possible use in the production or manufacture of narcotic drugs or psychotropic substances or to the provisions of any International Convention, by notification in the Official Gazette, declare to be a controlled substance]; (viii) "Conveyance" means a conveyance of any description whatsoever and includes any aircraft, vessel; (viiia) "Ilicit traffic", in relation to narcotic drugs and psychotropic substances, means (i) Cultivating any coca plant or gathering any portion of coca plant; (ii) Cultivating the opium poppy or any cannabis plant;(iii) Engaging in the production, manufacture, possession, sale, purchase, transportation, warehousing, concealment, use or consu-mption, import inter-State, export inter-State, import into India export from India or transhipment, of narcotic drugs or psychotropic substances.

- Dealing in any activities in narcotic drugs or psychotropic substances other than those referred to in sub-clauses (i) to (iii);
- Handling or letting out any premises for the carrying on of any of the activities referred to in sub-clauses (i) to (iv),Other than those permitted under this Act, or any rule or order made, or any condition of any licence, term or authorisation issued, thereunder, and includes, -(1) Financing, directly or indirectly, any of the aforementioned activities;(2) Abetting or conspiring in the furtherance of or in support of doing any of the aforementioned activities; and (3) Harbouring persons engaged in any of the aforementioned activities];

International Convention" means (a) The Single Convention on Narcotic Drugs, 1961 adopted by the United Nations Conference at New York in March, 1961; (b) The Protocol, amending the Convention mentioned in sub-clause (a), adopted by the United Nations Conference at Geneva in March 1972; (c) The Convention on Psychotropic Substances, 1971 adopted by the United nations Conference at Vienna in February, 1971; and (d) Any other international convention, or protocol, or other instrument amending an international convention, relating to narcotic drugs or psychotropic substances which may be ratified or acceded to by India after the commencement of this Act;-(x) "Manufacture", in relation to narcotic drugs or psychotropic substances, includes:

- All processes other than production by which such drugs or substances may be- obtained,
- Refining of such drugs or substances
- Making of preparation (otherwise than in a pharmacy on prescription) with or containing such drugs or substances;
- Manufactured drugs" mean

All coca derivatives, medicinal connabis, opium derivatives and poppy straw concentrate; Any other substance or preparation which the Central Government may, having regard to the available information as to its nature or to a decision, if any, under any International Convention, by notification in the Official Gazette, declare to be a manufactured drug.

But does not include any narcotic substance or preparation which the Central Government may, having regard to the available information as to its nature or to a decision, if any, under and International Convention, by notification in the Official Gazette, declare to be a manufactured drug.(xii) "Medical cannabis" that is, medicinal hemp, means any extract or tincture of cannabis (hemp);(xiii) "Narcotics Commissioner" means the Narcotics Commissioner appointed under Section 5; (xiv) "Narcotic drug" means coca leaf, cannabis (hemp), opium, poppy straw and includes all manufactured drugs; (xv) "Opium" means.

The coagulated juice of the opium poppy; and (b) Any mixture, with or without any neutral material, of the coagulated juice of the opium poppy, but does not include any preparation containing not more than 0.2 per cent, of morphine; (xvi) "Opium derivative" means (a) Medicinal opium, that is, opium which has undergone the processes necessary to adapt it for medicinal use in accordance with the requirements of the Indian Pharmacopoeia or any other Pharmacopoeia notified in this behalf by the Central Government whether in powder form or granulated or otherwise or mixed with neutral materials; (b) Prepared opium, that is, any product of opium obtained by any series of operations designed to transform opium into an extract suitable for smoking and the dross or other residue remaining after opium is smoked; (c) Phenanthrene alkaloids, namely, morphine, codeine, thebaine and theirs salts;(d) Diacetylmorphine that is, the alkaloid also known as diamorphine or heroin and its slats; and (e) All preparations containing more than 0.2 percent of morphine or containing any diacetylmorphine; (xvii) "Opium poppy" means-(a) The plant of the species papaver somniferum L; and (b) The plant of any other species of papaver from which opium or any phenanthrene alkaloid call be extracted and which the Central Government may, be notification in the Official Gazette, declare to be opium poppy for the purposes of this Act;

Poppy straw" means all parts (except the seeds) of the opium poppy after harvesting whether in their original form or cut, crushed or powdered and whether or not juice has been extracted therefrom; (xix) "Poppy straw concentrate" means the material arising when poppy straw has entered into a process for the concentration of its alkaloids;(xx) "Preparation" in relation to a narcotic drugs or psychotropic substance means any one or more such drugs or substances in dosage form or any solution or mixture, in whatever physical state, containing one or more such drugs or substances.

Prescribed means prescribed by rules made under this Act; (xxii) "Production" means the separation of opium, poppy straw, coca leaves or cannabis from the plants from which they are obtained; (xxiii) "Psychotropic substance" means any substance, natural or synthetic, or any natural material or any salt or preparation of such substance or material included in the list of psychotropic substances specified in the Schedule; [(xxiiia) "Small quantity", in relation to narcotic drugs and psychotropic substances, means any quantity lesser than the quantity specified by the Central Government by notification in the Official Gazette.]

To import inter-State" means to being into a State or Union territory in India from another State or Union territory in India; (xxv) "To import into India", with its grammatical variations and cognate expressions, means to being into India from a place outside India and includes the bringing into any port or airport or place in India of a narcotic drug or a psychotropic substances intended to be taken out of India without being removed from the vessel, aircraft, vehicle or any other conveyance in which it is being carried. Explanation.For the purposes of this clause and clause (xxvi), "India" includes the territorial waters of India; (xxvi) "To export from India", with its grammatical variations and cognate expressions, means to take out of India to a place outside India; (xxvii) "To export inter-State," means to take out of a State or Union territory in India to another State or Union territory in India;(xxviii) "To transport" means to take from one place to another within the same State or Union territory.

Relation to narcotic drugs and psychotropic substances, means any kind of use except personal consumption;] (xxix) Words and repressions used herein and not defined but defined in the Code of Criminal Procedure, 1973 have the meanings respectively assigned to them in that Code. Explanation: For the purpose of clauses (v), (iv), (xv),and (xvi) the percentages in the case of liquid preparations shall be calculated on the basis that a preparation containing one per cent of a substance means a preparation in which one gram of substance, if solid, or one mililitre of substance, if liquid, is contained in every one hundred mililitre of the preparation and so on in proportion for any greater or less percentage:

- Drugs and Magic Remedies (Objectionable Advertisements) Act 1954.
- Medicinal and Toilet Preparations (Excise Duties) Act 1955, Rules 1976.
- Poison Act.
- Factory Act.
- Delhi shops and Establishment Act.
- Medical termination of pregnancy Act.
- The Drug (price control) order.
- The Insecticide Act.
- Indian Patents Act as applicable to drugs and pharmaceuticals.
- AICTE Act, 1987.

Chapter 6

Freedom of Movement

OVERALL POSITION

Cyprus accepts and is in a position to implement the acquis with respect to the freedom of movement of persons, so that by the date of accession the Cyprus legislation, organisational structures and mechanisms required, will be in line with EU requirements.

No transitional period or derogation from the acquis is requested. As a working hypothesis the Government of the Republic of Cyprus considers that accession to the European Union will take place not later than 31 December 2002.

OVERVIEW OF ALIGNMENT WITH THE ACQUIS

CAPACITY TO IMPLEMENT THE ACQUIS

- Mutual recognition of qualifications.
- General Systems directives.
- Overview of Alignment with the Acquis.

As the University of Cyprus was established recently (in 1992) and its faculties are restricted in the sphere of economic and social sciences, a lot of academic qualifications (as well as professional training) are obtained abroad, mostly in E.U countries and the USA. This is the case for medical professions, for lawyers, for architects, for engineers, etc.

The prevailing legislative framework for the recognition of academic qualifications and professional training includes Law 11/85, which ratifies the UNESCO convention (Paris, 1979) on the recognition of studies, diplomas and degrees concerning higher education in the states belonging to the European region, Law 68(I) of 1996 (amended in 1998), which regulates matters concerning the recognition of higher and tertiary education qualifications and the provision of relevant information, and the Industrial Training Law of 1974. Cyprus is now in the process of ratifying the UNESCO/Council of Europe Convention on the recognition of Qualifications Concerning Higher Education in the European Region (Lisbon 1997).

Law 68(I) of 1996 provides for the establishment of the Cyprus Council for the Recognition of Higher Education Qualifications (KY.S.A.T.S.). The Regulations providing the framework for the functioning of the Council and setting up of explicit procedures and criteria for the recognition of qualifications were recently approved by the House of Representatives.

A number of professions is regulated in Cyprus but a lot of them, especially those for which a university degree is not required, are not. An indicative list of regulated professions under the General Systems Directives was given in the Harmonogram submitted during the screening process. Common features of most of the regulated professions are: (a) the requirement of Cypriot nationality, (b) the requirement of residence, (c) obligatory membership in professional bodies/associations, and (d) the recognition of academic qualifications, vested with the Council of Ministers, which decides on the basis of recommendations of the appropriate professional bodies/associations/ technical chamber, etc.

Full alignment with Directives 89/48/EEC and 92/51/EEC implies that all the above discriminatory provisions/restrictive requirements will be removed by the date of accession (1/1/2003). During the interim period Cyprus will create the necessary legal framework and will implement the necessary preparatory measures, including the definition of the role and responsibilities of the national authorities (and their relationship with the existing professional bodies/associations), the development of relations/linkages with national authorities of other member states, the training of personnel to be engaged in the provision of information and the processing of applications, and the dissemination of information to Cypriots and Europeans, with respect to both EU policies, and the prevailing legislation (in Cyprus and the Member States). The necessary institutional arrangements will be in place six months prior to the accession date (by 1/7/2002).

Issues such as the appointment of a national co-ordinator, and the commitment of a Member State to process the applications the soonest possible and communicate the decision of the competent authority the latest within 4 months from the submission of the application, and to provide for the necessary remedy measures, so that every applicant will have the right to lodge an appeal before a court in the host country, will be addressed in the legislation transposing the General Systems Directives. It will also be ensured that the provision of language, where retained, will not lead to discrimination against non-Cypriots and will not be disproportionate.

CAPACITY TO IMPLEMENT THE ACQUIS COMMUNAUTAIRE

The National Authorities which will be engaged in the implementation of the General System directives are, the Ministry of Education and Culture, supported by the Cyprus Council for the Recognition of Higher Education Qualifications (KYSATS) for Directive 89/48 and the Ministry of Labour and Social Insurance (in co-operation with the Industrial Training Authority) for the Directive 92/51.

The Cyprus Council for the Recognition of Higher Education Qualifications (KYSATS), an independent body, was established in 1997. The Council decides on issues of recognition of diplomas, and issues a relevant certificate, it advises the Minister of Education on issues relevant to the recognition of diplomas, it draws up suggestions on the preparation of national regulations relating to procedures, requirements and methodologies for recognition of diplomas, it appoints Committees of Experts for the examination of diplomas, and it decides on the matters proposed by the Committees of experts. For the recognition of equivalence and correspondence of a degree, the yardstick taken is the degree of the same discipline of the University of Cyprus, or other public educational institution of higher education of Cyprus. In the event that such degree is not conferred by these institutions, the yardstick is the degree of the same discipline of recognised educational institutions of E.U. countries.

The Ministry of Labour and Social Insurance will be the national authority for the implementation of Directive 92/51, in co-operation with the Industrial Training Authority.

Issues relating to the academic contents of training programmes and the recognition of educational qualifications will fall within the competence of the Ministry of Education and Culture.

- Sectoral directives
- Lawyers
- Overview of Alignment with the Acquis

The domestic legislation dealing with the legal profession in Cyprus is the Advocates Law, as amended, and the Regulations issued thereunder.

Only qualified advocates, members of the Cyprus Bar, may offer legal services. For an advocate to be qualified to practice law, he must be enrolled in "the Roll of Advocates", which is kept by the Chief Registrar of the Supreme Court. The prerequisites for enrolment are: (a) a Degree in Law, (b) twelve (12) months pupilage at the office of an advocate or at the office of the Attorney-General, (c) success in written examinations conducted by the Legal Board, (d) be over 21 years of age and of good character, and (e) Cypriot citizenship and residence.

Foreigners married to Cypriot citizens and residing in Cyprus are also entitled to be enrolled provided they satisfy all other criteria under the Law. Exceptionally, the Legal Board may grant a special permit to an advocate from abroad of acknowledged repute to appear before a Court in respect of a particular proceeding, cause or matter, provided he appears together with an advocate practising in the Republic.

It is noted that Cyprus is an observer member of the Council of the Bars and Law Societies of the European Communities.

The prevailing legislation and the existing institutions and practices provide the necessary framework and no problems are foreseen in adopting and implementing these directives. In order to ensure conformity, legislative changes will be introduced relating, inter alia, to the removal of citizenship requirement, the compliance of the migrant lawyer with the code of conduct of Cyprus, the registration and representa-tion of the migrant lawyer before the professional associations and the provision of remedies against any decision not to effect registration with the competent authority. The relevant amendments will be introduced by 1/1/2002, and the date for implementation will be 1/1/2003 (i.e. the date of accession to the E.U.).

Capacity to Implement the Acquis Communautaire

The Ministry of Justice and Public Order is acting as a co-ordinator for legislation. Furthermore, the following bodies established on the basis of the prevailing national legislation are the competent authorities for ensuring full compliance with the Community directives. The Legal Board, chaired by the Attorney-General, which has the power and responsibility for the admission to practice and the enrolment of advocates. The Cyprus Bar Council with powers and duties to maintain the honour and independence of the Bar and its defence in relation to the Judiciary and the Executive. Finally, all disciplinary matters of members of the Bar are exclusively within the competence of the Disciplinary Board. The Chief Registrar of the Supreme Court keeps the Roll of Advocates.

ARCHITECTS

Overview of Alignment with the Acquis

The professions of architecture, as well as of civil engineering, quantity surveying, mechanical and electrical engineering, electronic engineering, information technology, chemical engineering, mining engineering and geology, land valuation, topographical engineering and town planning and the profession of technician engineer are regulated by the Scientific and Technical Chamber Law No. 224 of 1990, as amended (1990-1997). According to the Law, access to these professions and the use of the corresponding professional title is restricted to the members of the Scientific and Technical Chamber (STC) only. To register as a member of the STC a person needs to be a citizen of the Republic of Cyprus and a permanent resident, he must be a holder of a university degree or other equivalent diploma recognised by the Council of Ministers, must have at least one year of professional experience, be over 21 years of age and without a criminal record. All provisions of legislation that are in conflict with the provisions of the relevant Community Directives will be amended, so that by accession national legislative instruments will be in full compliance with the acquis. The STC will continue to be the competent authority for the implementation of the Architects Directives.

Capacity to Implement the Acquis

The Ministry of Communications and Works is responsible for drafting the revised legislation, while the STC has responsibility for its implementation. The STC was established in 1991 under the Scientific and Technical Chamber Law No. 224 of 1990. It is a self-financed independent body with its General Council elected by its members. The STC is responsible for a variety of activities associated with regulating the architectural and engineering professions. These activities include: (a) the registration of members and the issue of licences for practising the relevant professions, (b) representation of its registered members, (c) the exercise of disciplinary control on its members, (d) the dissemination of information to the public on matters of its jurisdiction and (e) consultative role on engineering matters.

Health-Care Professionals

Overview of Alignment with the Acquis Communautaire The University of Cyprus has no faculty of Medicine,

Dentistry and Pharmacy and therefore Cypriot professionals in these fields receive their education abroad. The vast majority graduate from Greek Universities, and the rest, from universities of E.U. member countries as well as from the countries of Central and Eastern Europe.

Doctors (Directives 93/16, 97/50, 98/21, 98/63). The practice of Medicine and the recognition of diplomas, titles and other evidence of formal qualification in medicine and specialised medicine are regulated by law. The Medical Council, appointed by the Council of Ministers under the Law, Cap. 250 (the Medical Registration Law) is the competent authority for securing the right of establishment and the freedom to provide services for these professions. Registration within the Registry of the Medical Council and the local Medical Association is obligatory. The requirements for registration are (a) Cypriot citizenship, (b) a degree which provides evidence of qualification in a basic course of study of 6 year duration (theoretical and practical) at an approved University, (c) a certificate issued by the competent authority which provides for one-year internship (6 months Surgery and 6 months internal medicine) at a recognised hospital and (d) two references from medical consultants in Cyprus on the character of the applicant.

For specialists, with the exception of a one-year internship, all the above requirements must be met, and in addition, a diploma of specialisation issued by a University or a teaching Hospital is required. Full compliance with the acquis will be achieved by accession (1/1/2003). Towards this end, the necessary legislative changes will be introduced for the abolition of existing restrictive conditions, such as the requirement of Cypriot citizenship and the obligatory registration to the registry of the Medical Council, and the inclusion of provisions for the curricula of Doctors, the course of study of GP/s and the specific training in General Medicine, specialisations common to all Member States, diplomas not referred to in the directive, and qualifications awarded in third countries. Dentists (Directives 78/686 and 78/687). The practice of Dentistry, the recognition of diplomas in Dentistry and specialised Dentistry are subject to legislative provisions. The competent Authority for the exercise of the right of establishment and the freedom to provide services, is the Dental Council appointed by the Council of Ministers under the Law, Cap. 249 (Cyprus Dentists Registration Law).

Registration with the Registry of the Dental Council and the local Dental Association is obligatory. The requirements for registration are: (a) Cypriot citizenship and (b) a degree in Dentistry with evidence of qualification in a basic course of study in Dentistry of 5 years theoretical and practical instruction at an approved University. Regarding specialised dentistry, a diploma of specialisation with evidence of the training conditions must also be submitted.

The Dental Council recognises two specialisations in dentistry: Orthodontics and Dental Maxillo-facial surgery. The minimum duration of training studies to specialise in the above two areas is 2 years for orthodontics and three years for maxillofacial surgery.

For full compliance with the acquis, planned to be attained by accession (1/1/2003) all restrictive conditions (requirement of Cypriot citizenship and obligatory registration with the national Dental Association) will be abolished. Furthermore, the field of activity for dentists will be clearly defined in the Law, and the issues of dental and orthodontic specialisations, and the minimum training requirement (three years and five years) for oral maxillofacial surgery will be reconsidered.

Pharmacists (Directives 85/432, 85/433). The Pharmacy and Poisons Law Cap. 254, which is in partial compliance with the above directives, regulates the profession of pharmacists. Registration with the registry of the Pharmaceutical Council and the local association is obligatory. The requirements for registration are: (a) Cypriot citizenship, (b) a diploma in Pharmacy with evidence of qualification in a basic course of study of 4 years in pharmacy in an approved pharmaceutical faculty of a University, (c) evidence of practical training of 1 year in pharmacy open to the public or in a Hospital. The pharmacist must also pass an examination on forensic pharmacy. For full compliance with the acquis, legilslative changes will be introduced for the abolition of prevailing restrictive provisions (requirement of Cypriot citizenship, obligatory registration with the professional association, examination of forensic pharmacy). Full harmonisation will be achieved by accession (1/1/2003).

Nurses (Directives 77/452/EEC, 77/453/EEC) and Midwives (Directives 80/154/EEC, 80/155/EEC). Nursing and mid-wifery are regulated in Cyprus as two separate professions. The competent authority for the recognition of diplomas, the right of establishment and the right to provide services is the Nursing Council which is appointed by the Council of Ministers (as provided in the Nursing and Mid-Wifery Law of 1988 and its amendments).

The requirements to be registered as a Nurse for general care and to practice general Nursing are the following: (a) Cypriot citizenship and (b) a diploma with evidence of qualification in a basic course of study and a post-basic training course at an approved Nursing School consisting of a three year course or 4600 hours of theoretical and clinical instruction. Registration with the professional Association is obligatory.

The School of Nursing of the Ministry of Health provides basic and post-basic education of nurses and midwives, who are employed in the public or private sector. Students wishing to join the course are required to have a school-leaving certificate (Secondary Education) and to pass entrance examinations. The duration of the basic programme is 39 months. The School also offers a basic programme in Psychiatric Nursing (same duration), which deviates from the provisions of the relevant Directive.

For this purpose, as from next year, it will become a post basic programme. As far as midwifery is concerned, to register and to practice the profession, a diploma is required with evidence qualification in a basic course of study and a post-basic training course at an approved Nursing School comprising a three year course or 4600 hours of theoretical and clinical instruction (Nurse) and one year training in

Midwifery. As from 1999, the duration of the course was extended to 18 months in order to comply with the requirements of Directive 80/154/EEC. For full compliance with the Nurses and Midwives directives all restrictive provisions of the prevailing (i.e. requirement of Cypriot citizenship, obligatory registration to the professional association) will be abolished by 1/1/2003.

Veterinary Surgeons

Cypriot legislation is in partial conformity with directives 78/1026/EEC and 78/1027/EEC, through the Practice of Medicine and Registration of Veterinary Surgeons Law of 1990. A person is recognised as a veterinary surgeon after obtaining a diploma from a recognised academic institution offering studies in veterinary medicine and spending a period of six months of practical training in a government veterinary clinic. Cypriot citizenship is also required, although the registration of non-Cypriots may be allowed following a Council of Ministers decision.

The duration of studies for veterinary surgeons is in line with Community requirements. Content of studies is not specifically provided for in the Law and acceptance of academic qualifications depends on information and certifications received for each new case. Amendments to the existing Law in order to achieve full compliance with Community requirements, are scheduled to be introduced by accession.

Capacity to Implement the Acquis

The institutional and organisational structures, necessary to implement the directives relating to health care professions are already in place. The competent authorities for the professions covered above are, the Medical Council, the Dental Council, the Pharmaceutical Council and the Nursing and Midwives Council, all appointed by the Govern-ment. The administrative structures of the Ministry of Health will be enforced accordingly in order to cope with the additional functions relating to the dissemination of information to both

Cypriots and Europeans about opportunities offered and the requirements regarding the freedom to provide services in the medical field. The implementing body for the legislation relating to veterinary surgeons is the Veterinary Council, which is appointed by the Council of Ministers. The Veterinary Council maintains a register of qualified veterinary surgeons.

CITIZENS RIGHTS

VOTING RIGHTS

Overview of Alignment with the Acquis Communautaire Voting is compulsory for both Parliamentary elections and the Municipal elections and all Cypriot nationals over the age of 18 years are obliged to register in the Electoral lists provided they have been residing in Cyprus for six months. The penalty for failure to register, upon conviction, is up to 6 months imprisonment and/or a fine of not exceeding 450 Cyprus Pounds. The penalty for failure to exercise the right to vote is, upon conviction, a fine of not exceeding 200 Cyprus Pounds.

All Cypriot nationals may stand as candidates in Parliamentary and Municipal elections provided they have not been convicted of an offence involving dishonesty or moral turpitude or are of unsound mind. For Municipal Elections, the candidate must also be a permanent resident of the municipality.

For the transposition of Council Directive 93/109/EC allowing E.U. citizens residing in Cyprus (including Cypriot nationals) to exercise their right to vote and to stand as candidates in elections to the European Parliament, new legislation will be introduced.

In order to enable E.U. citizens residing in Cyprus to exercise their right to vote and stand as candidates in municipal elections, amendments to the existing legislation (The Municipal Corporations Law 1985 and Registration of the Electors and Register Law 1980) will be introduced to bring it in line with Council Directive 94/80/EC. It should be noted that no amendments to the Constitution would be required in order to grant EU citizens residing in Cyprus their rights under the voting rights directives.

Capacity to Implement the Acquis Communautaire

The authority responsible for implementing the legislation will be the Electoral Service of the Ministry of Interior. By the date of accession (1/1/2003), the necessary organisational/institutional structures will be operational and Cyprus will be in a position to implement the voting rights directives.

Right of Residence and Public Order

Overview of Alignment with the Acquis Communautaire

The Aliens and Immigration Law Cap. 105 as amended (1972-1998) and the Aliens and Immigration Regulations of 1972-1998 provide for the admission and residence in Cyprus. Currently, the Residence Permits are classified into Temporary Permits and Permanent Permits.

The former are valid for limited periods and are issued mainly for employment, studies, business, visit and medical treatment, whereas Permanent Permits are issued for self-employed persons in various sectors of economic activity such as in agriculture, in mining and quarrying, as entrepreneurs, as employees, and for retired persons, etc.

Permanent residence permits are approved by the Minister of Interior based on recommendation of the Immigration Control Board comprised of the Permanent Secretary of the Ministry of Interior (Chairman) and representatives of the Ministries of Foreign Affairs, Labour and Social Insurance and Commerce, Industry and Tourism. Temporary Residence Permits are approved by the Migration Officer.

The prevailing legislation provides for family reunification for the holders of a permanent residence permit, whereas for holders of temporary residence permit relevant applications are examined on a case by case basis. Children born in Cyprus are allowed to stay with their parents until the expiry of the parent's permit. For full compliance the existing Aliens and Immigration legislation will be replaced by a new Law in order to satisfy the requirements of the directives for both economically active and non-active individuals, as well as for the transposition of the public order directive. The new law will enter into force as from 1/1/2003.

Capacity to Implement the Acquis Communautaire

The competent authority for the implementation of the Aliens and Immigration legislation is the Ministry of Interior. By accession (1/1/2003), the necessary organisational/ institutional structures will be operational and Cyprus will have completed the necessary steps to address matters relating to the issuing of residence permits to EU nationals in accordance with the provisions of the relevant directives.

STUDENTS MOBILITY RIGHTS "GRAVIER RULING"

OVERVIEW OF ALIGNMENT WITH THE ACQUIS

The existing legislation is not in compliance with the principle of equal treatment. Deviations from this principle appear in tertiary education, both in state owned, as well as in private institutions. These mainly refer to differentiation in the level of tuition fees (Cypriots are entitled to free tuition at the University of Cyprus) and to quotas maintained for entry of foreign students. The subject has been discussed during the screening of Chapter 18: Education and Training and Cyprus has undertaken to eliminate all discrepancies and secure equal treatment between Cypriot and EU nationals upon accession. The Ministry of Education and Culture has already sent a circular to all public educational institutions of higher education, advising them to initiate the procedure for amending their administrative regulations in order to abolish any discriminatory provisions between nationals and EU students concerning fees and quotas for admission by 1/ 1/2003 (upon accession).

Capacity to Implement the Acquis Communautaire

The Ministry of Education and Culture is the competent authority in the field of education. The existing structures provide the capacity for adaptation to and the implementation of the relevant acquis. Tertiary level education is provided in three different types of institutions, namely in the University of Cyprus, in public schools, colleges or institutes and in private schools, collage or institutes.

Free Movement of Workers

For the effective implementation of the E.U. Regulation 1612/68, the above described structures need to be strengthened. To this end, the improvement of the relevant Unit will be promoted through computerisation and restructuring. Overview of Alignment with the Acquis Communaitaure The employment of foreign nationals is regulated by the Aliens and Immigration Law, Cap. 105 and the Aliens and Immigration Regulations (No. 242 of 1972) issued under this Law.

Cyprus has ratified the international instruments, which regulate the employment of foreign workers and provide for equal treatment of nationals and non-nationals as regards terms and conditions of employment. More specifically, Cyprus has ratified the ILO Convention No. 97 of 1949 on "Migration for Employment (Revised)", Convention No. 143 of 1975 on "Migrant Workers (Supplementary Provisions)" and Article 19 of the European Social Charter on "The Right of migrant workers and their families to protection and assistance". Hence, all foreigners employed in Cyprus enjoy equal treatment with nationals as regards conditions of work, salaries, social insurance benefits, income tax liabilities, etc.

Work Permits are currently classified as Temporary and Permanent. Permanent Work Permits may be issued after approval by the Minister of Interior on recommendation of the Immigration Control Board, to persons wishing to reside in Cyprus as self-employed professionals or to persons who have entered into employment agreement with Cypriot employers. Temporary Work Permits may be issued after approval by the Migration Officer only for specific positions/ jobs, basically to meet labour shortages in Cyprus and provided that no Cypriots are available. A Temporary Work Permit is valid only for the job for which the permit was issued and any change of employment or employer is treated as a new application.

Applications for Temporary Work Permits are submitted by the prospective Cypriot employer to the Ministry of Labour and Social Insurance, which recommends its approval or rejection to the Migration Officer, taking into account the labour market situation. A Temporary Work Permit, as a rule, may be issued provided that the foreign worker/applicant is outside the country, with the exception of nationals of E.U. member states, who are allowed to enter the country to seek employment in person, and then apply for a work permit. The duration of Temporary Work Permits may be up to four years and it is extended only in exceptional cases (for one further year only). For E.U. citizens there are no restrictions in respect of such extensions.

Capacity to Implement the Acquis Communautaire

The organisational structures necessary to implement the relevant E.U. regulation (1612/68) on the Freedom of Movement for Workers within the Community are already in place. Within the overall organisational set up of the Ministry of Labour and Social Insurance, the functions related to employment, including the employment of foreign workers, fall mainly within the sphere of responsibilities of the Department of Labour. Supplementary pension rights of workers moving within the Community in Cyprus supplementary schemes can be broadly distinguished in two categories: Provident Funds, which provide lump-sum benefits, and pension schemes which provide periodical benefits..Provident Funds are established within the system of free collective bargaining and are registered and operate in accordance with the Provident Fund legislation. Occupational Pension Schemes are established by Law for employees of the public and semi-public sector and local authorities. The existing legislation fulfils the requirements of the Directive since there is no discrimination regarding the preservation of vested rights for members of provident funds and occupational pension schemes in respect of whom contributions are no longer being made and remain in Cyprus and members in respect of whom contributions are no longer being made and move to another country. Moreover, no discrimination exists concerning the provision of information for pension rights to members of a supplementary scheme who move to another country. EURES network (European Employment Service) Overview of Alignment with the Acquis Communautaire. The existing system for the registration and processing of job vacancies and job applications is manual (both at national and at regional level) and relies on the use of standard forms for candidate registration, employer/vacancy registration and the collection of statistics.

Following the computerisation of the system, which is currently under way, Cyprus will not face any difficulties in participating in the EURES network and in disseminating information relating to vacancies and applications for Employment as well as information on the state and trends on the labour market, living and working conditions.

Capacity to Implement the Acquis Communautaire

The Employment Services of the Department of Labour (Ministry of Labour and Social Insurance), which is the authority responsible for the registration of job vacancies and job applications, shall also have the responsibility for the creation and the running of the EURES centre. Assistance from the European Commission is expected to be secured both for the setting up of the necessary infrastructure, as well as for the training of the Euro-adviser who will be appointed and the personnel to be involved.

COORDINATION OF SOCIAL SECURITY SCHEMES

Overview of Alignment with the Acquis Communautaire. The Cyprus legislation and in particular the Social

Insurance Law, the Social Pension Law, the Child Benefit Law and the Compensation of Victims of Violent Crimes Law apply to all branches of Social Security as specified under Article 4 of the Regulation 1408/71.

The Social Insurance legislation covers compulsorily every person gainfully occupied in Cyprus either as an employed or self-employed person. Voluntary insurance is available to persons, who wish to continue insurance after a prescribed period of compulsory insurance or to persons who work abroad in the service of Cypriot employers.

The Scheme is financed by contributions from the employers, the insured persons and the State. The rate of social insurance contributions for the employed persons is 16,6% and for the self-employed persons 15,6%. The Scheme provides cash benefits for marriage, maternity, sickness, unemployment, widowhood, invalidity, orphanhood, old age, death, and employment injury. The Scheme provides also free medical treatment for persons receiving invalidity pension and for employed persons who sustain injuries as a result of an accident at work or occupational disease.

Under the Social Insurance legislation the principle of equality of treatment between nationals and non-nationals is maintained and non-nationals have the same rights and obligations under the Scheme as nationals. The Social Insurance legislation allows the export of benefits to persons residing outside Cyprus, with the exception of sickness, maternity and unemployment benefits. The legislation will be amended in order to allow for the exportation of these benefits upon accession.

As regards the aggregation for insurance periods Cyprus already applies this principle in bilateral agreements. The principle of lex loci laboris applies to all benefits under the Social Insurance legislation. Regarding the healthcare system, draft legislation, which provides for the introduction of a National Insurance Health Scheme has been submitted to the House of Representatives and is now being discussed. The new Health Scheme will be providing universal coverage and its financing will be based on contributions of the social partners. It has been proposed that government contribution shall cover approximately 50% of the scheme's total budget, and the remaining 50% to be shared equally between employers and employees. Cyprus will enter into consultations with the European Commission in order to conclude the technical adaptations needed for the implementation of the Regulation, taking into account the characteristics of the national system and that certain non-contributory benefits currently provided, are directly funded from the government general budget.

Capacity to implement the Acquis Communautaire. By accession, Cyprus will be able to fully implement the Acquis in the area of co-ordination of Social Security Schemes without significant problems. The Department of Social Insurance, which administers the Social Insurance Scheme, the Social Pension Scheme, the Child Benefit Scheme and the Compensation of Victims of Violent Crimes Scheme, shall be the competent authority for the implementation of the Regulation.

This Department has gained substantial experience in the area of co-ordination of social security through the implementation of Social Insurance Bilateral Agreements. The Department of Social Insurance will be strengthened by additional duly trained staff in order to cope with the workload which will arise from the implementation of the Regulation. In order to make the appeal procedure in matters of Social Insurance more flexible, the setting up of Special Tribunals or the extension of the jurisdiction of the Industrial Disputes Court to cover such matters is under consideration.

Requests for Special Arrangements/Justification

No problems are foreseen in accepting the acquis and no derogation or transitional period is requested.

Chapter 7

Principles of Drugs

PRINCIPLES OF ANTIMICROBIAL THERAPY

Antimicrobial drugs are effective in the treatment of infections because of their selective toxicity-the ability to kill an invading microorganism without harming the cells of the host.

The selective toxicity is relative, rather than absolute, requiring that the concentration of the drug be carefully controlled to attack the microorganism while still being tolerated by the host. Selective antimicrobial therapy takes advantage of the biochemical differences that exist between microorganisms and human beings.

SELECTION OF ANTIMICROBIAL AGENTS

Depends on: (1) the identity of the organism and its sensitivity to a particular agent, (2) the site of infection, (3) the safety of the agent, and (4) patient factors.Identification and sensitivity of the organism is central to the selection of the proper drug. It is essential to obtain a sample culture of the organism prior to initiating treatment if possible.

Empiric Therapy Prior to Organism Identification

Acutely ill patients usually require immediate treatment (initiated after specimens for laboratory analyses are obtained but before the results of the culture are available). The choice of drug in the absence of sensitivity data is influenced by patient (e.g., age), location of the infection, and results of the Gram stain. Possible to initiate empiric therapy with an antibiotic or a combination of antibiotics covering infections by both gram-positive and gram-negative microorganisms.

The Site of the Infection

- *Effect of vascular perfusion:* Effective levels of antibiotic must reach the infection site »»» any change that diminishes access of the drug to the infected area may alter the effectiveness of the treatment (e.g., poor perfusion of an anatomic area, like the lower limbs of the diabetic, make infections in these regions difficult to treat).
- *Blood-brain barrier:* Treatment of infections of CNS (e.g. meningitis) depends on the ability of a drug to penetrate into the cerebrospinal fluid.

The blood-brain barrier ordinarily excludes many antibiotics. However, inflammation enhances penetrability and allows sufficient levels of many (but not all) antibiotics to enter the cerebrospinal fluid.

The Safety of the Agent

- *Inherent toxicity of the drug:* Many of the antibiotics (e.g. penicillins), are among to least toxic of all drugs because they interfere with a site unique to the growth of microorganisms. Other antimicrobial agents (e.g. chloramphenicol) are less specific and are reserved for life- threatening infections because of the drug s potential for serious toxicity.
- *Patient factors:* Safety is also related to patient factors that can predispose to toxicity.ad 4) Status of the patient
- *Immune system:* Elimination of infecting organisms from the body depends on an intact immune system. Antibacterial drugs decrease the microbial population (bactericidal), or inhibit further bacterial growth (bacteriostatic), but the host defenses must ultimately eliminate the invading organism.

Immunocompromised patients (weakened immune defenses) »»» higher than usual doses of bactericidal agents are required to eliminate the infective organism.

- *Renal dysfunction:* Poor kidney function (10% or less of normal) causes accumulation of antibiotics that are eliminated by this route »»» possibility of serious adverse effects (can be controlled by adjusting the dose or the dosage schedule).
  Note: The number of functioning nephrons decreases with age, making elderly patients particularly vulnerable.
- *Hepatic dysfunction:* Antibiotics that concentrate in the liver (e.g., erythromycin, tetracycline) are contraindicated in patients with liver disease.
- *Pregnancy:* All antibiotics cross the placenta. Adverse effects to the fetus are rare (except for tooth dysplasia and inhibition of bone growth with the tetracyclines). However, some anthelmintics are embryotoxic and teratogenic.
- *Lactation:* A nursing infant can receive antibiotics (as well as other drugs) administered to the mother via the breast milk. Even though the concentration of an antibiotics in breast milk is usually low, the total dose may be enough to cause problems.

BACTERIOSTATIC VERSUS BACTERICIDAL DRUGS

Bacteriostatic drugs arrest the growth and replication of bacteria at serum levels achievable in the patient, thus limiting the spread of infection while the body's immune system attacks, immobilizes, and eliminates the pathogens.

If the drug is removed before the immune system has scavenged the organism, enough viable organism may remain to begin a second cycle of infection. Bactericidal agents kill bacteria.

CHEMOTHERAPEUTIC SPECTRA

The chemotherapeutic spectrum of a drug refers to the species of microorganisms affected by that drug.

- Narrow spectrum (chemotherapeutic agents acting only on a single or a limited group of microorganisms, e.g. isoniazid is active only against mycobacteria).

- Extended spectrum (agents that are effective against gram-positive organisms and also against a significant number of gram-negative bacteria (e.g., ampicillin is considered to have an extended spectrum because it acts against gram-positive and gram-negative bacteria).
- Broad spectrum (drug such as tetracycline and chloramphenicol affect a wide variety of microbial species and are referred to as broad spectrum antibiotics. Administration of broad-spectrum antibiotics can drastically alter the nature of the normal bacterial flora and can precipitate a superinfection of an organism, e.g., candida whose growth is normally kept in check by the presence of other microorganism).

COMBINATIONS OF ANTRIMICROBIAL DRUGS

Therapeutically advisable to treat with the single agent that is most specific for the infecting organism. This strategy reduces the possibility of superinfection and decreases the occurrence of resistant organisms.

However, situations in which combinations of drugs are employed do exist (e.g. the treatment of tuberculosis). Treatment with a combination of drugs may lead to the emergence of superinfection antagonism between the drug, or an increased incidence of toxicity.

DRUG RESISTANCE

Resistance in bacteria spread at three levels:

1. By transfer of bacteria between people
2. By transfer of resistance genes between bacteria (usually on plasmides, i.e. on extrachromosomal genetic elements that can replicate independently and can carry genes coding for resistance to antibiotics/r genes/)
3. By transfer of resistance genes between genetic

elements within bacteria, on transposons (stretches of DNA that can be transported from one plasmid to another, and also from plasmid to chromosome and vice versa)

Bacteria are said to be resistant if their growth is not halted by the maximum level of an antibiotic that is tolerated by the host. Microbial species may develop strains resistant to that agent. This is usually accomplished through an alteration of their chromosomal or extrachromosomal (plasmid) DNA, followed by selection for resistant strains. Furthermore, these special plasmids (R-factors), which carry genes for resistance to one or more antimicrobial drug, can be transferred from one organism to another either by transduction or conjugation.

Multiple drug resistance spread by this mechanism - clinically significant problem (e.g., methicillin-resistant Staphylococcus aureus is also resistant to all antibiotics except vancomycin and possibly ciprofloxacin, rifampin and imipenem/cilastatin).

Biochemical mechanisms of resistance to antibiotics:

- Production of enzymes that inactivate the drug (e.g. Đ-lactamases inactivate penicillin, acetyltransferases inactivate chloramphenicol, kinases and other inactivate aminoglycosides)
- Alteration of the drug-binding sites, which are binding sites for antibiotics (e.g. sites of ribosomes) Occurs with aminoglycosides, erythromycin, penicillin
- Reduction of drug uptake by the bacterium (e.g. tetracyclines)
- Alteration of enzymes (e.g. dihydrofolate reductase becomes insensitive to trimethoprim)

PROPHYLACTIC ANTIBIOTICS

Certain clinical situation requires the use of antibiotics for the prevention rather than the treatment of infections. The indiscriminate use of antimicrobial agents can result in bacterial resistance and superinfection »»» prophylactic use is restricted to clinical situations where benefits outweigh the potential risks.

Uses:

- Prevention of streptococcal infections in patients with a history of rheumatic heart disease.
- Pretreatment of patients undergoing dental extractions who have implanted prosthetic devices (e.g. artificial heart valves).
- Prevention of tuberculosis or meningitis among individuals who are in close contact with infected patients.
- Presurgical treatment in gastrointestinal procedures, vaginal hysterectomy, cesarean section, joint replacement, and open fracture surgery.

COMPLICATIONS OF ANTIBIOTIC THERAPY

Selective toxicity to the invading organism does not insure the host against adverse effects (drug may produce an allergic response or be toxic in ways unrelated to the drug's antimicrobial activity.

HyperSensitivity

Reactions to antimicrobial drugs or their metabolic products frequently occur (e.g. the penicillins can cause serious hypersensitivity problems, from rashes (urticaria) to anaphylactic shock).

Direct Toxicity

High serum levels of antibiotic may cause toxicity by affecting cellular processes in the host (e.g. aminoglycosides can cause ototoxicity by interfering with membrane function in the hair cells of the organ of Corti).

Super Infections

Therapy (particularly with broad spectrum antimicrobials or combinations of agents) can lead to alterations of the normal microbial flora of the upper respiratory, intestinal and genitourinary tracts »»» the overgrowth of opportunistic organisms, especially fungi. These infections can involve resistant organisms and are often difficult to treat.

ANTIBIOTICS AFFECTING THE BACTERIAL CELL WALL

GENERAL PRINCIPLES OF ANTIMICROBIAL DRUG THERAPY

Definitions

- *Antibiotic:*
  - Relating to antibiosis.
  - Prejudicial to life.
  - A soluble substance derived from a mold or bacterium that inhibits the growth of other micro-organisms.
  - Relating to such an action.
- *Antimicrobial:* Tending to destroy microbes, to prevent their multiplication or growth, or to prevent their pathogenic action.
- *Antibacterial:* Destructive to or preventing the growth of bacteria.

Taken from Stedman's Medical Dictionary. 26th Edition. It is the structure of the antimicrobial that determines the its mechanism of action, toxicity, and metabolism.

Some desirable properties in a antimicrobial are: selective toxicity, bactericidal rather than bacterostatic action, low rate of resistance development, low toxicity, low rate of hypersensitivity reactions, water soluble, activity in a wide variety of chemical environments, wide distribution, and low cost. Antibiotics often target processes in the microbe that are significantly different or nonexistent in animal cells.

By exploiting the difference between microbial and animal cells antibiotics can be used to treat infections without harming host. This is known as selective toxicity. Selective toxicity is the corner stone of effective antimicrobial therapy. Penicillins are a classic example of excellent selective toxicity. This class of antibiotic interferes with bacterial cell wall synthesis and repair. Animal cells do not have a cell wall and penicillins have remarkably low direct toxicity to humans, while being highly deleterious to bacteria.

However, antibiotic therapy is never without risks, even with compounds with high selective toxicity. All antibiotics have potential to cause harm. Penicillins for one can illicit serious allergic reactions. Understanding the likely toxicity associated with each antibiotic class is imperative for responsible antibiotic use. Therapeutic index (or therapeutic window) relates to the dose of a drug required to produced the desired effect to the dose associated with toxicity.

Often an antibiotic is given to a patient before the organism infecting the patient is identified. This is known as empiric therapy. The choice of drug is guided by knowing which organisms are likely to be causing the specific infection. For instance, community-acquired pneumonia is often caused by *S. pneumoniae, M. pneumoniae,* and *C. pneumoniae, Legionella, M.catarrhalis,* or *H. influenzae* usually cause. The uncomplicated pneumonia is often empirically treated with macrolides, which has a good activity against these organisms.

Empiric therapy should be followed as much as possible by directed narrow spectrum therapy once the organism's identity and sensitivity to different antibiotics are established. Organism identification relies on a combination of macroscopic (e.g., colony morphology), microscopic, biochemical, and immunologic characteristics.

More recently molecular genetics methods (e.g., PCR) are also contributing to organism identification. With the organism isolated, the sensitivity to different antibiotics can be established to help guide therapy. As we will discuss later antibiotic resistance is a growing problem which underscores the need for sensitivity determination.

Some antibiotics do not kill bacteria at achievable serum concentrations and these are called bacterostatic. These drugs inhibit bacterial growth, but growth is resumed upon drug withdrawal. Drugs that kill bacteria are called bactericidal. In patients with immunologic compromise or life-threatening infection a bactericidal antibiotic should be given.

Bactericidal drugs are also highly desirable in infections characterized by poor regional host defenses, such as endocarditis and meningitis. Bacterostatic drugs are appropriate when the host's immune system is able to finish the job. Penicillins and the other beta-lactam are examples of bactericidal drugs; tetracyclines and sulfonamides are bacterostatic.

When one drug's mechanism of action makes another drug more effective, they are said to work in synergy. For instance, penicillins by making the bacterial cell wall more permeable facilitate the action of aminoglycosides that work intracellularly and must gain entry into the cell. In addition to understanding the drug's mechanism of action and spectrum of activity, the clinician should know about drug absorption, distribution, metabolism, and excretion.

These characteristics are essential in determining aspects of therapy like route of administration and dosing interval. In order to be effective the drug must reach the microbe and survive in the chemical environment at the site of infection. Some sites in the body are 'privileged' like the central nervous system, prostate, joints and eyes.

Infection in these sites must be treated with antibiotics that can penetrate them. Abscess are encapsulated and have harsh chemical environments (e.g., pH, redux potentials) limiting the penetration and actions of antibiotics. Abscess must for these reason be incised and drained, as antibiotic therapy alone is not appropriate. In patients with renal or hepatic failure, it is often necessary to readjust drug dosing if the antibiotic is metabolized or excreted by one of these organs.

BACTERIAL STRUCTURE & ANTIBIOTIC ACTION

Antibiotics are commonly classified according to their mechanism of action. Understanding an antibiotic's mechanism of action can frequently suggest the drug's spectrum of activity and side effects. Antibiotics target processes in the bacteria that are significantly different or nonexistent in mammalian cells.

THE BACTERIAL CELL WALL

Bacterial cells have a rigid outer layer, the cell wall, which surrounds the cytoplasmic membrane. It maintains the shape of the cell, and prevents the bacteria from bursting from the high osmotic pressure generated by its cytoplasm. The cell wall is composed of repeating units of a cross-linked peptidoglycan. This peptidoglycan (murein) is unique to bacteria and is responsible for its shape and rigidity.

The peptidoglycan unit is composed of a disaccharide of N-acetylglucosamine (G) and N-acetylmuramic acid (M). These are cross-linked into a linear polymer. The carboxyl group of N-acetylmuramic acid (M) is linked to a tetrapeptide. These tetrapeptides can be cross-linked to one another, thereby, joining adjacent glycan chains and forming a strong and rigid structure. Beta-lactam drugs (penicillins, carbapenems, cephalosporins and monobactams) act at the level of the bacterial cell wall and interfere with the cross-linking of the peptidoglycan chains.

They also activate autolytic enzymes that destroy the cell wall, leading to cell death. Beta-lactam drugs are a large group of compounds with a broad spectrum of activity. Bacitracin and vancomycin inhibit early steps in peptidoglycan biosynthesis. Vancomycin is only active against gram positive organisms.

PROTEIN SYNTHESIS

Bacterial protein synthesis is significantly different from eukaryotic protein synthesis. The major target of action of antibiotics is the bacterial ribosome. While mammalians have an 80S ribosome, the bacterial ribosome is a 70S. The bacterial ribosome is composed of a 30S and a 50S subunit. These are made up of three types of rRNA (5S, 16S, and 23S) and some 56 proteins. Protein synthesis takes place in the cytoplasm of the bacterial cell, and the number of ribosomes can be correlated with the rate of growth of the cell. In contrast to eukaryotic cells, many ribosomes can translate at the same time the same mRNA forming a structure known as a polysome.

Antibiotics that Bind at the 30S Subunit of the Bacterial Ribosome

Aminoglycosides (gentamicin, tobramycin, amikacin, streptomycin, neomycin) bind to the 30S ribosomal subunit and interfere with mRNA reading. Aminoglycosides are primarily effective against gram negative aerobes and mycobacteria.

Tetracyclines (tetracycline, doxycycline) bind to the 30S subunit and block polypeptide chain elongation by preventing the attachment of charged aminacyl-tRNA. They are effective against gram-positive cocci, chlamydia, mycoplasma, and rickettsia.

Antibiotics that Bind at the 50S Subunit of the Bacterial Ribosome

Chloramphenicol attaches to the 50S subunit and inhibits peptidyl transferase, stopping the binding of new amino acids to the nascent polypeptide chain. They have good coverage of most gram-positive and gram-negative bacteria including anaerobes.

Macrolides (erythromycin, clarithromcycin, and azithromycin) bind to the 50S subunit, and may act by interfering with ribosomal initiation complex formation or aminoacyl translocation.

They cover Mycoplasma, Legionella, Chlamydia, Treponema, Helicobacter pylori, Staphylococci, Streptococci, and other gram-positives. Lincosamines (clindamycin and lincomycins) bind to the 50S subunit and resemble macrolides in binding site and mechanism of action. They cover gram positives and most anaerobes.

NUCLEIC ACID SYNTHESIS

Drugs that interfere with bacterial DNA synthesis might target enzymes not found in the animal cell like the bacterial DNA girase (topoisomerase II) that pack and unpack supercoiled bacterial DNA. Some antibiotics also target the bacterial DNA-dependent RNA polymerase, and still others interfere with metabolites essential for DNA synthesis and repair. The bacterial genome is in the form of one circular double stranded chromosome. In contrast to eukaryotic cells, bacteria do not have a nucleus and the chromosome resides in the cytoplasm. As will be discussed in the section on resistance, there are also extra-chromosomal genetic elements named plasmids.

Otherwise the basic mechanism of DNA replication, and RNA transcription is similar to eukaryotic cells. Nonetheless, the enzymes involved in bacterial processes have diverged from the eukaryotic equivalents enough so as to be selective inhibited by the antibiotics discussed below.

Some inhibitors of DNA synthesis actually block the metabolism of tetrahydrofolic acid. Tetrahydrofolic acid is essential for the synthesis of purines, pyrimidines and some amino acids. Antimetabolites interfere with tetrahydrofolic acid synthesis and, therefore, inhibit DNA synthesis.

DNA Synthesis Inhibitors

Rifampin binds strongly to the DNA-dependent RNA polymerase, inhibiting RNA synthesis. This drug covers gram-positive cocci, many gram-negative bacilli, and most mycobacterium species. Quinolones and fluoroquinolones block the action of DNA gyrase. They cover enteric gram-negative bacilli, some gram positives, and have unreliable activity against Streptococcus pneumoniae. They have no anaerobic coverage.

Antimetabolites

The chemical structure of sulfonamides resembles that of para-aminobenzoic acid (PABA) a precursor in folic acid synthesis. Sulfonamides compete with PABA for the enzyme dihydropteroate synthase. Animals cannot synthesize folic acid and depend on exogenous sources. Therefore, animal cells are not inhibited by sulfonamides.

Trimethoprim selective inhibits the dihydrofolic acid reductase of bacteria, which converts dihydrofolic acid to tetrahydrofolic acid, a precursor of purines and, therefore, DNA synthesis. The combination of trimethoprim-sulfamethoxazole has a broad spectrum of action against gram-positive and gram-negative bacteria and Pneumocystis carinni.

ANTIBIOTIC RESISTANCE

With the advent of antibiotic therapy came the problem of antibiotic resistance. Resistance to antibiotics existed in the wild before the widespread use of antibiotics in medical practice.

These antibiotic resistance genes were designed to combat naturally occurring antibiotics commonly found in nature. However, the tremendous selective pressure of the prevalent antibiotic use and the various mutational and recombinant capabilities of bacteria, has transformed multidrug resistance into a real threat in our time.

In the 1940s all isolates of S. Aureus were sensitive to penicillin G, by 1951 approximately 75% of isolates were resistant. Penicillin resistant streptococcus pneumoniae (PRSP) accounted for approximately 2% of all S. pneumoniae isolates in the late 1980s. This number had risen to 11.7% in 1995.There is no question today that the rapid emergence of drug resistance is the product of human use of antibiotics in medicine and agriculture.

Some of the most troublesome multidrug resistant bacteria today are Vancomycin resistant enterococcus and Methicillin resistant Staphylococcus Aureus in the hospital setting; Penicillin resistant streptococcus pneumoniae in the community; and multidrug resistant TB, especially in the immune-compromised population.

ORIGIN OF ANTIBIOTIC RESISTANCE

Antibiotic resistance can be of genetic origin or of non-genetic change. Non-genetic antibiotic resistance is often due to natural resistance, such as with E.coli resistance to vancomycin, or mycoplasma resistance to penicillins. In these examples the drug mechanism of action does not affect the bacteria. A form of acquired non-genetic drug resistance is metabolic inactivity. As most antibiotics interfere with bacterial metabolic processes, metabolic inactive bacteria are not harmed. With resumption of normal growth these bacteria will be susceptible again.

Genetic origin of resistance implies genetic changes and subsequent environmental selection for the mutated bacteria. Although bacteria multiple by binary fusion, they have multiple mechanisms facilitating genetic exchange which occurs even between different bacterial species.

Genetic Change Can Occur Through

Spontaneous mutation of the bacterial chromosome affecting a 'susceptibility gene'. Spontaneous mutations occur with a frequency of 10 X -12 to 10X -7. However, it can happen with a much higher frequency, as is the case with rifampin chromosomal mutants that occur at a frequency of 10 X-7 to 10 X -5. Treatment of infections with rifampin as the sole medication usually results in resistance.

Transposition refers to the recombination of genetic material through the action oftransposons. Transposons are DNA segments which have specialized insertion sequences at each end. These insertion sequences enable transposons to migrate between DNA molecules within the same bacterium (e.g., from plasmid to chromosome, from chromosome to bacteriophage DNA).

The DNA between the two insertion sequences of transposons can code for various genes, such as genes that facilitate transposition and antibiotic resistance genes. Genetic resistance can also occur through the acquisition of extrachromosomal genetic elements named plasmids. Plasmids are circular DNA molecules much smaller than the bacterial chromosome.

They may be found as an independent element or integrated in the bacterial chromosome. Some plasmids carry their own gene of replication and transfer. R or resistance plasmids carry genes for bacterial antimicrobial resistance, often these genes work by inactivating an antibiotic. Examples are B-lactamases, and enzymes that acetylate, adenylate or phosphorylate aminoglycosides.

Plasmids can be Transferred Among Bacteria by Various Processes

- *Transduction*: Plasmid DNA is transferred from one bacteria to another of the same species by a bacterial virus.
- *Conjugation*: Unilateral transfer of genetic material between bacteria of the same of different species occurring during 'mating'. This is an important way of plasmid resistance spread.
- *Transformation:* Describes the take up of naked DNA into a bacterium from the environment. This can occur in the wild, as well as, through laboratory manipulation and is often used in recombinant DNA technology.

MECHANISMS OF ANTIBIOTIC RESISTANCE

Antibiotic modification - In this case the bacteria avoids the antibiotic's deleterious affects by inactivating the antibiotic. An example is the production of B lactamases by bacteria, which destroys the beta lactam ring of penicillins and cephalosporins.

Prevention of antibiotic entry into the cell - In gram negative bacteria porins are transmembrane proteins that allow for the diffusion of antibiotics through their highly impermeable outer membrane. Modification of the porins can bring about antibiotic resistance, as is the case of Pseudomonas aeruginosa resistance to imipenem.

Active efflux of antibiotic - Bacteria can actively pump out the antibiotic from the cell. An example would be the energy dependent efflux of tetracyclines widely seen in enterobacteriaceae.

Alteration of drug target - Bacteria can also evade antibiotic action through the alteration of the compound's target. For instance, Streptococcus pneumoniae modified penicillin-binding protein (PBP) which renders them resistant to penicillins. Bypassing drug's action - Finally the bacteria can bypass the deleterious effect of the drug while not stopping the production of the original sensitive target.

Examples are the alternative PBP produced by MRSA in addition to the normal PBB; and some sulfonamide-resistant bacteria that have become able to use environmental folic acid like mammalian cells, and in this way bypass the sulfonamide inhibition of folic acid synthesis.

CIRCUMVENTING ANTIBIOTIC RESISTANCE

One way to circumvent the origin of antibiotic resistance is to treat an infection with multiple drugs. Such drug combinations like trimethoprim-sulfamethoxazole can inhibit the development of antibiotic resistance. Perhaps of greater importance is the realization that widespread antibiotic resistance is a product of how we use antibiotics, and it can be decreased by changes in antibiotic prescription practices.

Antibiotics are often prescribed for mostly viral infections such as colds and acute bronchitis. Another problem is the sale of antibiotics as over the counter drugs in certain countries and the widespread use of antibiotics in agriculture.Changes in antibiotic prescribing practices can have a tremendous impact. In Finland, for instance, a nationwide effort was undertaken to fight the rapid increase in the prevalence of group A streptococci resistant to macrolides.

The total consumption of these antibiotics was decreased from 2 daily doses per 1000 inhabitants to 1.4 in 1992, subsequently the prevalence of group A streptococci resistance to macrolides declined from 19% in 1993 to 0.6% in 1996.

DRUGS TREATING URINARY TRACT INFECTIONS

Urinary tract infections are a serious health problem affecting millions of people each year. Infections of the urinary tract are the second most common type of infection in the body. Urinary tract infections (UTIs) account for about 8.3 million doctor visits each year.* Women are especially prone to UTIs for reasons that are not yet well understood. One woman in five develops a UTI during her lifetime. UTIs in men are not as common as in women but can be very serious when they do occur. The urinary system consists of the kidneys, ureters, bladder, and urethra. The key elements in the system are the kidneys, a pair of purplish-brown organs located below the ribs toward the middle of the back. The kidneys remove excess liquid and wastes from the blood in the form of urine, keep a stable balance of salts and other substances in the blood, and produce a hormone that aids the formation of red blood cells.

Narrow tubes called ureters carry urine from the kidneys to the bladder, a sack-like organ in the lower abdomen. Urine is stored in the bladder and emptied through the urethra. The average adult passes about a quart and a half of urine each day. The amount of urine varies, depending on the fluids and foods a person consumes. The volume formed at night is about half that formed in the daytime.

CAUSES OF UTI

Normally, urine is sterile. It is usually free of bacteria, viruses, and fungi but does contain fluids, salts, and waste products. An infection occurs when tiny organisms, usually bacteria from the digestive tract, cling to the opening of the urethra and begin to multiply. The urethra is the tube that carries urine from the bladder to outside the body. Most infections arise from one type of bacteria, *Escherichia coli (E. coli)*, which normally lives in the colon.

In many cases, bacteria first travel to the urethra. When bacteria multiply, an infection can occur. An infection limited to the urethra is called urethritis. If bacteria move to the bladder and multiply, a bladder infection, called cystitis, results. If the infection is not treated promptly, bacteria may then travel further up the ureters to multiply and infect the kidneys. A kidney infection is called pyelonephritis. Microorganisms called *Chlamydia* and *Mycoplasma* may also cause UTIs in both men and women, but these infections tend to remain limited to the urethra and reproductive system. Unlike *E. coli*, *Chlamydia* and *Mycoplasma* may be sexually transmitted, and infections require treatment of both partners.

The urinary system is structured in a way that helps ward off infection. The ureters and bladder normally prevent urine from backing up toward the kidneys, and the flow of urine from the bladder helps wash bacteria out of the body. In men, the prostate gland produces secretions that slow bacterial growth. In both sexes, immune defenses also prevent infection. But despite these safeguards, infections still occur.

RISK

Some people are more prone to getting a UTI than others. Any abnormality of the urinary tract that obstructs the flow of urine (a kidney stone, for example) sets the stage for an infection. An enlarged prostate gland also can slow the flow of urine, thus raising the risk of infection. A common source of infection is catheters, or tubes, placed in the urethra and bladder. A person who cannot void or who is unconscious or critically ill often needs a catheter that stays in place for a long time.

Some people, especially the elderly or those with nervous system disorders who lose bladder control, may need a catheter for life. Bacteria on the catheter can infect the bladder, so hospital staff take special care to keep the catheter clean and remove it as soon as possible. People with diabetes have a higher risk of a UTI because of changes in the immune system. Any other disorder that suppresses the immune system raises the risk of a urinary infection.

UTIs may occur in infants, both boys and girls, who are born with abnormalities of the urinary tract, which sometimes need to be corrected with surgery. UTIs are more rare in boys and young men. In adult women, though, the rate of UTIs gradually increases with age. Scientists are not sure why women have more urinary infections than men. One factor may be that a woman's urethra is short, allowing bacteria quick access to the bladder.

Also, a woman's urethral opening is near sources of bacteria from the anus and vagina. For many women, sexual intercourse seems to trigger an infection, although the reasons for this linkage are unclear. According to several studies, women who use a diaphragm are more likely to develop a UTI than women who use other forms of birth control. Recently, researchers found that women whose partners use a condom with spermicidal foam also tend to have growth of *E. coli* bacteria in the vagina.

Recurrent Infections

Many women suffer from frequent UTIs. Nearly 20 per cent of women who have a UTI will have another, and 30 per cent of those will have yet another. Of the last group, 80 per cent will have recurrences.

Usually, the latest infection stems from a strain or type of bacteria that is different from the infection before it, indicating a separate infection. Even when several UTIs in a row are due to *E. coli,* slight differences in the bacteria indicate distinct infections. Research funded by the National Institutes of Health (NIH) suggests that one factor behind recurrent UTIs may be the ability of bacteria to attach to cells lining the urinary tract.

A recent NIH-funded study found that bacteria formed a protective film on the inner lining of the bladder in mice. If a similar process can be demonstrated in humans, the discovery may lead to new treatments to prevent recurrent UTIs.

Another line of research has indicated that women who are "non-secretors" of certain blood group antigens may be more prone to recurrent UTIs because the cells lining the vagina and urethra may allow bacteria to attach more easily. Further research will show whether this association is sound and proves useful in identifying women at high risk for UTIs.

Infections in Pregnancy

Pregnant women seem no more prone to UTIs than other women. However, when a UTI does occur in a pregnant woman, it is more likely to travel to the kidneys.

According to some reports, about 2 to 4 per cent of pregnant women develop a urinary infection. Scientists think that hormonal changes and shifts in the position of the urinary tract during pregnancy make it easier for bacteria to travel up the ureters to the kidneys. For this reason, many doctors recommend periodic testing of urine during pregnancy.

SYMPTOMS OF UTI

Not everyone with a UTI has symptoms, but most people get at least some symptoms. These may include a frequent urge to urinate and a painful, burning feeling in the area of the bladder or urethra during urination. It is not unusual to feel bad all over—tired, shaky, washed out—and to feel pain even when not urinating. Often women feel an uncomfortable pressure above the pubic bone, and some men experience a fullness in the rectum.

It is common for a person with a urinary infection to complain that, despite the urge to urinate, only a small amount of urine is passed. The urine itself may look milky or cloudy, even reddish if blood is present. Normally, a UTI does not cause fever if it is in the bladder or urethra. A fever may mean that the infection has reached the kidneys. Other symptoms of a kidney infection include pain in the back or side below the ribs, nausea, or vomiting.

In children, symptoms of a urinary infection may be overlooked or attributed to another disorder. A UTI should be considered when a child or infant seems irritable, is not eating normally, has an unexplained fever that does not go away, has incontinence or loose bowels, or is not thriving. Unlike adults, children are more likely to have fever and no other symptoms. This can happen to both boys and girls. The child should be seen by a doctor if there are any questions about these symptoms, especially a change in the child's urinary pattern.

UTI DIAGNOSED

To find out whether you have a UTI, your doctor will test a sample of urine for pus and bacteria. You will be asked to give a "clean catch" urine sample by washing the genital area and collecting a "midstream" sample of urine in a sterile container. This method of collecting urine helps prevent bacteria around the genital area from getting into the sample and confusing the test results. Usually, the sample is sent to a laboratory, although some doctors' offices are equipped to do the testing.

In the urinalysis test, the urine is examined for white and red blood cells and bacteria. Then the bacteria are grown in a culture and tested against different antibiotics to see which drug best destroys the bacteria. This last step is called a sensitivity test.

Some microbes, like *Chlamydia* and *Mycoplasma*, can be detected only with special bacterial cultures. A doctor suspects one of these infections when a person has symptoms of a UTI and pus in the urine, but a standard culture fails to grow any bacteria. When an infection does not clear up with treatment and is traced to the same strain of bacteria, the doctor may order some tests to determine if your system is normal.

One of these tests is an intravenous pyelogram, which gives x-ray images of the bladder, kidneys, and ureters. An opaque dye visible on x-ray film is injected into a vein, and a series of x rays is taken. The film shows an outline of the urinary tract, revealing even small changes in the structure of the tract.

If you have recurrent infections, your doctor also may recommend an ultrasound exam, which gives pictures from the echo patterns of soundwaves bounced back from internal organs. Another useful test is cystoscopy. A cystoscope is an instrument made of a hollow tube with several lenses and a light source, which allows the doctor to see inside the bladder from the urethra.

UTI TREATMENT

UTIs are treated with antibacterial drugs. The choice of drug and length of treatment depend on the patient's history and the urine tests that identify the offending bacteria. The sensitivity test is especially useful in helping the doctor select the most effective drug. The drugs most often used to treat routine, uncomplicated UTIs are trimethoprim (Trimpex), trimethoprim/sulfamethoxazole (Bactrim, Septra, Cotrim), amoxicillin (Amoxil, Trimox, Wymox), nitrofurantoin (Macrodantin, Furadantin), and ampicillin (Omnipen, Polycillin, Principen, Totacillin). A class of drugs called quinolones includes four drugs approved in recent years for treating UTI.

These drugs include ofloxacin (Floxin), norfloxacin (Noroxin), ciprofloxacin (Cipro), and trovafloxin (Trovan). Often, a UTI can be cured with 1 or 2 days of treatment if the infection is not complicated by an obstruction or other disorder. Still, many doctors ask their patients to take antibiotics for a week or two to ensure that the infection has been cured.

Single-dose treatment is not recommended for some groups of patients, for example, those who have delayed treatment or have signs of a kidney infection, patients with diabetes or structural abnormalities, or men who have prostate infections. Longer treatment is also needed by patients with infections caused by *Mycoplasma or Chlamydia,* which are usually treated with tetracycline, trimethoprim/ sulfamethoxazole (TMP/SMZ), or doxycycline.

A followup urinalysis helps to confirm that the urinary tract is infection-free. It is important to take the full course of treatment because symptoms may disappear before the infection is fully cleared.Severely ill patients with kidney infections may be hospitalized until they can take fluids and needed drugs on their own. Kidney infections generally require several weeks of antibiotic treatment.

Researchers at the University of Washington found that 2-week therapy with TMP/SMZ was as effective as 6 weeks of treatment with the same drug in women with kidney infections that did not involve an obstruction or nervous system disorder. In such cases, kidney infections rarely lead to kidney damage or kidney failure unless they go untreated. Various drugs are available to relieve the pain of a UTI.

A heating pad may also help. Most doctors suggest that drinking plenty of water helps cleanse the urinary tract of bacteria. During treatment, it is best to avoid coffee, alcohol, and spicy foods. And one of the best things a smoker can do for his or her bladder is to quit smoking. Smoking is the major known cause of bladder cancer.

Recurrent Infections in Women

Women who have had three UTIs are likely to continue having them. Four out of five such women get another within 18 months of the last UTI. Many women have them even more often.

A woman who has frequent recurrences (three or more a year) can ask her doctor about one of the following treatment options:

- Take low doses of an antibiotic such as TMP/SMZ or nitrofurantoin daily for 6 months or longer. If taken at bedtime, the drug remains in the bladder longer and may be more effective. NIH-supported research at the University of Washington has shown this therapy to be effective without causing serious side effects.
- Take a single dose of an antibiotic after sexual intercourse.
- Take a short course (1 or 2 days) of antibiotics when symptoms appear.

Dipsticks that change colour when an infection is present are now available without a prescription. The strips detect nitrite, which is formed when bacteria change nitrate in the urine to nitrite. The test can detect about 90 per cent of UTIs when used with the first morning urine specimen and may be useful for women who have recurrent infections.

Doctors suggest some additional steps that a woman can take on her own to avoid an infection:

- Drink plenty of water every day.
- Urinate when you feel the need; don't resist the urge to urinate.
- Wipe from front to back to prevent bacteria around the anus from entering the vagina or urethra.
- Take showers instead of tub baths.
- Cleanse the genital area before sexual intercourse.
- Avoid using feminine hygiene sprays and scented

douches, which may irritate the urethra. Some doctors suggest drinking cranberry juice.

Complicated Infections

Curing infections that stem from a urinary obstruction or other systemic disorders depends on finding and correcting the underlying problem, sometimes with surgery. If the root cause goes untreated, this group of patients is at risk of kidney damage.

Also, such infections tend to arise from a wider range of bacteria, and sometimes from more than one type of bacteria at a time.

Infections in Men

UTIs in men are often a result of an obstruction—for example, a urinary stone or enlarged prostate—or from a medical procedure involving a catheter. The first step is to identify the infecting organism and the drugs to which it is sensitive.

Usually, doctors recommend lengthier therapy in men than in women, in part to prevent infections of the prostate gland. Prostate infections (chronic bacterial prostatitis) are harder to cure because antibiotics are unable to penetrate infected prostate tissue effectively.

For this reason, men with prostatitis often need long-term treatment with a carefully selected antibiotic. UTIs in older men are frequently associated with acute bacterial prostatitis, which can have serious consequences if not treated urgently.

VACCINE TO PREVENT RECURRENT UTIS

In the future, scientists may develop a vaccine that can prevent UTIs from coming back. Researchers in different studies have found that children and women who tend to get UTIs repeatedly are likely to lack proteins called immunoglobulins, which fight infection.

Children and women who do not get UTIs are more likely to have normal levels of immunoglobulins in their genital and urinary tracts. Early tests indicate that a vaccine helps patients build up their own natural infection-fighting powers. The dead bacteria in the vaccine do not spread like an infection; instead, they prompt the body to produce antibodies that can later fight against live organisms.

Researchers are testing injected and oral vaccines to see which works best. Another method being considered for women is to apply the vaccine directly as a suppository in the vagina.

URINARY TRACT INFECTIONS IN CHILDREN

Aside from unexpected wetting, the most common urinary problem among children is infections. An estimated 3 per cent of girls and 1 per cent of boys have had a urinary tract infection (UTI) by the age of 11. Some researchers believe these estimates are low because many cases of UTI go undetected.

The symptoms are not always obvious to parents, and younger children are usually unable to describe how they feel. Recognizing and treating urinary tract infections is important. Untreated UTIs can lead to serious kidney problems that could threaten the life of your child.

URINARY TRACT NORMALLY FUNCTION

The kidneys filter and remove waste and water from the blood to produce urine. They get rid of about 11/2 to 2 quarts of urine per day in an adult and less in a child, depending on the child's age.

The urine travels from the kidneys down two narrow tubes called the ureters. The urine is then stored in a balloon-like container called the bladder. In a child, the bladder can hold about 1 to 11/2 ounces of urine for each year of the child's age. So, the bladder of a 4-year-old child may hold about 4 to 6 ounces (less than 1 cup); an 8-year-old can hold 8 to 12 ounces.

When the bladder empties, urine flows out of the body through the urethra, a tube at the bottom of the bladder. The opening of the urethra is at the end of the penis in boys and in front of the vagina in girls.

URINARY TRACT BECOME INFECTED

Normal urine contains no bacteria (germs). Bacteria may, at times, get into the urinary tract (and the urine) from the skin around the rectum and genitals by traveling up the urethra into the bladder.

When this happens, the bacteria can infect and inflame the bladder, resulting in swelling and pain in the lower abdomen and side. This is called "cystitis." If the bacteria travel further up through the ureters to the kidneys, a kidney infection can develop. The infection is usually accompanied by pain and fever. Kidney infections are much more serious than bladder infections. In some children a urinary tract infection may be a sign of an abnormal urinary tract that may be prone to repeated problems.

For this reason, when a child is found to have a urinary infection, additional tests are often recommended. In other cases, children develop urinary tract infections because they are prone to such infections the way, for example, other children are prone to getting coughs, colds, or ear infections. Or a child may happen to get an infection with a type of bacteria that has a special ability to cause urinary tract infections.

SIGNS OF URINARY TRACT INFECTION

The lining of the bladder, urethra, ureters, and kidneys become irritated with a urinary tract infection, just like the inside of the nose or throat with a cold. If your child is an infant or is only a few years old, the signs of a urinary tract infection may not be clear, since children that young cannot tell you just how they feel.

Your child may have a high fever, be irritable, or not eat. An older child with bladder irritation may complain of pain in the abdomen and pelvic area. Your child may urinate often. If the kidney is infected, your child may complain of pain under the side of the rib cage (the flank) or low back pain.

Crying or complaining that it hurts to urinate and producing only a few drops of urine at a time are other signs of urinary tract infection. Your child may have difficulty controlling the urine and may leak urine into clothing or bedsheets. The urine may smell unusual or look cloudy.

URINARY TRACT INFECTION

Only by consulting a health care provider can you find out for certain whether your child has a urinary tract infection. Some of your child's urine will be collected and examined. The way urine is collected may depend on how old your child is. The health care provider may place a plastic collection bag over your child's genital area (sealed to the skin with an adhesive strip) if the child is not yet toilet trained. An older child may be asked to urinate into a container.

The sample needs to come as directly into the container as possible to avoid picking up bacteria from the skin or rectal area. A doctor or nurse may need to pass a small tube into the urethra. Urine will drain directly from the bladder into a clean container through this tube (called a catheter). Sometimes the best way to get the urine is by placing a needle directly into the bladder through the skin of the lower abdomen. Getting urine through the tube or needle will make sure that the urine collected is pure. Some of the urine will be examined under a microscope. If an infection is present, bacteria and sometimes pus will be in the urine. If the bacteria from the sample are hard to see at first, the health care provider may place the sample in a tube or dish with a substance that encourages any bacteria present to grow.

Once the germs have multiplied, they can be then identified and tested to see which medications will provide the most effective treatment. The process of growing bacteria in the laboratory is known as performing a culture and often takes a day or more to complete. The reliability of the culture depends on how long the urine stands before the culture is started. If you collect your child's urine at home, it should be refrigerated as soon as collected and the container should be transported in a plastic bag filled with ice.

URINARY TRACT INFECTIONS TREATED

Urinary tract infections are treated with antibiotics

(infection-fighting drugs). After a urine sample is obtained, the health care provider may begin treatment with a drug that treats the bacteria most likely to be causing the infection. Once culture results are known, the health care provider may switch your child to another antibiotic, if necessary.

The way the antibiotic is given and the number of days that it must be taken depends in part on the type of infection and how severe it is. When a child is sick or not able to drink fluids, the antibiotic may need to be put directly into the bloodstream through a vein in the arm or hand. Otherwise, the medicine (liquid or pills) may be given by mouth or by shots.

The medicine is given for at least 3 to 5 days and possibly for as long as several weeks. The daily treatment schedule recommended depends on the specific drug prescribed: the schedule may call for a single dose each day or up to four doses each day.

In some cases, your child will need to take the medicine until further tests are finished. After a few doses of the antibiotic, your child may appear much better, but often several days may pass before all symptoms are gone. In any case, your child should take the medicine for as long as the doctor says.

Do not stop medications because the symptoms have gone away. Infections may return, and germs can resist future treatment if the drug is stopped too soon. Children should drink fluids when they wish. Make sure your child drinks what he or she needs, but do not force your child to drink large amounts of fluid. The health care provider needs to know if the child is not interested in drinking.

TESTS NEEDED AFTER THE INFECTION IS GONE

Once the infection has cleared, additional tests may be recommended to check for abnormalities in the urinary tract. Repeated infections in abnormal urinary tracts may cause kidney damage. The kinds of tests ordered will depend on your child and the type of urinary infection. Because no single test can tell everything about the urinary tract that might be important to know, more than one of the following tests may be needed:

- *Kidney and bladder ultrasound*: A test that examines the kidney and bladder using sound waves. This test shows shadows of the kidney and bladder that may point out certain abnormalities; this test cannot reveal all important urinary abnormalities. It also cannot measure how well a kidney works.
- *Voiding cystourethrogram (VCUG)*: A test that examines the urethra and bladder while the bladder fills and empties. A liquid that can be seen on x-rays is placed into the bladder through a catheter. The bladder is filled until the child urinates. This test can reveal abnormalities of the inside of the urethra and bladder. The test can also determine whether the flow of urine is normal when the bladder empties.
- *Intravenous pyelogram*: A test that examines the whole urinary tract. A liquid that can be seen on x-rays is injected into a vein. The substance travels into the kidneys and bladder, revealing possible obstructions.
- *Nuclear scans*: A number of tests using radioactive materials that are usually injected into a vein to show how well the kidneys work, the shape of the kidneys, and whether urine empties from the kidneys in a normal way. The many kinds of nuclear scans each give different information about the kidneys and bladder. Nuclear scans expose a child to no more radiation than he or she would receive from a conventional x-ray. At times, it can even be less.

ABNORMALITIES LEAD TO URINARY PROBLEMS

Many children who get urinary tract infections have normal kidneys and bladders, but children who have an abnormality need to have it detected as early as possible in life to try to protect their kidneys against damage. Abnormalities that could occur include the following:

- Vesicoureteral reflux. Urine normally flows from the kidneys down the ureters to the bladder in one direction. With reflux, when the bladder fills, the urine may also flow backward from the bladder up the ureters to the kidneys. This abnormality is common in children with urinary infections.

- Urinary obstruction. Blockages to urinary flow may occur at many sites in the urinary tract. Blockages usually occur if the ureter or urethra is too narrow or a kidney stone at some point stops the urinary flow from leaving the body. Occasionally, the ureter may join the kidney or bladder at the wrong place, preventing urine from leaving the kidney in a normal way.

ANTI-MYCOBACTERIAL TREATMENT AND CROHN'S DISEASE

The rationale for antibiotic therapy of infectious bacterial disease is this. If the disease is caused by bacteria, then by eradicating the bacteria, the disease should end. Bacteria are "attacked" with a combination of drugs that are hopefully effective against them.

For more thorough discussions, please read the "Related info" links to the right of this page. It is important to bear in mind that both of the papers "Crohn's disease and the Mycobacterioses:- a review and comparison of two disease entities" and"Ruminant paratuberculosis:- current status and future prospects" were both written before the development of macrolideantibiotics, which have since been shown to be the most effective antibiotics against Mycobacterium paratuberculosis.

CONDUCTING A CLINICAL TRIAL

Clinical trials are designed to test whether a drug or combination of drugs is effective against any given disease. The test population in a clinical trial is divided into two groups, one of which receives the actual drug treatment under test and the other, known as the control group, which receives a "placebo" drug, which is known not to have any effect on the disease. If those taking the real drug treatment improve and the control group does not improve, then the trial is deemed to have proved that the drug treatment is successful at treating the disease. It is difficult to judge the results of the trial if the people taking part in it are receiving other treatment for the same disease, but outside the trial. If patients are, for example, taking a course of drugs that maintains the disease, or are having surgery during the trial, it becomes difficult to judge improvements or lack of them.

This seems to be further complicated in the case of Crohn's Disease, since there are different views on what the disease actually is. Its symptoms vary widely from patient to patient, with treatment regimes differing greatly for each.

CHOICE OF DRUGS

All of the studies below have tested the use of antibiotic drugs for the treatment of Crohn's Disease. The drugs chosen are ones that are known to be effective against well known mycobacterial infections, such as tuberculosis or leprosy.

It is theorised that Crohn's disease is caused by mycobacteria that live inside host cells, i.e. they are intracellular mycobacteria. Hence, to be effective against them, the drugs chosen must have intracellular activity. Few antibiotics have intracellular activity. It is only in recent years that antibiotics have been developed that are active against intracellular mycobacteria.

These antibiotics are known as macrolide antibiotics. One of these macrolide antibiotics is clarithromycin, which has been shown to be effective in treating Mycobacterium avium intracellulare, an intracellular mycobacterium that commonly infects immuno-compromised AIDS patients.

MULTI-DRUG REGIMES

When treating mycobacterial diseases, it is important to use multi-drug regimes. The reason for this is that mycobacteria have the ability to develop resistance to inividual drugs. If a single drug regime is used, then there is a possibility that the organism may become resistant to that one drug, and thus the treatment may fail.

LONG TREATMENT TIMES[H]

Also, mycobacteria can exist in an inactive state, in which they do not metabolise. Antibiotics can only be effective against bacteria that are actively metabolising. Therefore, treatment duration must not only be long enough to destroy all active bacteria, but also long enough to destroy the inactive bacteria as they "re-activate".

Since these periods of inactivity can be as long as many months, antibiotic treatment duration must be at least as long as this, and it is possible that the target mycobacteria may never be eradicated.

POLAR MANIFESTATIONS OF THE DISEASE

Mycobacterial diseases present in two forms, the contained and aggressive forms. If it is not recognised that the population to be treated under a trial should be split between these two forms, the trial may yield incorrect results. It is theorised that Crohn's disease may present in two "polar" forms. Individual patients usually do not suffer from the extremes mentioned below, but display symptoms that are somewhere between the two extremes. The aggressive "perforating" form.

This form of Crohn's is experienced by sufferers if they do not mount an immune response that is strong enough to control the Mycobacterium paratuberculosis infection. In this group, the population of infecting mycobacteria would be uncontrolled by the immune system, and would cause extensive damage to the intestines.

The symptoms of this form are perforation of the intestinal wall and fistulisation, the formation of abnormal connections between the intestines and other internal organs. Crohn's patients with the aggressive perforating form would greatly benefit from treatment with antibiotics, since they are unable to control the bacterial infection by themselves.

- The contained "nonperforating" form. This form of Crohn's comes about when the immune system of the sufferer is strong enough to control the mycobacterial infection. However, this immune success comes at a high cost, since inflammation and granulomas are the result. Granulomas are formed when the immune system seals the mycobacteria inside hard shells. Over time, as the body is exposed to infection by Mycobacterium paratuberculosis again and again, more and more of these granulomas form in the intestines, eventually leading to obstruction (blockage) of the intestines. Crohn's patients with the contained nonperforating form of Crohn's disease may not benefit as much from treatment with antibiotics, since their infection may already be under control.

All of the studies listed below were complete or still in progress when attention was drawn, to the possibility that Anti-mycobacterial treatment studies may fail if the study population is not first divided up into the perforating and nonperforating forms of Crohn's disease. This is because patients with the perforating form will show a strong improvement, whereas those with the nonperforating form will show less improvement. These two groups will be lumped together, leading to incorrect statistical analysis of the results.

DRUGS TREATING FUNGAL INFECTIONS

Invasive fungal infection is an increasingly common cause of mortality and morbidity in preterm infants. The increase in incidence over the past 20 years is likely to be due to the improved survival rates for very small and immature infants and the invasive and intensive nature of the care that these infants need. The estimated incidence of invasive fungal infection is 2% in very low birth weight infants.

In extremely low birth weight infants, the incidence has been estimated to be as high as 10%. Other specific risk factors for invasive fungal infection include fungal colonisation, severe illness at birth, the use of multiple courses of antibiotics, the use of parenteral nutrition, the presence of a central venous catheter, and the use of histamine receptor subtype 2 antagonists. Systemic fungal infection accounts for about 10% of all cases of sepsis diagnosed in infants more than 72 hours old. The estimated attributable mortality is about 25%, much higher than that associated with invasive bacterial infection. Systemic fungal infection is also associated with increased short and long term morbidity in preterm infants. In particular, fungal infection of the central nervous system has a significant impact on long term neurodevelopmental outcome.

The clinical presentation of invasive fungal and bacterial infection is similar, and this may lead to a delay in diagnosis and treatment. In addition to fungaemia, infants may present with pneumonia, meningitis, renal tract infection, ophthalmitis, osteomyelitis, endocarditis, liver abscesses, and skin abscesses. The diagnosis may be further delayed due to an inability to consistently recover the organism from blood, cerebro-spinal fluid, or urine.

A high index of suspicion and the use of additional laboratory and clinical tests, including retinal examination, echocardiography, and renal ultrasonography, may be needed to confirm the suspected diagnosis. Given the high mortality and difficulty in establishing an early diagnosis, systemic antifungal therapy is often given prior to the establishment of a confirmed diagnosis.

In some centres, prophylactic antifungal therapy is given to preterm infants at high risk of invasive fungal infection. The evidence of effect of this practice has been evaluated in other Cochrane reviews. A number of antifungal drugs are available for treating preterm infants with invasive fungal infection. Prescribing practice varies between neonatal units. The most commonly used drug is amphotericin B, a polyene antifungal agent that reacts with sterols in cell membranes to cause cell lysis.

Amphotericin B is poorly absorbed via the enteral route and is only available as an intravenous preparation. Drug toxicity, particularly nephrotoxicity, is a significant problem as amphotericin B also damages mammalian cell membranes. These adverse effects limit the total dose that may be given.

The newer lipid complex formulations of amphotericin B deliver the active drug directly to the site of action on the fungal cell membrane. Because the lipid complex is more stable in mammalian cells, toxicity is reduced. Consequently, amphotericin B lipid complex can be given at higher total doses.

There is good evidence of reduced nephrotoxicity with the lipid complex formulations compared with conventional amphotericin B in some groups of patients, for example, cancer patients with neutropaenia. There are also some observational data to suggest less toxicity in preterm infants. However, the lipid complex formulations are very much more expensive than conventional amphotericin B.

In current neonatal practice use is often restricted to infants who are intolerant of, or do not respond to, conventional amphotericin B. Amphotericin B is highly protein bound and does not achieve good penetration into extra-cellular fluid spaces, including cerebro-spinal fluid. Another drug is often used instead of, or in addition to, amphotericin B to treat preterm infants with suspected or confirmed fungal meningitis.

The most commonly used additional agent is 5-fluorocytosine (flucytosine), a fluorinated pyrimidine anti-metabolite that competitively inhibits nucleic acid synthesis. 5-fluorocytosine achieves very good penetration into the cerebro-spinal fluid. Since monotherapy is thought to increase the risk of the development of stable antifungal resistance, 5-fluorocytosine is usually prescribed with amphotericin B or another antifungal agent.

Amphotericin B and 5-fluorocytosine are not antagonistic, but the evidence for synergism is inconsistent, and depends on the laboratory assessment method used. 5-fluorocytosine is very well absorbed via the enteral route. Oral and intravenous preparations are available.

The known side effects of 5-fluorocytosine include hepatic toxicity and transient neutropaenia, although more significant bone marrow suppression has also been reported. The other major class of antifungal agents available for treating preterm infants with invasive fungal infection is the azole group of drugs. These include the triazoles (fluconazole, itraconazole) and the imidazoles (miconazole, ketoconazole). These drugs bind preferentially to the fungal cytochromes P450 and interfere with ergosterol synthesis in the cell membrane. There are two potential advantages of using an azole drug compared with amphotericin B.

The first advantage is that the azoles are well absorbed after enteral administration. A prolonged treatment course can therefore be given without the presence of an intravenous catheter, a potential risk factor for invasive fungal infection. Secondly, evidence from systematic reviews of randomised controlled trials in adult populations suggests that the azole drugs are less toxic than conventional amphotericin B. However, these findings may have been biased by methodological flaws in some of the included trials.

There appears to be limited experience with the systemic use of imidazole drugs in preterm infants, although there are reports of apparent treatment success, and of apparent treatment failure. However, the triazoles, particularly fluconazole, are increasingly used in neonatal practice. Fluconazole has appeared to be a safe treatment for preterm infants with invasive fungal infection, including fungal meningitis. The only relatively common side effect is mild and transient elevation of plasma levels of creatinine or hepatic enzymes, described in about 5% of preterm infants treated with fluconazole. There are, however, rare important side effects, such as Stevens-Johnson syndrome, reported in other populations of patients. Additionally, as highlighted by other authors, there is a potential risk of adverse effects as a result of drug interactions with medications that are prescribed for preterm infants, including cisapride, theophylline, and thiazide diuretics.

A major consideration with antimicrobial drug use is the potential for the emergence of stable resistance to the antimicrobial agent. Some species of fungi, for example Candida glabrata or Candida krusei, are intrinsically resistant to fluconazole. There has been some concern, although not any definite evidence, that fluconazole is poorer than amphotericin B in eradicating these non-albicans Candida species in adults.

The potential clinical consequences at the population level of altering the pattern of antifungal resistance must be considered. However, these consequences are difficult to define in controlled trials that do not use a neonatal nursery/ unit/centre as the unit of randomisation. Given the potential for the choice of systemic antifungal therapy to affect outcomes for preterm infants with invasive fungal infection, we reviewed the available evidence to determine if there are any implications for current practice or for future research.

OBJECTIVES

In preterm infants (less than 37 weeks' gestation) with suspected or confirmed invasive fungal infection, does treatment with newer systemic antifungal drugs or drug combinations, versus conventional amphotericin B alone, reduce mortality and adverse neurodevelopmental outcomes?

We planned to examine the following intervention comparisons:

- Amphotericin B lipid complex versus amphotericin B. We intended to undertake subgroup analyses of the individual lipid complex formulations (for example, "AmBisome", "Abelcet", "Amphocil").
- Azole antifungal agents versus amphotericin B (including amphotericin B lipid complex). We intended to undertake subgroup analyses of:
  - The individual azole drugs (fluconazole, itraconazole, ketoconazole, miconazole)
  - Conventional and lipid formulations of amphotericin B
- Amphotericin B plus 5-fluorocytosine versus amphotericin B alone. We intended to undertake subgroup analyses of the trials that only included infants treated for confirmed or suspected fungal meningitis.

For all of the above, we intended to undertake subgroup analyses of trials that specifically recruited only infants with confirmed invasive fungal infection (defined in types of participants).

CRITERIA FOR CONSIDERING STUDIES FOR THIS REVIEW

- Controlled trials utilizing either random or quasi-random patient allocation.
- Cluster randomised trials, where the unit of randomisation is the neonatal nursery/unit/centre.

Types of Participants

Preterm (less than 37 weeks' gestation) infants with confirmed or suspected invasive fungal infection cared for in a hospital setting.

We defined "confirmed" invasive fungal infection as:

- Culture of fungus from a sterile site- cerebrospinal fluid, blood, urine, bone or joint, peritoneum, pleural space. Blood cultures should have been obtained from peripheral sites, not from indwelling catheters. Urine samples should have been obtained from sterile urethral catheterisation or suprapubic aspiration of the bladder, not from indwelling catheters or from urine "bag" samples (since organisms isolated from these may represent perineal contamination).
- Findings on ophthalmological examination consistent with fungal ophthalmitis or retinitis
- Pathognomonic findings on renal ultrasound examination: "renal fungal balls"

We defined "suspected" invasive fungal infection pragmatically as an individual clinician's choice to prescribe a systemic antifungal agent based on the clinical suspicion of invasive fungal infection, but in the absence of a confirmed diagnosis as described above. We did not include trials of antifungal prophylaxis, or trials where systemic antifungal therapy is given to treat superficial mucosal or skin infection.

Types of Interventions

- Amphotericin B

- Amphotericin B lipid complex formulations (for example, "AmBisome", "Abelcet", "Amphocil").
- Azole antifungal agents (for example, fluconazole, itraconazole, ketoconazole, miconazole)
- Amphotericin B plus 5-fluorocytosine

Types of Outcome Measures

Primary outcomes:

- Death (all cause) prior to hospital discharge. We did not use death attributed to fungal infection as an outcome measure, as this information may be unreliable and prone to bias.
- Neurodevelopmental outcomes during infancy and beyond using validated assessment tools such as Bayley Scales of Infant Development, and classifications of disability, including auditory and visual disability. Severe neurodevelopmental disability was defined as any one or combination of the following: non-ambulant cerebral palsy, developmental delay (developmental quotient less than 70), auditory and visual impairment.

Secondary outcomes:

- Clinically significant adverse reactions attributed to the antifungal agent that resulted in discontinuation of the therapy, for example:
  - Abnormal hepatic function
  - Abnormal renal function
  - Gastrointestinal disturbance such as diarrhoea, feeding intolerance, or necrotising enterocolitis that results in cessation of enteral feeding
  - Hypokalaemia
  - Cardiac dysrhythmias
  - Thrombophlebitis
  - Rash (including Stevens-Johnson reactions)
  - Seizures
  - Anaphylaxis
- Emergence of organisms resistant to anti-fungal agents, as detected in infants enrolled in the study,

or, in cluster-randomised studies, on surveillance of other infants in the same unit in the study centre (including infants who are admitted to the unit following completion of the study).

SEARCH STRATEGY FOR IDENTIFICATION OF STUDIES

We used the standard search strategy of the Cochrane Neonatal Review Group, including electronic searches of the Cochrane Controlled Trials Register, MEDLINE and EMBASE. We did not apply any language restriction. The search strategy included the following text words and MeSH subject headings: Infant-Newborn, Infant-Low Birth Weight, Infant-Premature, infan$, neonat$, newborn, premature, low birth weight, LBW, fungi, fungemia, fungaemia, candidiasis, Candida albicans, anti fungal agents, fluconazole, azoles, amphotericin B, ABLC, AmBisome, Abelcet, Amphocil, 5-fluorocytosine, 5FC, flucytosine.

We did not apply any language restriction. The search outputs were limited with the relevant search filters for clinical trials. We examined references in previous reviews and in studies identified as potentially relevant. We hand searched the abstracts presented at Society for Pediatric Research and European Society for Pediatric Research, published in the journal Pediatric Research between 1984 and 2002 inclusive.

Trials that have been reported only as abstracts were eligible if sufficient information was available from the report, or from contact with the authors, to fulfill the inclusion criteria.

We undertook a search of Science Citation Index from 1996 until 2003 to try to identify any potentially relevant trials that cited the included study. We did not identify any further trials with this search.

We contacted all of the manufacturers of anti-fungal agents that are listed in the current edition of the British National Formulary: Bristol-Myers Squibb Pharmaceuticals Limited, Cambridge Laboratories, Elan Pharma Limited,

Gilead Sciences Limited, ICN Pharmaceuticals Limited, Pfizer Limited). We did not obtain any information on any relevant reports that were not already available from public sources.

METHODS OF THE REVIEW

- The first reviewer screened the title and abstract of all studies identified by the above search strategy. Both reviewers re-screened the full text of the report of each study identified as of potential relevance. Only the studies that met all of the pre-specified inclusion criteria were eligible for inclusion. The reviewers resolved any disagreements by discussion until consensus was achieved.
- We used the criteria and standard methods of the Cochrane Neonatal Review Group to assess the methodological quality of the included trials. The quality of the trials was evaluated in terms of allocation concealment, blinding of parents or carers and assessors to intervention, and completeness of assessment in all randomised individuals. We requested additional information from the authors of each trial to clarify methodology and results as necessary.
- We used a data collection form to aid extraction of relevant information and data from each included study. Each reviewer extracted the data separately, compared data, and resolved differences by consensus.
- We used the standard methods of the Cochrane Neonatal Review Group to analyse and synthesize the data. For categorical data, we have expressed effects as relative risk, risk difference, and number needed to treat, with respective 95% confidence intervals. For continuous data, we planned to express the effects as weighted mean difference and 95% confidence interval.
- We contacted the author to establish the outcomes of the preterm infants included in the study.

DESCRIPTION OF STUDIES

We identified only one study which appeared relevant after the first round of screening. This study fulfilled the inclusion criteria and is described in the table 'Characteristics of Included Studies'. The study was undertaken between June 1992 to June 1993 in two tertiary neonatal centres in South Africa. Infants with proven fungal septicaemia, aged less than 3 months of age, were eligible for inclusion.

Infants were randomised to receive either fluconazole or amphotericin B or, if meningitis was present, either fluconazole or amphotericin B plus 5-fluorocytosine. Treatment was continued in both groups until cultures were negative for one week and there was no laboratory evidence of infection. Twenty-four infants were enrolled to the study. Thirteen infants were randomised to receive Fluconazole. The trial investigators excluded one infant in this group as the infant was found not to have invasive fungal infection. Of the remaining 12 infants in the fluconazole group, we excluded one term infant from the analysis for this review. Of the 11 infants randomised to receive Amphotericin, 10 were preterm.

Death before hospital discharge was reported. Eight of 22 preterm infants enrolled in the study died, but one of these infants died after hospital discharge. There were not any longer term data on outcomes after discharge. Data on adverse reactions to treatment including gastro-intestinal disturbance or thrombophlebitis were recorded throughout the study period. The investigators monitored the infants' renal, hepatic, and haematological function weekly throughout the study period.

METHODOLOGICAL QUALITY OF INCLUDED STUDIES

Randomisation was computer generated independently for the two centres and via a sealed envelope system for individual case allocation. Both preterm infants and term infants were eligible for inclusion in the trial, and these groups were not randomised separately.

There were not any statistically significant differences between treatment groups in infant characteristics at trial entry. Follow-up was complete. The carers and assessors were blinded to randomisation. However, due to differences in the drug preparations, the carers and investigators were likely to be aware which drug each infant received.

RESULTS

Primary outcomes:

- Death prior to hospital discharge: three of the 11 preterm infants in the fluconazole group died before discharge versus four of 10 in the amphotericin group: Relative risk (RR) 0.68 (95% confidence interval 0.20, 2.33), Risk Difference -0.13 (95% confidence interval -0.53, 0.27).
- Neurodevelopmental outcome is not reported by this study.

Secondary outcomes:

- This study reports adverse reactions. However, none of these resulted in discontinuation of treatment.
  - Hepatic function: There was not any statistically significant difference in the plasma levels of liver enzymes gamma-glutamyl transpeptidase, aspartate aminotransferase and alanine aminotransferase between the fluconazole and amphotericin groups at the end of treatment.
  - Thrombophlebitis: One infant in the fluconazole group and five infants in the amphotericin group had evidence of thrombophlebitis resulting in skin abscesses (but not in discontinuation of treatment): RR 0.17 (95% CI 0.02, 1.24), Risk Difference -0.38 (95% confidence interval -0.71, -0.05). This analysis includes the two term infants recruited in the trial.
  - Gastrointestinal disturbance: One infant in the fluconazole group had severe vomiting. However this infant also had a disorder of branch chain amino acid metabolism.

- Emergence of antifungal resistance is not reported in this study

We were unable to undertake subgroup analysis of the azole antifungals, Amphotericin B versus lipid complex, or drugs in combination. We were also unable to analyse data for subgroups of confirmed versus suspected invasive fungal infection.

DISCUSSION

We identified only one eligible study. The included trial compared fluconazole with amphotericin B as treatment for preterm infants with invasive fungal infection. Although the study was of good methodological quality, the trial was very small (total of 22 preterm infants) and it is not possible to draw meaningful conclusions from the data. We did not find any studies which compared the use of amphotericin B with liposomal amphotericin B.

Consequently, we do not know if treating preterm infants with invasive fungal infection with the newer antifungal agents compared with conventional amphotericin B improves clinical outcomes. In the particular case of suspected or confirmed fungal meningitis, the use of another agent which is known to cross the blood brain barrier should still be considered instead of or in combination with Amphotericin B.

Our pre-specified outcomes did not include any specific measure of convenience of drug administration or of the cost of the treatment course, although these may be related to the incidences of side-effects that result in discontinuation of therapy. The incidence of thrombophlebitis was statistically significantly lower in the group treated with fluconazole compared to amphotericin B, but this complication did not result in discontinuation of treatment.

In the included study, there were no other instances of adverse events resulting in discontinuation of therapy. The trial also found that there were not any statistically significant differences in duration of treatment, days in hospital after enrollment to the study, or duration of need for a central venous line. However, the mean duration of intravenous antifungal therapy was statistically significantly lower for the fluconazole group (which is well absorbed orally and was prescribed enterally for part of the treatment course) compared with amphotericin B.

DRUGS TREATING VIRAL INFECTIONS

We live in a time of rapid development of antiviral compounds. For selective chemotherapy of viral infections, a drug should inhibit virus replication when used at concentrations not detrimental to the host. A number of antiviral drugs have been formally licensed and are widely used for the chemotherapy of specific viral infections. Other antiviral agents are being developed. These fall primarily in three classes: anti-herpesvirus, anti-retrovirus, and, to a lesser extent, anti-rhinovirus compounds. The mechanisms of action targeting virus-specific events are being studied. Antiviral chemotherapy offers a decisive approach to the control of virus, notwithstanding some current limitations.

BASIC MECHANISMS

Specificity against virus replication is the key issue in chemotherapy. Because of the close interaction between virus replication and normal cellular metabolism, it was originally thought too difficult to interrupt the virus replicative cycle without adversely affecting the host cell metabolism.

It is now clear, however, that several events in the virus replicative cycle either do not occur in normal uninfected cells or are controlled by virus-specified enzymes that differ structurally and functionally from the corresponding host cell enzymes. Quite schematically, the virus replicative cycle can be divided into 10 steps: (1) adsorption, (2) penetration, (3) uncoating, (4) early transcription, (5) early translation, (6) replication of the viral genome, (7) late transcription, (8) late translation, (9) assembly, and (10) release of new virus particles. Adsorption, penetration, and uncoating are typical examples of replicative events that are specific for virus infection and do not occur in uninfected cells. Examples of virus replication steps controlled by virus-specified enzymes are the transcription of positive-sense RNA to DNA (catalyzed by the reverse transcriptase associated with retroviruses), the replication of DNA to DNA (catalyzed by the DNA polymerases of herpesviruses), and the proteolytic cleavage of viral precursor proteins (catalyzed by the protease of human immunodeficiency virus).

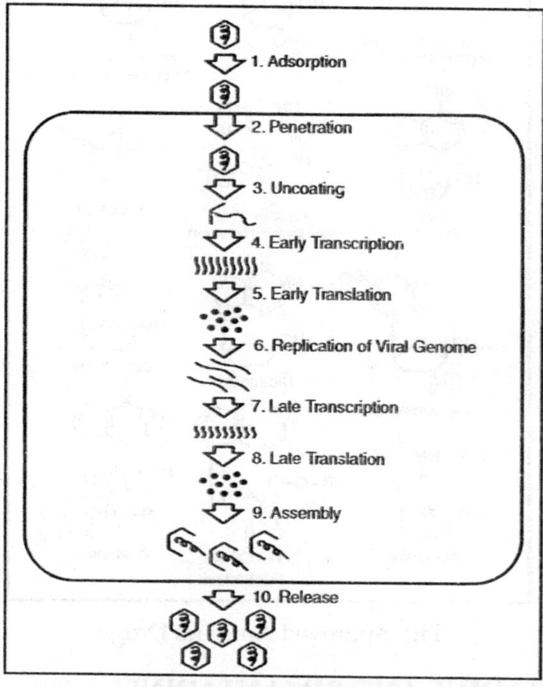

Fig. Virus Replicative Cycle.

The various steps in the replicative cycle at which the virus deviates from normal host processes are potential targets for chemotherapeutic intervention. It is not yet possible to tailor new antiviral agents to virus-specific target molecules. The molecular modes and targets of action for some of the approved antiviral drugs remain to be better defined.

APPROVED ANTIVIRAL DRUGS

Antiviral compounds that have been formally licensed for clinical use are amantadine, rimantadine, ribavirin,

idoxuridine, trifluridine, vidarabine, acyclovir, ganciclovir, foscarnet, zidovudine, didanosine, zalcitabine, stavudine, famciclovir and valaciclovir.

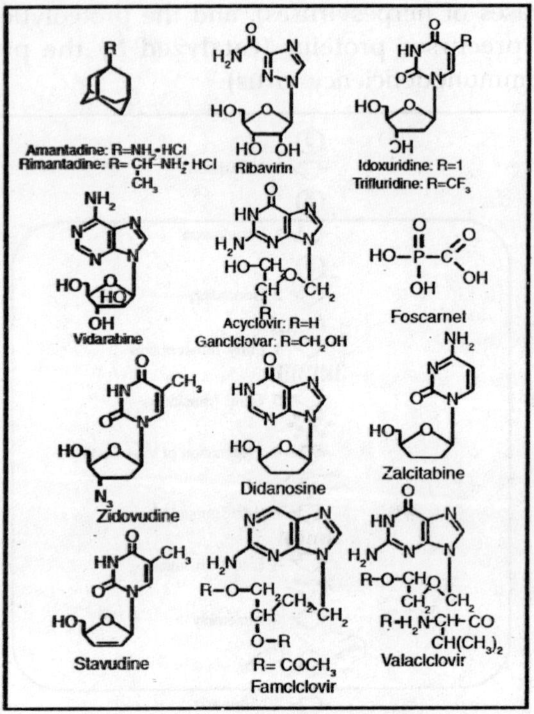

Fig. Approved Antiviral Drugs.

AMANTADINE AND RIMANTADINE

The clinical use of amantadine and rimantadine is restricted to the prophylaxis and early therapy of influenza A virus infections. Influenza prophylaxis is particularly indicated in immunodeficient patients, persons who are allergic to influenza vaccine, unvaccinated house contacts of high-risk patients, and residents of chronic care facilities where an outbreak of influenza A has been recognized.

Amantadine is noted for its central nervous system side effects, such as hallucinations and disorientation, which lead, for example, to a risk of falling. Rimantadine causes fewer

side effects than amantadine, when used at the same dosage (200 mg/day, perorally). Influenza A virus resistance to both amantadine and rimantadine has been described.

Ribavirin

Although active against ortho- and paramyxoviruses, ribavirin (Virazole) is approved only for the treatment of respiratory syncytial virus (RSV) infection in infants. The drug is administered as a small-particle aerosol (particle diameter, 1 to 3 μm) so that it can reach the lower respiratory tract. Aerosolized ribavirin treatment results in more rapid cessation of viral shedding and resolution of clinical symptoms without signs of systemic toxicity.

Idoxuridine and Trifluridine

Because of their myelosuppressive, mutagenic and teratogenic effects following systemic administration, idoxuridine and trifluridine are only suitable for topical use. Trifluridine is superior to idoxuridine when used in eyedrops for the topical treatment of herpetic keratitis. Idoxuridine can be formulated for topical treatment of herpetic skin lesions.

Vidarabine

Vidarabine (Vira-A) is used for both topical and systemic treatment of herpes simplex virus (HSV) infections. A serious drawback is the poor solubility of this drug in aqueous media, which means that intravenous administration requires a large volume of fluid. When vidarabine and acyclovir were compared for efficacy in treating herpetic encephalitis and varicella-zoster virus (VZV) infection in immunocompromised hosts, acyclovir proved clearly superior to vidarabine.

Vidarabine has various toxic side effects (i.e., tremor, ataxia, seizures, myalgia, nausea, vomiting, and diarrhea). Acyclovir is now generally preferred over vidarabine in the treatment of HSV and VZV infections.

Acyclovir, Valaciclovir and Famciclovir

Acyclovir (Zovirax) represents a major breakthrough in the treatment of herpesvirus infections. The main indications for its use are primary genital herpes, herpetic encephalitis and HSV and VZV infections in immunosuppressed patients. It can be used topically, intravenously, or perorally, although its oral absorption is only 20 per cent.

It offers limited benefit in the topical treatment of recurrent herpes labialis. It is also efficacious in preventing recurrent genital herpes, as well as in preventing HSV infections in renal allograft recipients. Based on an alteration of their thymidine kinase, HSV and VZV may develop resistance to acyclovir, particularly in immunocompromised patients.

Valaciclovir (Valtrex) and Famciclovir (Famvir) represent two orally bioavailable compounds for the treatment of HSV and VZV infections. Their main indication is herpes zoster. Valaciclovir and famciclovir act as prodrugs of acyclovir and penciclovir, respectively.

Penciclovir acts in a similar fashion as acyclovir, although it would generate higher intracellular levels of the triphosphate form, which is supposed to be the active metabolite for these compounds.

Ganciclovir, Foscarnet

Ganciclovir (Cytovene) is the preferred drug for treating cytomegalovirus (CMV) infections in patients with acquired immune deficiency syndrome (AIDS) or other immunodeficiencies. It has very poor oral bioavailability (3 per cent), and, therefore, mostly given intravenously. Of the various clinical manifestations of cytomegalovirus infection in immunosuppressed patients, cytomegalovirus retinitis responds best to ganciclovir therapy, but recurs after treatment is stopped.

The most frequent adverse side effects are granulocytopenia (neutropenia) and thrombocytopenia. Foscarnet (Foscavir) is the second drug used in the treatment of CMV infections, particularly CMV retinitis, in immunocompromised patients. It must be given intravenously, and it has proved effective in delaying progression of CMV retinitis compared to untreated controls.

Zidovadine, Didanosine, Zalcitabine and Stavudine

Zidovudine is licensed for patients infected with human immunodeficiency virus type 1 or 2 (HIV-1 or -2), the agent of AIDS. It appears to impede progression of the disease, to lower the mortality rate and to diminish the frequency of opportunistic infections.

The duration of the beneficial effects may be hampered by the emergence of resistant mutants. AZT is well absorbed orally (60 per cent) and readily crosses the blood-brain barrier. Serious side effects, particularly megaloblastic anemia and leukopenia, necessitate withdrawal of the drug in some patients.

In addition to zidovudine, three other dideoxynucleosides, *viz.* didanosine, zalcitabine and stavudine have been licensed for the treatment of patients with HIV infection. All these compounds act in a similar fashion in that they are targeted at the reverse transcriptase. They all cause toxic side effects, particularly peripheral neuropathy and pancreatitis (DDI).

As these adverse reactions are not overlapping with those of AZT, both DDI and DDC have been used in combination with AZT in attempts to obtain better efficacy with lower toxicity.

FUTURE ANTIVIRAL DRUGS

The importance of virus infections and the early successes with some antiviral drugs have prompted the search for new agents. This search has been focused on compounds that are active against herpesviruses, retroviruses, and rhino-viruses. These antiviral drugs of the future are expected to be useful in clinical settings in which the approved antiviral drugs are not sufficiently efficacious.

Among the yet to be approved antiviral compounds rank bromovinyldeoxyuridine (Helpin, BVDU) for the treatment of HSV-1 and VZV infections; cidofovir for the treatment of CMV infections (in particular CMV retinitis, where it confers a long-lasting suppression of the disease); and the HIV protease inhibitor saquinavir (Inverase) for the treatment of

AIDS, where it may be combined with the dideoxynucleoside analogues (i.e. AZT and DDC) to achieve maximal benefit.

MAIN TARGETS FOR ANTIVIRAL DRUGS

For rational drug design, the molecular targets (i.e., proteins or enzymes) should be identified first and then the drugs should be tailored on the basis of the molecular configuration and action of the target proteins. None of the antiviral drugs now available, or considered for clinical use, have been developed by rational drug design (except, to a certain extent, for the HIV protease inhibitors). Instead, their antiviral activity was found first, often by chance, and their molecular targets determined later.

Antiviral compounds can be divided into two categories: (1) those that can interact directly with their target and (2) those that must first be activated intracellularly by phosphorylation to the active (generally triphosphate) forms. Those approved compounds that do not require such activation are: amantadine, rimantadine, foscarnet and viral protease inhibitors.

They interact directly with their target (viral adsorption, penetration, uncoating, HIV-1 reverse transcriptase or HIV protease). In contrast, all nucleoside analogs, whether active as anti-herpesvirus agents (such as acyclovir, ganciclovir, penciclovir or bromovinyldeoxyuridine) or anti-retrovirus agents (such as zidovudine and other dideoxynucleoside analogs) must be activated through three consecutive phosphorylation steps (although only two phosphorylations are required for the acyclic nucleoside phosphonates) before they can interact with their target enzyme, the herpesvirus DNA polymerase or retrovirus reverse transcriptase.

The triphosphates of the nucleoside analogs then compete with the natural substrates of the DNA polymerase or reverse transcriptase reaction. They can inhibit the incorporation of the natural substrates (e.g., dTTP and dGTP) into the growing DNA chain or can themselves become incorporated into DNA. This has been clearly demonstrated with a number of nucleoside analogs, such as idoxuridine, bromovinyldeoxyuridine, acyclovir, penciclovir, ganciclovir and zidovudine. The incorporation of acyclovir, zidovudine and the other dideoxynucleosides into DNA leads to termination of chain elongation; therefore, these compounds act as chain terminators.

Antiviral selectivity may stem from the specific affinity of the antiviral compounds (or their activated forms) for their target protein (or enzyme). Alternatively, when phosphorylation is involved, antiviral selectivity may also evolve from the phosphorylation by a virus-encoded thymidine kinase.

Herpes simplex virus and varicella-zoster virus encode such virus-specific thymidine kinase, and since acyclovir and bromovinyldeoxyuridine are excellent substrates for the viral enzymes but poor substrates for the cellular thymidine kinase, their preferential phosphorylation by virus-infected cells, as compared to uninfected cells, significantly contributes to their selectivity as antiherpetic agents.

DRUGS TREATING HIV INFECTION AND AIDS

TREATMENTS AND DRUGS

When HIV was first identified in the early 1980s, there were few drugs to treat the virus and the opportunistic infections associated with it. Since then, a number of medications have been developed to treat both HIV/AIDS and opportunistic infections.

For many people, including children, these treatments have extended and improved their quality of life. Scientists at the National Institutes of Health estimate that since 1989, anti-retroviral medications have provided HIV-positive Americans with years of extended life.

But none of these drugs can cure HIV/AIDS, many have side effects that can be severe, and most are expensive. What's more, after 20 years on AIDS drugs, scme people develop resistance to the drugs and no longer respond to treatment. Newer drugs are being researched and created to help this group of people.

Treatment Guidelines

A panel of leading AIDS specialists has developed recommendations for the use of anti-retroviral medications in people with HIV. These recommendations are based on the best information available at the time they were developed. AIDSinfo, a programme of the Department of Health and Human Services, regularly refines and updates the recommendations as knowledge about HIV infection evolves.

According to current guidelines, treatment should focus on achieving the maximum suppression of symptoms for as long as possible. This aggressive approach is known as highly active anti-retroviral therapy (HAART). The aim of HAART is to reduce the amount of virus in your blood to very low or even nondetectable levels, although this doesn't mean the virus is gone. This is usually accomplished with a combination of three or more drugs.

But the treatment guidelines also emphasize the importance of quality of life. Thus the goal of AIDS treatment is to find the strongest possible regimen that is also simple and has the fewest side effects. If you have HIV/AIDS, it's important that you take an active role in treatment decisions. You and your doctor should discuss the risks and benefits of all therapies so that you can make an informed decision about what will likely be a complex and long-term treatment.

Anti-retroviral Drugs

Anti-retroviral drugs inhibit the growth and replication of HIV at various stages of its life cycle. Seven classes of these drugs are available:

- Nucleoside analogue reverse transcriptase inhibitors (NRTIs). NRTIs were the first anti-retroviral drugs to be developed. They inhibit the replication of an HIV enzyme called reverse transcriptase. They include zidovudine (Retrovir), lamivudine (Epivir), didanosine (Videx), stavudine (Zerit) and abacavir (Ziagen). A newer drug, emtricitabine (Emtriva), which must be used in combination with at least two other AIDS medications, treats both HIV and hepatitis B.

The major side effect of zidovudine is bone marrow suppression, which causes a decrease in the number of red and white blood cells. Approximately 5 per cent of people treated with abacavir experience hypersensitivity reactions such as a rash, fever, fatigue, nausea, vomiting, diarrhea and abdominal pain. Symptoms usually appear within the first six weeks of treatment and generally disappear when the drug is discontinued. If you've had a hypersensitivity reaction to abacavir, avoid taking the drug again. Side effects of emtricitabine include skin discoloration.

- Protease inhibitors (PIs). PIs interrupt HIV replication at a later stage in its life cycle by interfering with an enzyme known as HIV protease. This causes HIV particles in your body to become structurally disorganized and noninfectious. Among these drugs are saquinavir (Invirase), ritonavir (Norvir), indinavir (Crixivan), nelfinavir (Viracept), amprenavir (Agenerase), lopinavir/ritonavir (Kaletra), atazanavir (Reyataz) and tipranavir (Aptivus). Darunavir (Prezista) is intended for people who haven't responded to treatment with other drugs. Darunavir is used with ritonavir and other anti-HIV medications. Protease inhibitors are usually prescribed with other medications, to help avoid drug resistance.

The most common side effects of protease inhibitors include nausea, diarrhea and other digestive tract problems. PIs can also cause a significant number of side effects when they interact with certain other medications.

That's because all PIs, to one degree or another, affect an enzyme system in your liver that is responsible for metabolizing a large number of drugs. Newer side effects have also appeared with the continuing and widespread use of protease inhibitors.

These include elevated triglyceride levels and problems with sugar metabolism that may sometimes progress to diabetes. There may also be abnormalities in the way fat is metabolized and deposited in your body. Some people lose much of their total body fat. Others gain excess fat on the back between their shoulders (buffalo hump) or in the stomach (protease paunch). No one knows exactly why these abnormalities occur. In fact, it's not even certain whether these problems are a direct result of treatment with protease inhibitors or due to some other cause that has yet to be identified. Similar metabolic abnormalities have occurred in people on anti-retroviral therapy that doesn't include PIs. Although these body changes can be distressing, the possibility they may occur should not stop you from getting treatment for HIV/AIDS.

- *Non-nucleoside reverse transcriptase inhibitors (NNRTIs):*These drugs bind directly to the enzyme reverse transcriptase. Four NNRTIs are approved for clinical use: nevirapine (Viramune), delavirdine (Rescriptor), efavirenz (Sustiva) and etravirine (Intelence). A major side effect of all NNRTIs is a rash. In addition, people taking efavirenz may have side effects such as abnormal and worsening of underlying mood disorders.
- *Nucleotide reverse transcriptase inhibitors (NtRTIs):* NtRTIs work much like nucleoside analogs They interfere with the replication of reverse transcriptase and prevent the virus from inserting its genetic material into cells. But NtRTIs act more quickly than NRTIs do. The only approved drug in this class, tenofovir (Viread), inhibits both HIV and hepatitis B and appears to be effective in people who are resistant to NRTIs. The most common side effects of tenofovir, when used in combination with other anti-retrovirals, are nausea, vomiting, diarrhea and gas. As with all reverse transcriptase inhibitors, the possibility of severe, and even fatal, liver damage exists.
- *Fusion inhibitors:* One of the most alarming developments in the AIDS epidemic is the emergence

of drug-resistant strains of HIV. Worldwide, a majority of people receiving treatment for HIV are resistant to at least one drug, and many don't respond to a typical three-drug combination. But a drug called enfuvirtide (Fuzeon), the first in a new class of drugs called fusion inhibitors, appears to suppress resistant strains of HIV. Fusion inhibitors stop the virus from replicating by preventing its membrane from fusing with the membrane surrounding healthy cells. Fuzeon is used in combination with other HIV drugs for people who have advanced infection and who have developed resistance to other drugs. Doctors administer Fuzeon by injection.

- *Integrase inhibitors:* These drugs are aimed at treating those who become resistant to other treatments. The only drug in this class, raltegravir (Isentress), is intended to be used in combination with other anti-retroviral drugs rather than alone. This is the first class of drugs that blocks replication of the HIV integrase enzyme, which keeps HIV DNA from inserting itself into human DNA. Common side effects include diarrhea, nausea, headache and fever.
- *Chemokine co-receptor inhibitors*: Chemokine co-receptor inhibitors (CCR5 antagonists) make up a new class of drugs used to treat a particulapr type of HIV infection called CCR5-tropic HIV-1. The only drug in this class — maraviroc (Selzentry) — is for treatment of CCR5-tropic HIV-1 in adults. Maraviroc is the first drug that targets a human protein rather than components of the HIV virus itself.

Maraviroc is used in combination with other anti-retroviral drugs for the treatment of adults with CCR5-tropic HIV-1 who have elevated levels of HIV (high viral load) in their blood despite treatment with other HIV medications. Maraviroc reduces viral load by preventing HIV from entering uninfected white blood cells. It does this by blocking CCR5, a major route of entry into the cells. CCR5 is a protein found on the surface of some immune cells, and maraviroc blocks the CCR5 co-receptor from accepting HIV. During two large clinical trials, approximately twice as many people with CCR5-tropic HIV-1 infection who received maraviroc had undetectable viral loads after 24 weeks as did those who received more standard therapy in the control groups.Side effects of maraviroc may include liver and cardiovascular problems, as well as cough, fever, upper respiratory tract infections, rash and abdominal pain.

Treatment Response

Your response to any treatment is measured by viral load. Viral load should be tested at the start of treatment and then every three to four months while you're undergoing therapy. In some cases, you may be tested even more often.

Short-Term Side Effects

I'm a prime example of someone whose body and mind are not the least bit compatible with mind-altering drugs. For example, if I take a stimulant such as a mild appetite suppressor or even a cup of coffee, I will develop tachycardia (rapid heartbeat) and an arrhythmia (irregular heartbeat) that lasts anywhere from hours to days.

This is dangerous, to say the least-not to mention unpleasant. When I am in this altered, medicated state, I am unable to focus my thoughts or do any constructive work. If I ingest a tranquilizer (a downer), I am zonked out for a day and a half.

To give you an idea, when I was an intern, I once took a 10 milligram (mg) Valium (diazepam), a commonly prescribed class of drug called benzodiazepine, before going to work. After taking this anti-anxiety agent, I literally was unable to get off the couch for a full day. I had to call in sick-the only day of my entire internship that I missed. Psychoactive drugs and I simply do not get along.

Many of my patients have experienced the same adverse effect with benzodiazepines. Along with the drowsiness, they have reported slurred speech and dizziness. One patient, thirty-two-year-old Victoria, said she was unable to wake up until noon after taking medication the night before for mild anxiety. When she awoke, she discovered that her two preschoolers had unlocked the front door and were playing in the front yard near a busy highway. I'm sure Victoria's mild anxiety turned into outright panic when she thought of what could have happened to her unsupervised young children.

Another woman, Caroline, age forty-seven, took Valium to help ease anxiety during a lengthy divorce. She came to me for a natural therapy, saying the tranquilizer made her so numb that she was devoid of all emotions. "The drug calmed my anxiety," Caroline said, "but after taking it for a week, it also dulled any joy or enthusiasm I had for life."

People who do not have problems with drugs are often puzzled by or suspicious of those who say they can't take mind-altering medications. To them I say, why not see this for what it is-one extreme along the spectrum of responses to chemicals. At the other extreme are those who never feel normal without drugs. These people can easily become abusers. In between, we find the average person, who can tolerate the majority of drugs pretty well. Still, there is more to the problem of taking drugs than simple tolerance.

Long-Term Adverse Effects

Along with the short-term uncomfortable side effects of drug therapy, there can be long-term adverse effects that can sometimes be toxic. Any drug that acts on the central nervous system (such as an analgesic, a stimulant, or a depressant) is potentially able to cause noxious side effects such as cognitive impairment, dependence, habituation, or neurological disorders.

In fact, up to 10 per cent of patients using psychotropic drugs report serious side effects, including hepatitis, dermatitis, low white blood cell count, amnesia, paradoxical excitation, changes in vision, hearing alterations, breathing problems, hypertension, low blood pressure, fast or slow heartbeat, palpitations, and headaches, among others.

Today there are thousands of studies on the toxic effects and resulting adverse reactions to psychotropic medications. There are hundreds of studies on suicides, overdoses, and deaths from use of these drugs, not including driving accidents and memory impairment.

Drug therapy for anxiety usually consists of using anti-panic drugs for immediate symptom relief while attempting to find the most appropriate mix of drugs from several different categories, including antidepressants, anti-seizure and anti-anxiety medications. Yet, drugs, and especially psychotropic drugs, are not as specific in their actions as you may think. For example, the benzodiazepines (tranquilizers such as Valium, Ativan, and Xanax) have five major therapeutic qualities:

- Anxiety reduction (anxiolytic)
- Hypnotic (sleep-inducing)
- Muscle relaxant
- Anti-epileptic
- Amnesic (ability to ignore or forget unfavorable events)

Benzodiazepines such as Valium act by enhancing the effects of gamma-aminobutyric acid (GABA) in the brain. GABA is a neurotransmitter, a chemical that nerves in the brain use to send messages to one another. GABA inhibits activity in many of the nerves of the brain, and it is thought that this excessive activity is what causes anxiety or other psychological disorders.

Patients who take this class of drug may be subject to all of the above-mentioned treatment actions, along with any other adverse effects that may result, including rebound anxiety or insomnia (a major surge of anxiety or insomnia immediately after a drug that controlled the anxiety or insomnia is discontinued), aches and pains, epileptic seizures, and memory problems, among many others.

In fact, most people are unaware that more than 500 different types of adverse reactions to benzodiazepines have been reported to the FDA. Because there are so many chemical effects and because benzodiazepines are fat-soluble and thus remain in the body, no part of the body or brain is exempt. Yes, the expected benefit may occur with these medications; but there is always the potential for an enhancement of any preexisting psychological or physical problem in addition to possible new problems.

Virtually every doctor recognizes individual variability in therapeutic and adverse effects. For example, a strong prescription might affect you and yet have no effect at all on a family member. Benzodiazepines accumulate in the body and brain at different speeds and different levels in each person.

With the long-term use of psychotropic drugs, mental and emotional impairment, if it occurs, comes on gradually and is often barely noticed by the patient. It is of interest to note that patients who have become dependent on the drugs are unlikely to ever respond normally to those drugs again, once they are discontinued.

Big Pharma Promotes Expensive Options

Prescription drugs are driven by what is known as Big Pharma, the big-business pharmaceutical industry. In fact, many of the so-called latest and greatest breakthrough medical studies are funded by the pharmaceutical industry and thus the outcomes reported can sometimes be biased. Deserved or not, Big Pharma often gains power and respectability from the government through lobbying and financial contributions.

Consequently, legislation and government agencies such as the Food and Drug Administration often reflect the interests of these companies.Most doctors get their drug information from well-paid sales reps who work for Big Pharma and don't have time to explore other remedies, specifically the healing benefits of natural (and inexpensive) therapies that are less known. These doctors have little time to explain the possible risks of these medications to patients or to teach them key lifestyle changes that might benefit the patient's overall health. This is problematic because the consumer often receives pricey and sometimes ineffective pharmaceuticals when a natural therapy might work just as well and cost a lot less without all the deleterious side effects. Natural approaches often do not make big money for powerful drug companies and do not get the testing, FDA approval, and the million-dollar advertising budget that drugs produced by Big Pharma receive.

Post-Withdrawal Symptoms After Long-Term Benzodiazepine Use During the 1980s, there were substantial long-term studies related to latent physical and psychological symptoms that resulted from discontinuation of psychotropic drugs. The effects were not exclusive to acute withdrawal but also were seen after discontinuation of long-term benzodiazepine use.

These symptoms would not be occurring had there not been a semipermanent or even permanent change in the brain's neurochemical or neurological system. While it is true that some people who use psychotropic drugs do not experience post-withdrawal symptoms, the risk is still there for many others.

- Behavioral disorders
- Bursting head feeling
- Delusions
- Depression
- Gastrointestinal problems
- Headache
- Increased anxiety
- Insomnia
- Irritability
- Malaise
- Moodiness
- Neck tension
- Neuromuscular problems
- Numbness in extremities

Chapter 8

Diagnostic Language

INTRODUCTION

Much effort is directed towards optimising doctor-patient communication and avoiding misunderstandings. The language of everyday diagnostic reasoning as it routinely occurs among doctors in teaching hospitals could benefit from similar attention. Although interest in evidence based medicine has increased in recent years, and it is taught in most medical schools, evidence based strategies have been adopted inconsistently into routine care.

One aspect of evidence based medicine involves understanding the limitations of inherently imperfect diagnostic tests. Many trainees appreciate the concepts of sensitivity and specificity and learn how to combine the "art" of the history and physical exam (pre-test probability of disease) with the "science" of diagnostic testing (post-test probability of disease) without explicit use of quantitative probability theory.

Nevertheless, it seems that quantitative reasoning is neither intuitive nor well understood. As diagnostic testing is a common and critical component of evaluating patients, it is worth considering whether the manner in which we verbally communicate these ideas may represent a fundamental (yet reparable) hindrance to diagnostic reasoning. We discuss common examples of diagnostic language that do not accurately reflect the underlying theory, and review the evidence for inadequate clinical application of bayesian strategies.

GENERALISATIONS

As trainees, we can all recall hearing pearls of wisdom conveyed in the form of: "Any patient presenting with this sign/symptom is assumed to have disease *X* until proved otherwise." The common mnemonic "SPin/SNout" is used to indicate that positive results from specific tests rule in disease, while negative results from sensitive tests rule out disease.

One may hear sensitivity or specificity discussed in isolation ("that test is so sensitive that a negative result rules out disease") or, more commonly, of a test having good positive or negative predictive value. Certain findings are called "non-specific" because they manifest in multiple diseases. Although this language seems to capture simple diagnostic generalisations, does it actually reflect the bayesian logic that underlies diagnostic reasoning?

The accuracy of such language is easily overlooked because in common practice test results agree with clinical suspicion and the details of sensitivity, specificity, and predictive value become arguably less important.

BASICS OF BAYESIAN LOGIC

To interpret any diagnostic test, one must have information not only about the test's characteristics but also about the patient (or a population with similar characteristics). Few tests are inherently accurate enough to "rule in" or "rule out" disease effectively in all cases. We should look at results as altering disease probability. This requires estimation of a pre-test probability that will be adjusted up or down by the test results.

This is bayesian logic, which uses an adjustment factor called the likelihood ratio (LR) to convert a pretest probability into a post-test probability (fig). The upward adjustment of the probability after a positive result is called the LR(+) and is a number > 1, while the downward adjustment after a negative result is the LR(-) and is a fraction < 1. The key feature of the likelihood ratio is that it incorporates both the sensitivity and the specificity. Ruling disease in or out (or considering subsequent decisions on management) depends on a comparison of post-test probability with thresholds for further action based on factors such as severity of disease, risks of further testing, or side effects of treatment.

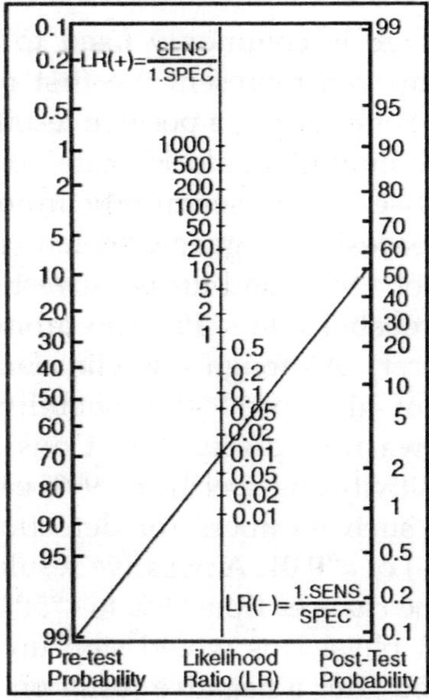

Nomogram to convert pre-test probability to post-test probability using the likelihood ratio. The line refers to a text example. Simply remembering that the likelihood ratio incorporates both sensitivity and specificity protects against the common misconception that sensitivity and specificity can be considered in isolation. Although it is true in general that sensitivity impacts LR(-) more than specificity (and specificity impacts LR(+) more than sensitivity), the likelihood ratio is derived from both measurements. In fact, for every sensitivity (or specificity) less than 100%, there is a specificity (or sensitivity) that renders the LR = 1 (that is, no change in probability of disease).

The fact that most tests are imperfect and therefore do nothing more than adjust probability (which may or may not "rule in" or "rule out" the disease depending on the situation) protects against the misconception that a result can be interpreted without considering pre-test probability. Several studies have shown deficiencies in using pre-test probability when interpreting test results.

"AFFECTED UNTIL PROVED OTHERWISE"

This language is commonly used to emphasise that certain symptoms can represent the first presentation of a serious disease. For example, a positive result on faecal occult blood testing in an adult could indicate "colon cancer until proved otherwise." This seemingly innocent statement translates into bayesian language: "colon cancer has a pre-test probability of > 99%, and further investigation is needed to reduce its probability to < 1%" (an arbitrary certainty of not having cancer). Although few clinicians use this strict interpretation of high pre-test probability, the bayesian consequences warrant discussion. Consider a test with exceptional sensitivity and specificity: 99% each. Colonoscopy may approach such numbers for detection of neoplasm, yielding an LR(-) of <"0.01. A negative result on colonoscopy would reduce the chances from 99% to <"50%—hardly ruling it out. Yet most physicians would stop investigating stools positive for blood after a negative result on colonoscopy.

The gap between the language and the practice is that the actual pre-test probability of colon cancer in the example is far less than 100%, so the negative colonoscopy is informative. The intended message of "affected until proved otherwise" is actually that the threshold for further evaluation is low, not that the pre-test probability is high. It is worth considering more realistic numbers. A negative result from what might be called a "good" test, with 90% sensitivity and 90% specificity, would reduce the disease probability only slightly, from 99% to <"90%.

For a single test with such characteristics (LR(-)of <"0.1) to render disease probability < 1%, the nomogram shows that pre-test probability would have to be no greater than 10%. Negative results from two independent tests with exceptional sensitivity and specificity (99% each) would be needed to reduce disease probability from 99% to 1%, or four consecutive negative results from independent tests with sensitivity and specificity of 90% each. Test independence means that the result from one test cannot bias the outcome of the next, such that the post-test probability after one test becomes the pre-test probability of the subsequent test.

PREDICTIVE VALUE

The language of predictive value is more problematic, yet understanding predictive value is critical for moving beyond the simplicity of sensitivity and specificity for interpretation of test results. Referring generally to the "predictive value of a test" gives the false impression that a test's predictive power stands alone (in the same way, theoretically, as its sensitivity or specificity) and therefore can be applied to any patient.

In fact, the predictive value is a reflection of the pre-test probability as well as the discriminative power (sensitivity and specificity) of the test. Therefore, the predictive value is a characteristic of a test result in a specific patient (or representative population) not of the test result in general, nor of the test itself. It is inappropriate, for example, to describe a negative d-dimer test result as having good negative predictive value for pulmonary embolism.

Doing so ignores the impact of pre-test probability—that is, it ignores the information provided by clinical judgment. If the pre-test probability of pulmonary embolism were high, then the negative d-dimer result would not rule out pulmonary embolism, and thus the d-dimer test is most useful in the setting of lower pre-test probability.

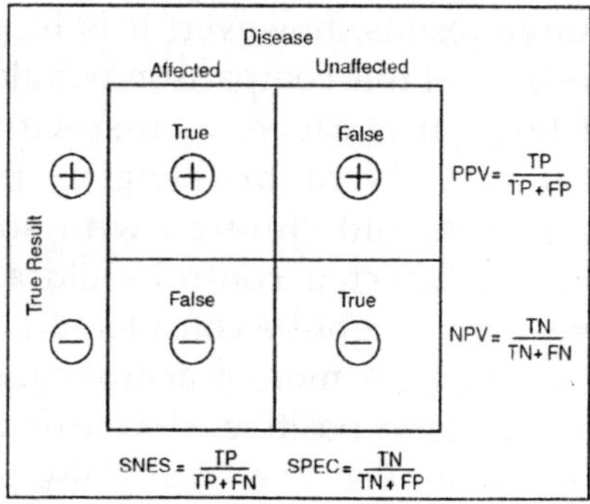

Standard 2×2 box illustrating the determination of sensitivity, specificity, and predictive value for a dichotomous test. One of the potentially confusing aspects of predictive value is that it seems to be determined by simple calculations with the 2×2 box, similar to sensitivity and specificity, and therefore it may be misconstrued as a characteristic of the test itself.

Whereas the calculations of sensitivity and specificity are unaffected by the proportion of affected versus unaffected patients, this is not the case for predictive value ("horizontal" calculations), which depends heavily on the disease prevalence.

Thus, test results cannot be said to have predictive value; only a test result in a given patient (or population) has predictive value. Rather than a mere semantic distinction, this fundamental issue in test interpretation has been reported to be deficient at all levels of training.

CONTROL POPULATION

The concept of specificity itself presents hidden challenges. One may refer to a test as being either "specific for a disease," to indicate that few other diseases could produce a positive test result, or as "non-specific," to indicate that it may yield positive results in multiple diseases (or in health). Specificity, like sensitivity, is often considered an intrinsic property of a test and therefore independent of the population under study.

As specificity is determined by unaffected individuals who have positive results, however, it is in fact dependent on the characteristics of this comparison population. Consider the finding of fever: it is called "non-specific" for obvious reasons, but if a study of pharyngitis investigated a population of 10 year old children with sore throat it is unlikely that the unaffected control children would have fever. Therefore, fever might be considered a highly specific finding in such a study. A more practical challenge involves the mechanism of a false positive: stochastic assay variation (no biological meaning) versus a "real" false positive, arising from a different disease present in some members of the control population. Consider next the finding of oligoclonal bands in the cerebrospinal fluid of a patient suspected of having multiple sclerosis.

While several texts and reviews report 92-98% specificity (comparing patients with multiple sclerosis with "normal" controls), is that value relevant if the clinician is also considering alternative diagnoses such as lupus or Sjogren's, which can also manifest with oligoclonal bands in cerebrospinal fluid? In this situation, it cannot be said that oligoclonal bands are "specific for multiple sclerosis," regardless of the reported specificity as previous control populations might not have contained patients with lupus or Sjogren's.

Conversely, it has been suggested that the 14-3-3 protein assay in cerebrospinal fluid is not specific for Creutzfeldt-Jakob disease because the protein can also occur with other diseases, including central nervous system malignancy, infection, or stroke. If imaging and evaluation of the cerebrospinal fluid can reduce the likelihood of such confounding conditions, however, a positive 14-3-3 in that setting might then be considered more "specific."

Interpretation of specificity requires careful attention not only to the control population but also to the test's performance in other diseases that are being considered. Specificity should not be considered an intrinsic property of a test because it depends in part on the characteristics (even subclinical) of the control population from which it was derived.

It is therefore critical to evaluate the study design from which the specificity of a test has been determined and to consider whether the test can be used more appropriately to distinguish one disease from another or to distinguish the presence or absence of disease.

STANDARDIZED LANGUAGES

Public health nurses have provided care to individuals, families and communities for over a century. Their work is

A standardized nursing language is a structured vocabulary that provides nurses with a common means of communication. A standardized language ensures that when a nurse talks about a stage III pressure area, another nurse fully understands what the first nurse is describing. Nurses should use a standardized language in the same way physicians do (ie, to describe diagnoses or problems, interventions, and outcomes).

Imagine the communication problems that would arise among physicians if the term appendicitis did not have the same meaning each time it is used. Language in nursing has never been clear, precise, or consistent for the same clinical problems and treatment. For example, pressure ulcers have been described as decubitus ulcers, bedsores, or skin breakdown.

In addition, nurses never have been consistent in the ways they discuss clinical processes. Operating rooms across the country use similar terms (eg, turnover time, start time); however, the definition of those terms can vary widely from one institution to another despite national efforts to standardize the definitions for these processes. Inconsistency of language and meaning makes it almost impossible to draw comparisons or attempt to benchmark one facility to another.

A standardized language consists of a collection of data elements. In the PNDS, the data elements include perioperative nursing diagnoses, interventions, outcomes, and structural definitions. A data element is a "unit of data for which the definition, identification, representation and permissible values are specified by means of a set of attributes."(2) Data elements are characterized by being the smallest unit of information that retains meaning.

Data elements allow for standardization of a language and also permit the language to be more easily managed in an electronic format. Nursing terminology is key to the development of a nursing information system. Computerized patient records provide opportunities to meet the medical-legal standards for documentation, support clinical decision making, develop and analyse databases, and improve care and communication. Currently, standardized nursing languages provide a structure to manage nursing data in a computerized patient record. The data elements that compose the various nursing standardized languages provide discrete facts or atomic-level data that can be managed electronically.

CLASSIFICATION

Classification and language efforts in nursing have their origins in disease classification systems. Most nurses are familiar with the International Classification of Disease, the Standard Diagnostic Statistical Manual of Mental Disorders, and the Systematized Nomenclature of Medicine. All of these classifications provide uniformity in naming and defining specific health and illness conditions.

Early efforts in medical classification were limited to the causes of death. Obviously, there were reasons to expand that language beyond causes of death. In 1860, Florence Nightingale recommended to the fourth International Statistical Congress in London that nonfatal conditions also be included in the existing classification system.

The first standardized language that most nurses learn in school traditionally has been derived from medical diagnostic classifications. In fact, much of nursing education and practice has been organized according to medical conditions. The reliance on medical language has contributed to the limited availability and acceptance of a standardized nursing language; however, as the role of the professional nurse has expanded, the need for a standardized nursing language has emerged.

Two nursing classification systems were introduced in the mid-twentieth century—these included Abdellah's classification system of nursing problems that described nursing goals and Henderson's classification of basic functional health problems focused on patient needs.(4) Both of these early classification efforts were used as frameworks for nursing curricula and provided a helpful tool in organizing and delivering patient care. During this time, a focus on the nursing process in both practice and education developed.(5)

Nurses were defining more clearly the various domains of professional nursing practice. Since then, there have been a number of initiatives to develop standardized languages for nursing practice. Some of the reasons for these efforts reflect the fact that

- Nurses, as professionals, have become more aware of the need to name and describe their contributions to health care;
- Clinical information systems require standardized terms and definitions to help clinicians in electronic documentation;
- Nurses have recognized that, as professionals, they need common languages for communication purposes;
- Nursing science, theory, and research has resulted in knowledge gain that supports the development of nursing language and classification systems.

The National League of Nursing and the ANA have supported efforts related to nursing classification systems at both the professional, educational, and organizational levels. In addition to providing leadership on the issue of standardized language, the ANA also has established criteria for recognizing nursing classifications and standardized languages.

The ANA has worked closely with the National Library of Medicine and other organizations so that recognized languages can be mapped into the Unified Medical Language System. The ANA also has taken a leadership role in developing and maintaining relationships with the standard development organizations and organizations collaborating on multidisciplinary health care terminologies.

In addition, the ANA has promoted opportunities to interface with policy makers and legislators on issues pertinent to standardized language and the computerized medical record.

Nursing languages for clinical practice that have been recognized by the ANA Committee for Nursing Practice Information Infrastructure include the

- North American Nursing Diagnosis Association Taxonomy,
- Omaha System,
- Home Health Care Classification,
- Nursing Intervention Classification,
- Nursing Outcome Classification,
- Patient Care Data Set, and
- PNDS.

The ANA Committee for Nursing Practice Information Infrastructure requires that languages meet certain criteria, including

- the language provides a clinically useful terminology and a rationale for development;
- the language consists of clear and unambiguous terms;
- the developer provides evidence of reliability, validity, and utility; and
- the language includes a unique identifier for each term.

North American Nursing Diagnosis Association (NANDA) Taxonomy. Since 1973, the NANDA has been involved in a systematic process to identify and label the phenomena of concern to nurses. The NANDA Taxonomy was the first language system recognized by ANA and is integrated in other data sets (ie, Home Health Care Classification, Patient Care Data Set, PNDS).

The NANDA Taxonomy includes 150 diagnostic categories with etiologies, risk factors, and defining characteristics (ie, signs and symptoms). Nursing diagnoses have been widely used by nurses in a number of clinical settings and have been published in most major nursing textbooks. Nursing diagnoses also provide the framework for many educational programs in nursing.

Omaha System. The Omaha System was derived from clinical practice to improve community health practice, document care in community and health care systems, and provide management data. Developed by community health nurses, it has been successfully implemented in numerous community and home health care agencies. This system consists of 42 nursing diagnoses, nursing interventions, and a problem-rating scale for outcomes.

The concepts in this language are similar to other nursing classification systems, but the terms and classification structure reflect areas of community health practice. The four major domains are environmental, psychosocial, physiological, and health-related problems.Home Health Care Classification (HHCC).

The HHCC, developed by Virginia Saba, RN, EdD, FAAN, FACMI, a scholar and language developer at Georgetown University, Washington, DC, is used in numerous home health agencies providing health care services in the home and community as well as thousands of ambulatory care settings, including ambulatory outpatient clinics, health maintenance organizations, and other facilities.

This vocabulary consists of 145 nursing diagnoses and 160 interventions developed to code, index, classify, document, track, and analyse clinical care processes. The nursing diagnoses and interventions are classified according to 20 care components to facilitate computerization and provide an organizing framework. The HHCC provides one framework for comparing patients' assessed needs to the use of home health resources.

Nursing Intervention Classification (NIC). The third edition of the NIC consists of 486 direct and indirect interventions assigned to one of seven domains and 30 classes. Each intervention includes a concept label, definition, and activities. This comprehensive classification of interventions provides a framework for clinical documentation and communication.

The interventions include nurse- and physician-initiated treatments as well as daily essential functions. The NIC has been used by numerous health care agencies for use in nursing care plans, standards, nursing information systems, and nursing educational programs.Nursing Outcome Classification (NOC). The second edition of the NOC contains 260 outcomes, including seven family unit and six community level outcomes. The NOC is a comprehensive standardized language designed to help clinicians evaluate the effectiveness of nursing interventions. Each outcome statement includes a definition and a rating scale to assess a patient's progress based on specific indicators.

The NOC classification has been used in a number of clinical and educational settings. Both the NIC and NOC systems provide the framework for analyzing nursing care, patient outcomes, and the use of clinical nursing resources. Patient Care Data Set (PCDS).

The development of the PCDS was spearheaded by Judy Ozbolt, RN, PhD, FAAN, professor of nursing and biomedical informatics at Vanderbilt University, Nashville, in her work with a number of clinical agencies. It is composed of a data dictionary, 363 nursing diagnoses, 1,357 patient care actions, and 311 patient care goals. Some of the diagnostic categories are derived from the NANDA Taxonomy and the HHCC.

The 20 care components of the HHCC and two additional components that reflect the needs of the acutely ill client serve as the framework for organizing the PCDS. The data set is used in a number of acute care health care agencies. The PCDS was developed, in part, from a multidisciplinary perspective and also is used by health care practitioners in disciplines other than nursing.

Perioperative Nursing Data Set (PNDS). The PNDS is a nomenclature that describes perioperative nursing practice and consists of 64 nursing diagnoses, 127 nursing interventions, and 29 patient outcomes. This standardized language is organized in four domains—safety, physiologic response to surgery, patient and family behavioursal response to surgery, and health care system.

The PNDS was the first nursing language developed by a nursing specialty recognized by the ANA. Currently, the PNDS is being incorporated into computerized documentation tools by at least two software vendors. International Council of Nurses (ICN). Another important, long-term classification effort is the ICN project, the International Classification of Nursing Practice (ICNP). One purpose of this project is to describe nursing practice in various clinical settings worldwide using a common language.

Additional purposes include enhancing nurses' ability to compare clinical data, advancing nursing knowledge, and improving the quality and cost-effectiveness of nursing care. To date, the ICNP includes three components—nursing phenomena, outcomes, and actions. The project is in a beta one version and is being translated and validated in more than 20 countries.

CLASSIFICATION AND STANDARDIZED

Classifications, which have existed since early times, help to promote the knowledge base of a field of study by identifying the underlying principles of what is known about the field. Classifications also identify gaps in knowledge, which can then be addressed by research, and help to achieve economy of memory and facilitate communications.

There are several existing classification systems for nursing including: the Omaha System, a client focused taxonomy of nursing diagnoses related to community health nursing; an intervention taxonomy for home health care; a system of outcome measures of service quality related to home care; Henderson's components of basic nursing ambulatory care nursing taxonomy; the eight domains of nursing described; and Sigma Theta Tau's International Classification of Nursing Knowledge.

Language standardization involves assignment of a single term or phrase to a phenomenon that can be described by several different words or phrases. In standardizing nursing interventions, the phenomena being classified are the nurse behaviourss or activities that are directed toward maintaining or improving the client's health status.

Labeling discrete sets of activities and defining the assigned label improves communication and understanding among nurses and between nurses and other professionals. It allows nurses to communicate both the unique and complementary functions of nursing. In addition to improving communication, language standardization can foster the expansion of nursing knowledge, enhance development of health information systems, facilitate determining the cost of nursing services, plan for resource needs, and improve nursing education.

When multiple labels exist that describe similar interventions, documenting and comparing nursing treatments becomes very complex requiring enormous investments of time and resources.

Standardization increases comparability when observing or measuring phenomena across individuals or groups, or across different settings. This is particularly useful in public health where there are a variety of care providers and care settings.

The Interventions Classification

The development of a standardized language used to describe activities performed by nurses is outlined in the first edition of a comprehensive publication, Nursing Interventions Classification (NIC), a book that documents the development of a standardized language for nursing interventions. The NIC work initiated and continued by McCloskey and Bulechek represents the first major effort to describe and standardize systematically the treatments performed by nurses.

The 2nd edition of the Nursing Interventions Classification contains 433 interventions, each with a definition and a detailed set of activities that describe what it is a nurse does to implement the intervention. Each intervention is coded with a unique number. The interventions are organized in 27 classes and 6 domains.

The Nursing Intervention Classification (NIC) was developed using a multidimensional research approach including content analysis, expert survey, focus group review, similarity analysis, hierarchical clustering, multidimensional scaling and clinical field-testing. Research teams of faculty and clinicians used inductive methods to developed nursing interventions and activities based on current practice as reflected in textbooks, journal articles, care planning guides, and clinical documentation systems. More than 1000 nurses and 50 professional organizations have provided input on the classification. Of particular interest to nurses whose practice encompasses the community beyond institutional walls is the current NIC teamwork, which has resulted in the development of community interventions.

The third edition of NIC includes a new domain in the taxonomy called *Community* having two classes: Community Health Promotion and Community Risk Management. This edition includes 16 new community interventions.

Overall, the third edition of NIC has 58 new interventions, 10 label name changes, 32 substantive intervention changes and 58 minor intervention changes. Five interventions included in the second edition have been deleted for the third edition by replacement or in combination to form new interventions.

VALUE OF STANDARDIZED LANGUAGES

Each of these languages has made its unique contributions to knowledge development in nursing. In comparing the languages, one would note either overlapping or similar terms and clinical processes. At this time, it appears that no one language has captured nursing practice in its entirety. Each language is in the process of revision and further development, and each language appears to have applications for other health care providers, including physical, occupational, and speech therapists and social workers.

From an informatics perspective, the language developers have been collaborating to develop consensus regarding strategies to enhance the processes required to map the different languages to each other. From a standardized language and informatics perspective, nursing is on the cutting edge and is well positioned to be part of the computerized medical record.

Learning more about and working with standardized nursing languages will ensure that nursing contributions are an integral component of any computerized medical record.

Understanding those nursing contributions through research and teaching will help in further defining the scope of nursing practice.

Standardized language, teaching, clinical practice, and research are interrelated as nursing moves forward as a profession into the twenty-first century.

STANDARDIZED LANGUAGE IN PUBLIC HEALTH

Public health nurses have been recognized for their accomplishments for over a century and have consistently been identified with the struggles of communities to meet the needs of particularly vulnerable populations. Their services, although effective when measured, were and may still be invisible to the public and even to other care providers.

The current changes in health care delivery which focus on cost containment, managed care and home-based service have caused public health nurses to once again focus on their unique contributions to the care of communities. Clarification of that care is essential to recognizing the work of public health nurses and to assuring that their work will continue and will be recognized as effective.

The public health core functions of assessment, policy development and assurance reflect the practice of all public health professionals including public health nurses. These functions are evident in public health interventions and are broad enough to meet individual, population, community and system needs.

Assessment includes activities associated with community diagnosis; policy development includes the process by which society makes decisions about problems and their solutions; and assurance involves the necessary services to reach agreed upon goals based on the specified level of services.

As authors explore the roles and functions of public health nurses, it is evident that their efforts cover a wide range of concerns associated with the naming, describing and evaluating what it is that public health nurses do. There also continues to be an on-going discussion to differentiate the roles of community health nurses and public health nurses. Such a distinction focuses on the nurse's educational preparation, location of practice and individual versus population focused care.

Although there is clearly an attempt in the literature to make a distinction between community and public health nurses, the task of naming what it is that these nurses do is not dependent on whether they are called community health or public health nurses.

The distinction between roles is more at the level of care to be provided. In other words, care focused at the individual or family levels versus care focused at the community or health system levels. These levels at which public health nurses provide care are the focus of additional literature describing their scope of practice.

Some authors identify the work of public health nurses, which is focused on the individual client or family unit as one level, to be part of the role but not that which distinguishes the public health nurse's specialty. The distinctive role of the public health nurse is at the level of interacting with populations or communities and with health systems or the context of care.

Public health nurses are also recognized for their expertise in well-defined specialty areas working with vulnerable populations. Although their efforts may be focused on individual clients or families with vulnerabilities such as AIDS, drug abuse, adolescent pregnancy or chronic disease, the distinctive practice of public health nurses is again at the population, community and systems levels.

The language for care provided to individuals and families is well developed. The language, which refers to care of vulnerable populations in communities and through systems, is the current work of the NIC team.

Along with efforts to name what it is that public health nurses do, there is an urgent need to identify the effectiveness of such efforts. Many authors have attempted to measure the effectiveness of the nurses' interventions, primarily at the individual/family level; however, such efforts are inconsistent and may not lend themselves to generalization across levels or populations. The early efforts of the Nursing Sensitive Outcomes Classification (NOC) team have started to clarify the language and process of measuring outcomes applicable to all health care settings.

Knowing that interest is building for developing a language to describe and evaluate the unique interventions of public health nurses prompted these authors to propose a new domain, Community, in NIC which can be clearly integrated with the Core Public Health Functions. This integration will enhance the language of interventions and outcomes to better define the scope of public health nursing practice.

CORE PUBLIC HEALTH FUNCTIONS

The Community Intervention and Public Health Core Functions Matrix depicts the relationship between the core public health functions and NIC community health interventions. The matrix also shows the relationship of selected interventions in the NIC classification to the level of care provided and how the three core functions of assessment, policy development and assurance are represented by NIC.

Public Health Functions

The core public health functions are the underpinnings of public health nursing practice, serving as a framework for nursing interventions in the community. The current functions include assessment, policy development, and assurance. First defined in the Institute of Medicine report (IOM, 1988), the core functions characterize the major phases of public problem solving including problem identification, mobilization of necessary effort and resources, and assurance that vital conditions are in place and that crucial services are received.

Assessment includes activities such as surveillance, needs identification, case finding, monitoring, and forecasting. This function facilitates decision-making in both the private and public sectors (IOM, 1988, p. 44). Examples of policy development are policy leadership, advocacy; convening, negotiating, brokering; mobilizing resources; training, constituency building and provision of public information.

The assurance function in public health involves insuring the implementation of legislative mandates as well as maintaining statutory responsibilities. This function is carried out through developing adequate responses to crises, supporting crucial services, regulating services and products in both the public and private sector, and maintaining accountability to the people by setting objectives and reporting on progress. The current core functions represent a broader view of public health activities than has existed in the past.

Community Health Interventions

"A community (or public) health intervention is targeted to promote and preserve the health of populations. Community interventions emphasize health promotion, health maintenance, and disease prevention of populations and include strategies to address the social and political climate in which the population resides". In the 3rd edition of NIC, there is a separate community domain that contains interventions reflecting "care that supports the health of the community".

This new domain has two classes, community health promotion, interventions that promote the health of the whole community, and community risk management, interventions that assist in detecting or preventing health risks to the whole community. Figure presents an example of the community intervention, "programme development."

Nursing Interventions and Levels of Care

Community health nurses provide care to individuals, families, aggregates, and communities. They also impact community health status by indirect services that affect the health system or the context in which health care is delivered. Currently, there are several community level interventions in NIC including environmental management: community, environmental management: worker safety, health education, health policy monitoring, health screening, risk identification, and teaching: group. There are also interventions that can be used in community nursing practice at the individual and family levels of care. Examples of interventions for individuals in the community include abuse protection: child, patient rights protection and immunization/vaccination administration.

Additional interventions such as developmental enhancement, caregiver support and parent education: adolescent are examples of family-level interventions that could be used in community health practice.

Further work of the NIC team will be to develop additional interventions at the health system level such as collaboration enhancement. The NIC team has developed several additional community and health system level interventions which are included in the current edition of the classification.

They are case management, communicable disease management, community disaster preparedness, community health development, consultation, cost containment, environmental risk protection, financial resource assistance, fiscal resource management, programme development, surveillance: community, and vehicle safety promotion. Additional community-level interventions, including advocacy, collaboration, health promotion and staff/provider education are being developed.

CONCLUSION

The efforts of the NIC team to incorporate community health interventions are necessary and helpful as one examines the context and content of the professional work of community/public health nurses. Integrating these interventions with those of the IOM's Public Health Core Functions illustrates the unique work of public health professionals and the ability of the standardized language of NIC to address the specific activities of public health nurses. As public health professionals strive to clarify their roles and functions in the rapidly changing health care arena, with emphasis on health promotion, disease prevention and community-based or system level care, a standardized language will describe the mission of public health nurses more clearly and make it more visible to consumers and providers.

Evaluating the outcomes of public health nursing interventions remains an essential element of determining effectiveness and will continue to be the work of the NOC team as they develop and apply meaningful measures of the interventions of nurses in all settings.

CLASSIFICATION SYSTEMS

Classification research conducted at Iowa is unique and crucial to the documentation and study of nursing care and to the articulation of nursing care with that of other providers. For nearly a decade the University of Nursing has been a leader in developing standardized languages to describe the work of nursing. The Centre for Nursing Classification, established in 1995, facilitates the continued development of this important work.

The purposes of the Centre for Nursing Classification are to:

- Facilitate the continued development of the Nursing Interventions Classification and the Nursing Outcomes Classification to reflect current nursing practices
- Conduct the review processes and procedures for updating the Classifications
- Produce and disseminate materials related to the Classifications
- Assist faculty investigators in writing grants and obtaining funding
- Provide education and research experience opportunities for student research assistants and fellows

NURSING INTERVENTIONS CLASSIFICATION

The Nursing Interventions Classification (NIC) describes the treatments that nurses perform. NIC is useful to nurses in all specialties and in all settings. The classification contains a standardized list of 433 interventions, each with a definition, a set of activities that a nurse performs to carry out the intervention, and a short list of background readings.

The interventions are coded and organized in a three-level taxonomic structure which makes it easier to select an intervention and use the classification on a computer. Examples of interventions include the physiological (Acid-Base Management), the psychosocial (Anxiety Reduction), those used for illness treatment (Shock Management), for illness prevention (Fall Prevention), and to promote health (Exercise Promotion). Indirect care interventions (Emergency Cart Checking) are also included.

NURSING INTERVENTIONS CLASSIFICATION

The *Nursing Interventions Classification* (NIC) is a comprehensive, standardized language describing treatments that nurses perform in all settings and in all specialties. NIC interventions include both the physiological (e.g. Acid-Base Management) and the psychosocial (e.g. Anxiety Reduction). There are interventions for illness treatment (e.g. Hyperglycemia Management), illness prevention (e.g. Fall Prevention), and health promotion (e.g. Exercise Promotion). Interventions are for individuals or for families (e.g. Family Integrity Promotion).

Indirect care interventions (e.g. Emergency Cart Checking) and some interventions for communities (e.g. Environmental Management: Community) are also included. Each NIC intervention has a unique number which can facilitate computerization. NIC interventions have been linked with NANDA nursing diagnoses and the Omaha System problems and are in the process of being linked with Nursing Outcomes Classification (NOC) patient outcomes. There is a form and a review system for submitting suggestions for new or modified interventions.

Developing Organization

The classification work is part of the Centre for Nursing Classification at the University of Iowa College of Nursing.

Research methods used to develop the Classification include content analysis, expert survey, focus group review, similarity analysis, hierarchical cluster analysis, multidimensional scaling, and field testing.

More than 40 national nursing organizations have reviewed NIC and assisted with intervention development and validation and taxonomy construction and validation. The research, conducted by a large team of investigators, has been partially supported for the past seven years by the National Institute of Nursing Research, National Institutes of Health.

Description

NIC contains 433 interventions each with a definition and a detailed set of activities that describes what it is a nurse does to implement the intervention. Each intervention is coded with a unique number. The interventions are organized in 27 classes and 6 domains. NIC facilitates the implementation of a Nursing Minimum Data Set. The use of NIC to plan and document care will facilitate the collection of large databases which will allow us to study the effectiveness and cost of nursing treatments.

The use of standardized language provides for the continuity of care and enhances communication among nurses and between nurses and other providers. NIC provides nursing with the treatment language that is essential for the computerized health care record. The domains and classes provide a description of the essence of nursing. NIC is helpful in representing nursing to the public and in socializing students to the profession.

The coded interventions can be used in documentation and in reimbursement. The language is comprehensive and can be used by nurses in all settings and in all specialties. In addition, there are numerous journal publications about NIC that detail aspects of development or use. An anthology of NIC publications and an implementation manual containing helpful guides and forms related to implementation from selected user agencies are available from the Centre for Nursing Classification.

Indicator of Market Acceptance

NIC is recognized by the American Nurses Association and is included in the National Library of Medicine's Metathesaurus for a Unified Medical Language. Both the Cumulative Index to Nursing Literature (CINAHL) and SilverPlatter have added NIC to their nursing indexes. NIC is included in the Joint Commission on Accreditation for Health Care Organization's (JCAHO) as one nursing classification system that can be used to meet the standard on uniform data.

The National League for Nursing has made a 40-minute video about NIC to facilitate teaching of NIC to nursing students and practicing nurses. Many health care agencies are adopting NIC for use in standards, care plans, and nursing information systems; nursing education programs are beginning to use NIC; authors of major texts are beginning to use NIC to discuss nursing treatments; and researchers are using NIC to study the effectiveness of nursing care.

OUTCOMES CLASSIFICATION

The Nursing Outcomes Classification (NOC) describes patient outcomes sensitive to nursing intervention. NOC evaluates the effects of nursing care as a part of health care. Standardized patient outcomes are essential to ensure that nursing becomes a full participant in clinical evaluation science along with other health disciplines.

The classification contains 190 outcomes, each with a label, definition, and a set of indicators and measures to determine achievement of the outcome. Examples of outcomes influenced by nursing interventions include: Ambulation, Caregiver Emotional Health, Mobility Level, Nutritional Status, and Cognitive Orientation.

Since August 1991, a research team consisting of 43 nurses representing service agencies and nursing education has been conducting a study of nursing-sensitive patient outcomes. The purposes of the research are to: 1) identify, label, validate, and classify nursing-sensitive patient outcomes and indicators, 2) evaluate the validity and usefulness of the classification in clinical field testing, and 3) define and test measurement procedures for the outcomes and indicators.

The classification contains patient outcome categories and indicators at four levels of abstraction and empirical measurement scales. The taxonomy of domains and labels can be obtained from the NOC project office at the University of Iowa.

Most Abstract	Nursing-Sensitive Outcomes Domains
High-Middle Level Abstraction	Nursing-Sensitive Outcome Classes
Middle Level Abstraction	Nursing-Sensitive Outcome Labels
Low Level Abstraction	Nursing-Sensitive Outcome Indicators
Empirical Level	Measurement Activities for Outcomes

An inductive approach was used to extract outcomes, indicators, and measures from current literature, instruments, and information systems. Combined inductive and deductive approaches were used to label and define outcomes, specify indicators for the outcomes, and develop the classification

For purposes of this study, a nursing-sensitive patient outcome is defined as a variable patient or family state, behaviours or perception, responsive to nursing interventions and conceptualized at middle levels of abstraction. Thus outcomes are stated as concepts which are measured along a continuum rather than as goals. Each outcome has an associated group of indicators which are used to determine the outcome.

The following illustrates an outcome label, it's definition and 2 example indicators with the measurement scale.

Indicators:	Severe	Substantial	Moderate	Slight	None
Restlessness	1	2	3	4	5
Appetite loss	1	2	3	4	5

Surveys of random samples of masters prepared nurses, representing diverse areas of practice, were used to validate each outcome and its associated indicators as well as their sensitivity to nursing interventions.

Nurses were asked to rate the importance of each indicator for assessing the outcome and the contribution of nursing to the outcome. Fehring's methodology for assessing content validity of nursing diagnoses was used with minor revisions to estimate content validity and sensitivity to nursing interventions. The NOC is being tested in a tertiary care setting, a community hospital, a nursing home, and a home care setting.

NOC provides one of the elements necessary to complete the Nursing Minimum Data Set. NOC has major implications for nursing administrative practice and care delivery. It provides the first standardized language and measurement for nursing-sensitive patient outcomes.

The use of standardized language allows nurses to compare outcomes for large numbers of patients across settings, diagnoses, age groups, or other aggregates of interest. Development of outcomes as neutral statements that are measured on a continuum rather than as "expected outcomes," facilitates the identification and analysis of patient states actually being achieved for specific populations and/or settings.

It also enables the evaluation of nursing care over a care continuum as well as at one point in time. However, if goals are needed they can be defined as a desired point on the outcome continuum. A book describing the research and containing the outcomes is available from Mosby Publication.

Benefits of NIC and NOC

The Classifications will benefit health care providers, patients, and third-party payers in many ways. They will:

- Provide a standardized language for nursing.
- Facilitate appropriate selection of nursing interventions.
- Define and predict outcomes nurses can achieve with patients.
- Facilitate communication of nursing treatments to other nurses and other providers.
- Standardize and define the knowledge base for nursing curricula and practice.
- Facilitate the teaching of clinical decision-making to novice nurses.

- Assist administrators in effectively planning for staff and equipment resources.
- Enable researchers to examine the effectiveness and cost of nursing care.
- Assist educators in developing curricula that better conform with clinical practice.
- Promote the development of a reimbursement system for nursing services.
- Facilitate the development of computerized information systems.
- Communicate the nature of nursing to the public.

EXISTING TAXONOMIES

Nursing is recognized as an integral member of the interdisciplinary team providing inpatient rehabilitation for individuals with spinal cord injury (SCI). Rehabilitation nurses in acute SCI inpatient settings provide a myriad of interventions, including direct patient care, collaborative medical care, patient and caregiver education, care management, and psychosocial support for patients and families.

They carry over what was done in the therapies, including practice and reinforcement of such activities as bed mobility, transfers, and activities of daily living (ADLs). Yet despite the substantial contributions of nurses to the rehabilitation of individuals with SCI, there is a dearth of information to document nursing interventions in SCI rehabilitation and their impact on patient outcomes.

Additionally, the specialty practice of rehabilitation nursing lacks standards of care for nursing interventions for individuals receiving rehabilitation for SCI. Furthermore, although there are taxonomies of nursing care interventions and outcomes documented in the literature, no formal taxonomy exists to specifically describe rehabilitation nursing or SCI nursing interventions and outcomes.

Although there is a tremendous amount of literature related to nursing care of patients with SCI, there is a paucity of literature that focuses on how nursing care during rehabilitation influences outcomes, including length of stay, complications, and quality of life. The Consortium for Spinal Cord Medicine identified 4 domains of outcomes for patients with traumatic SCI: motor recovery, functional independence, social integration, and quality of life.

Nursing interventions perhaps have the most significant impact ir the domains of functional independence, social reintegration, and quality of life. In a qualitative study that examined how the nursing role is perceived in SCI rehabilitation, Pellatt concluded that patients value nurses' contributions more as a means of emotional and physical support and less as a serious input in the rehabilitation process.

Nurses saw themselves as the "bedrock" of rehabilitation, although some felt that nursing might be perceived as the "low-profile aspect of rehabilitation". The patients in this study felt that "rehabilitation was therapy, with nursing care appearing to be compartmentalized into something complementary to rehabilitation rather than a rehabilitation intervention in its own right".

However, patients identified nurses as their main source for learning skin care, medication, and bladder management and acknowledged the nurse as being the core professional who has a global perspective on the rehabilitation programme. Nurses were seen as the first point of contact for the rehabilitation patient and as the team members who gave them most of the information they needed during their hospitalization.

This may be an invaluable, although unrecognized, advantage that nurses might have in influencing patient learning and, ultimately, in affecting patient outcomes. May et al examined education of the patient with SCI with regard to the domains of knowledge, problem solving, and perceived importance of the information that is taught.

They concluded that even though a patient may perceive a topic as important, increased knowledge did not necessarily translate into better problem-solving capabilities. They suggest that this might indicate the need to interject active learning strategies into programme curricula to accomplish knowledge transfer in everyday situations.

May and colleagues suggest that it might be "difficult to implement within a lecture format of teaching" the learning principle of the adult as independent learner. Although group learning develops the patient's knowledge base, the "active" learning necessary for cementing concepts and tasks is less attainable in the traditional classes that most programs utilize.

In Pellatt's study, patients attested to the efficacy of nurse interaction in their learning process. Ralph et al define outcomes of nursing practice as "those end products of the nursing care process that can be linked to specific structural and procedural nursing-sensitive variables". They also state that nursing-sensitive outcomes for SCI provide a system for measuring the quality of nursing care and present the basis for improved care.

In this study, which aimed to examine nursing-sensitive outcomes in patients with SCI, bowel elimination and urinary elimination were ranked as the top 2 nurse-sensitive outcomes as perceived by experienced SCI nurse clinicians. These were followed by ambulation and tissue integrity. The authors suggest that these 4 outcomes strongly relate to individuals' ability to provide or direct self-care and enable them to be independent.

In the study by May, patients consistently ranked bladder, bowel, and skin care as highly important to them during their rehabilitation. Nurses are in the unique position to mold behaviours through teaching and reinforcing actions that are important in the areas of bladder, bowel, and skin, as well as complementing and supporting the education on which other interdisciplinary team members focus their interventions.

Olinzock undertook a qualitative study to develop a model for assessment of learner readiness for self-direction of care in individuals with SCI. This model addresses levels of dependency of the patient (from dependent to self-direction) and role of the nurse from authority to consultant. Although this model has not been tested widely, the fundamental premise of the model lies in the concept of patient engagement. The assumption is that as patient engagement increases, so does readiness to learn and therefore movement towards independence in self-directed care.

Patient engagement is characterized as a dynamic and selective process, with the role of the nurse to surrender control of patient care as the patient moves towards independence in self-directed care.

SCIREHAB PROJECT

The SCIRehab Project is a 5-year research effort designed to determine which SCI rehabilitation interventions, including nursing interventions, are associated most strongly with positive outcomes at 1-year after SCI.

Outcome measures include functional independence, medical complications, rehospitalizations, social integration, and quality of life. The first article on SCIRehab in this series describes the SCIRehab study in greater detail and sets forth the importance of the practice-based evidence methodology utilized in this study.

Gassaway et al (second article in this series) outlines the multiple data sources being used to obtain project data, including the medical record. Although other disciplines were not confident that reliable, detailed intervention data would be present in traditional documentation, such as the medical record, nursing leaders from the 6 participating centres were convinced that most nursing-related intervention data, including information on skin assessment/wound care, bladder management, and bowel management, were contained in nursing care narrative notes, flow sheets, and other forms of nursing documentation.

The nurse leaders acknowledged practice differences among the 6 participating centres relative to these fundamental nursing care practices but were confident that practices were described adequately in existing nursing documentation.

However, they did recognize there were 2 key areas of nursing interventions that were not documented adequately in traditional nursing records: (a) time spent by nurses in direct patient education on various topics and (b) time spent by nurses in the care management process (differentiated from "case management" described below).

Therefore, the decision was made to augment traditional nursing documentation with point-of-care documentation in these two areas.

PATIENT AND CAREGIVER EDUCATION

Patient and caregiver education is an integral component of every area of nursing intervention in the SCI rehabilitation setting. Education is provided in short informal sessions, longer organized one-on-one individual patient/caregiver education sessions, and broader group-oriented classroom activities.

Group classes and other formal methods of patient and caregiver education are captured separately for the SCIRehab study. These formal methods of education are not the exclusive responsibility of nursing, and, in some centres, nursing is minimally involved; therefore, only the ongoing one-on-one education provided "bedside" by nurses is the focus for the nursing taxonomy.

In developing this classification, each SCIRehab centre's patient education programme and nursing documentation tools were reviewed for points of commonality and differences. A spreadsheet containing about 100 different education topics was created.

The project nursing leaders determined which education topics were covered almost exclusively by nursing and not in group education formats and consolidated these into 10 main areas.

The resulting education topic list is outlined in Table. The group postulated that more intensive nursing involvement in education would be associated with better rehabilitation outcomes but concurred that this intensity may be difficult to obtain from current medical record data. Thus, intensity (or dose) of patient and caregiver education is quantified using time. SCIRehab nursing documentation captures "blocks" of education time in 10-minute increments. Shorter periods of education are not added together to equal 10 minutes, because the focus is on capturing more significant education sessions.

Most of the education topics are routine SCI rehabilitation interventions (eg, medication, bowel, bladder, skin). However, 2 topics bear further explanation: complications and therapy carry over. Patients may develop complications, which diminish or eliminate their ability to take advantage of therapeutic interventions and effectively progress through rehabilitation.

Nurses often have to explain and provide education to patients and family members about such medical complications as autonomic dysreflexia, fevers, and infections. Therapy carry over is an integral part of nursing function in the rehabilitation setting.

On a daily basis, nurses reinforce activities and/or topics that are taught initially by other disciplines: education on splint application, use of bowel management devices and equipment, transfer techniques, ADLs, feeding, etc.

CARE MANAGEMENT

Care management, which includes discharge planning, psychosocial support, and team process, is a critical component of the role of SCI rehabilitation nurses, consumes a great deal of nursing time, and has the potential to have a significant impact on patient outcomes.

The care management functions of SCI nurses are supplementary to the role of the case manager or social worker. Nurses undertake care management activities to communicate with other members of the rehabilitation team, the primary and consulting medical staff, the nursing team during shifts and at shift change, and patients and caregivers/ families.

These care management activities may include informal meetings and discussions about care planning but do not include team meetings, patient/family conferences, or other formal care/case planning meetings. These formal meetings/

conferences are being collected in the social worker/case management point-of-care system.

Discharge Planning

Nurses play a major role in preparing patients for discharge. This comprehensive process begins at admission to the rehabilitation centre; includes educating home care providers, providing instructions for medications, and ordering supplies; and ends with the final discharge from the centre.

Completion of thorough and accurate discharge instructions is essential to the continuation of quality patient care after discharge from initial rehabilitation. The discharge planning process also includes an assessment of what information the patient or family member has retained for functioning in the community.

Psychosocial Support

Spinal cord injury brings with it a plethora of psychological and social adjustments for patients and potential caregivers. Nurses, who are present throughout most of the patient's day, often spend a great deal of time listening to and coaching patients and families through challenging emotional times; they are the sounding board for real fears and dilemmas that develop.

Psychosocial support entails the listening process and gleaning of information for referral to the appropriate professional; it does not include in-depth counseling, which may be undertaken by the psychologist, psychiatrist, rehabilitation counselor, social worker, or case manager.

Team Process

All interactions between a nurse and other members of the interdisciplinary team (eg, physician report, collaboration with specialists, planning with therapists or nursing technicians) related to their common patients are included in team process care management. Intensity of team process, even informal hallway discussions, which frequently happen in SCI rehabilitation units, may influence patient outcomes. Team process, in this context, does not include team rounds or conferences, which is captured elsewhere by the SCIRehab team.

COLLECTION OF TAXONOMIC

Capturing the Data

Extensive nursing care data are contained within the medical record for every patient enrolled in the study and will be captured using medical chart abstracting. Methods used to capture supplemental nursing education and care process data vary among the 6 centres. Two centres were able to update current computerized documentation in a timely manner to integrate the SCIRehab nursing data set into existing electronic records and meet study implementa-tion timelines for data collection.

The additional information became part of the shift-by-shift computerized nursing documentation. Nurses at 4 centres, in which electronic nursing records do not yet exist or there was less flexibility to modify existing records, were required to use handheld personal digital assistants (PDAs), as do the other disciplines collecting SCIRehab data, to capture the supplemental nursing data.

Staff Education and Implementation

Implementation of the supplemental nursing data capture methods required extensive staff education. A variety of methods were utilized for staff education; nursing leaders at each centre were responsible for coordinating the education. Content of the nursing staff education was similar at each centre.

An introduction to the study purpose provided a description of nursing participation in the large, interdisciplinary, multicentre study. Emphasis was placed on the importance of accurate and timely nursing documentation. Details of documentation that would be extracted from the medical record were included so that nurses would understand the full scope of nursing information that would be included in the study. Quantifying patient education delivered, by topic and time, was new for nurses. The nurses needed to understand how to categorize time increments correctly.

The minimum time increment to include in the documentation was 10 minutes. Although nursing staff routinely spend significant time on team process activities, documenting these efforts in time intervals was also new. Another major (and new) focus of staff education was the participation scale.

Differentiating between the participation categories is sometimes difficult, and assigning a single participation value to a patient who varied his involvement and interests during a full nursing shift of 8 or 12 hours can be challenging.

Reliability of Documentation

Reliability audits are completed to ensure consistency of documentation between the 6 centres and among individual nurses at each centre. Case studies written by the project nurse leaders outline a hypothetical patient's care for a nursing shift. Each case study indicates what education and/or care management were delivered, to whom (patient and/or caregiver), and for how long, along with a description of the patient's participation in all activities.

All nurses participating in the SCIRehab study at the 6 centres are asked to complete the reliability case studies. Achieving a high completion rate was the first challenge. The number of nurses working on the 6 study units ranges from 40 to 115.

Although the clinical leaders who wrote case scenarios thought them to be clear and concise, it became apparent that the reading of narrative descriptions leads to varied interpretation by staff nurses.

There are many changes within the course of a nursing shift, and, thus, although the case study was meant to be "black and white," the context in which staff nurses complete their patient care is much more complex. Over time, good reliability was achieved by reinforcing the concepts, creating consensus on the meaning of the point-of-care categories, etc.

SPIRITUAL DIAGNOSES

THE study of the soul in health and disease ought to be as much an object of scientific study and training as the health and diseases of the body. It has long been one of the favourite axioms of Apologetics, that a Christian life is the best argument for Christianity.

And, if an old argument, it is after all the best argument, for in these last days there is nothing in the philosophy of apologetical religion at all worth reviving compared with this living power of true lives.

A freethinker may go very far without meeting an argument to throw him back upon his own inner soul, but no one can live long, be he in high life or low life, without coming within the influence of a Christian man. The power of the individual, the value of the unit, the respect due to one human soul—this is the great truth for churches, for armies, and for empires.

Students of the new science of sociology may deny this truth as they will, and their great disciple, Herbert Spencer, may denounce what he calls the "great-man-theory of history" as only fit for savages gossiping round their camp fire, but it still remains a great and important truth (as he himself expresses it before failing to refute it) "that throughout the past of the human race the doings of conspicuous persons have been the only things worthy of remembrance."

The past has indeed no masses. *Men*, not masses, have done all that is great in history, in science, and in religion. The New Testament itself is but a brief biography; and many pages of the Old are marked by the lives of men. Yet it is just this truth which we require to be taught again to-day—to be content with aiming at units. Every atom in the universe can act on every other atom, but only through the atom next it. And if a man would act upon every other man, he can do so best by acting, one at a time, upon those beside him. The true worker's world is a unit. Recognise the personal glory and dignity of the unit as an agent. Work with units, but, above all, work *at* units. But the capacity of acting upon individuals is now almost a lost art. It is hard to learn again. We have spoilt ourselves by thinking to draw thousands by public work—by what people call "pulpit eloquence," by platform speeches, and by convocations and councils, Christian conferences, and by books of many editions.

We have been painting Madonnas and Ecce Homos and choirs of angels, like Raphael, and it is hard to condescend to the beggar boy of Murillo. Yet we must begin again, and begin far down. Christianity began with one.

We have forgotten the simple way of the Founder of the greatest influence the world has ever seen—how He ran away from cities, how He shirked mobs, how He lagged behind the rest at Samaria to have a quiet talk with *one* woman at a well, how He stole away from crowds and entered into the house of *one* humble Syro-Phoenician woman, "and would have no man know it."

In small groups of twos and threes He collected the early Church around Him. One by one the disciples were called—and there were only twelve in all. We all know well enough how to move the masses; we know how to draw a crowd round us, but to attract the units—that is the hard matter. Teach us how to fascinate the unit by our glance, by our conversational oratory, by our mystery of sympathy!

We know how to bring the mob about us, how to flash and storm in passion, how to work in the appeal at the right moment, how to play upon all the figures of rhetoric in succession, and how to throw in a calm when no one expects, but every one wants it.

Every one knows this, or can know it easily; but to draw souls one by one, to buttonhole them and steal from them the secret of their lives, to talk them clean out of themselves, to read them off like a page of print, to pervade them with your spiritual essence and make them transparent, this is the spiritual science which is so difficult to acquire and so hard to practise. "After a spirit of discernment," says an old French Sage (La Bruyere), "the next rarest thing in the world are diamonds and pearls." Of the three elements, body, mind, and soul, which make up a responsible human being, two only have been hitherto treated as fit subjects for scientific inquiry. From six thousand years of contemplation of the phenomena of human life and thought, only two sciences have emerged. Physiology has told us all that is possible of the human body; psychology, of the mind.

But the half is not accounted for. We wish, further, a spiritual psychology to tell us of the unseen realities of the soul. This is where our University training must be supplemented. It deals with man as a body and a mind. It forgets that man is a trinity. It is an extraordinary and momentous fact that by far the most important factor in human life has been up to this time all but altogether ignored by the thinking world.

Of course every religious writer has a few notions upon the subject, but notions are not enough. If the mind is large enough and varied enough to make a philosophy of mind possible, is the soul such a trifling part of man that it is not worth while seeking to frame a science of it?—a science of it which men can learn, and which can be a guide and help in practice to all who feel an interest in the deepest thing in human life?

It is no use to say there is no special soul—that there is a strange never-comprehended essence, half emotion, half affection, half reason, half unearthliness, to attempt to analyse which would only leave us, like Milton's philosophic angels, "in wandering mazes lost." But this is the mere concealment of ignorance in mystery. There *is* a soul, and there is a spiritual life. Plato knew it and called it, in his wonderment over it, "the soulish mind." Solomon knew it when he talked of "the hearing ear."

Addison knew it and defined it: "'Tis the divinity that stirs within us." And in "Culture and Religion" the Principal of St. Andrew's University charges his students "that there is a faculty of spiritual apprehension which is very different from those which are trained in schools and colleges, which must be educated and fed not less but more carefully than our lower faculties, else it will be starved and die." The same thoughtful writer has put the problem which we are endeavouring to meet in plain and forcible terms. "But because the primary truths of religion," he says, "refuse to be caught in the grip of the logical vice—because they are transcendent, and only mystically apprehended, are thinking men therefore either to give up these subjects as impossible to think about or to content themselves with a vague religiosity, an unreal sentimentalism?"

The Principal's question is a striking question. Are we content to let this great spiritual life work silently around us without attempting to know more about it, to analyse it, to make it more accessible to us and us to it? Are we to regard it as some weird element, unapproachable, mysterious, unstable, incomprehensible in its essence?

There is, it is true, an element about it which keeps us at our distance from it; but as its groundwork is human, may we not see the points where it touches the human, the changes it effects, the hindrances to the changes, and the wonderful complexity of action and interaction which it originates? Are there materials here for a philosophy, and is it lawful to reduce it to a science? Can there, in short, be a *science of spirituality?*

At first sight the idea is repulsive in the extreme. Yet a science is a classification of facts; and is there anything irreverent or presumptuous in attempting to classify the facts of the spiritual life? The facts, it may be answered, are too numerous; they are more than the sand of the sea. But so are the combinations of elements with which the chemist deals, and the modifications of morphological type with which the biologist deals, yet we have a chemistry and a biology.

That, then, is the least of the difficulty. But a great one, apparently an insurmountable one, lies just on the threshold. The facts of physical science lie in the order of the natural, and they are finite. The facts of spiritual science, if we may call it so, lie in the order of the supernatural, and they are infinite. They are pervaded by an element which no man can fathom. "The Spirit bloweth where it listeth." We look in a man's soul for that which we saw there yesterday, but the unseen influence has swept across the heart, and the spiritual scenery is changed. The man himself is the same, his passions unaltered in their strength, his foibles unchanged in their weakness, but the furniture of the soul has been moved, and the spiritual machinery goes on upon a new and suddenly developed principle.

Here, then, our investigations are stopped at the outset. Dare we approach no nearer? Often we would fain do so. Often we are placed in such circumstances that plainly we must do so. A friend is in trouble, we are in trouble. But how are we to proceed? What guide have we in ministering to a soul diseased?

Is there no guide-book upon the subject, no chart or table of the logical history of the spiritual life, no chair of Spiritual Diagnosis? We do not mean a table such as Doddridge has given us in "The Rise and Progress of Religion in the Soul." The fatal error of that style of work is to give the inquiring soul the idea of a certain mechanical process to be passed through before conversion can be attained.

But conversion does not always develop like a proposition in Euclid, or sensitized plate in photography. God the Creator will have no machine-made men in earth or heaven. And it is not His will that there should only be a few stereotyped forms of saints—the Richard Baxter type, the Jeremy Taylor type, and the Philip Doddridge type. Therefore it is a dangerous thing to put forms and processes, which exist only in the logical imagination, into the hands of the inquirer.

But when these works are put into the hands of the Christian teacher or minister, their utility is beyond all praise. He, as spiritual adviser, should be thoroughly acquainted with the *rationale* of conversion. He should know it as a physician his pharmacopoeia.

He should know every phase of the human soul, in health and disease, in the fulness of joy and the blackness of despair. He should know the "Pilgrim's Progress" better than Bunyan. The scheme of salvation, as we are accustomed to call it, should be ever clearly defined in his consciousness. The lower stages, the period of transition, its solemnity, its despairs, its glimmering light, its growing faith; and the Christian life begun, the laborious working out in fear and trembling, the slavish scrupulosity, still the fearfulness of fall, still remorse, more faith, more hope; and last of all the higher spiritual life, the realization of freedom, the disappearance of the slavish scrupulosity, the pervasion of the whole life with God.

Such a skeleton is easily made and easily remembered, and it is all that many have to perform their work with; but it is no more adequate for its great task than is the compass of a schoolboy's whistle to take in the sweep of Handel's "Messiah."

To fill up such an outline with all the exquisite tracery of thought and emotion and doubt, which develop within the mind of an inquiring soul, is a great and rare talent; and to apply such knowledge in the practice of daily life is a power which scarce one will be found to possess.

Let not any think that such knowledge is easily attained; nor have many attained it. The men to whom you or I would go if spiritual darkness spread across our souls, who are they? How few have penetration enough to diagnose our case, to observe our least apparent symptoms, to get out of us what we had resolved not to tell them, to see through and through us the evil and the good. Plenty there are to preach to us, but who will interview us, and anatomize us, and lay us bare to God's eye and our own? X won't be preached to along with Y and Z and Q; that won't do X any good, for he thinks it is all meant for Y, Z, and Q. But to take X by himself; to feel his pulse alone, and give him one particular earnest word—the only one word that would do—all to himself—this is the simple feat which we look in vain for men to perform.

There is a tendency piously to leave such matters to God, and say they are quite safe in His hands, who alone searcheth the heart. But He hath appointed us to be our brother's keeper, nor will He do for my brother what could be done by me. We cannot expect the Spirit's help to teach us what only laziness and personal indifference hinder us from learning;

and to despise a power which He gave us capacities to possess is not the way to show that we trust Him who gave it.

"Placeat homini quidquid Deo placet." This study of the soul, in which I am endeavouring to enlist your interest, is a difficult study. It is difficult, because the soul as far transcends the mind in complexity and in variety as the mind the body. The soul is an infinitely large subject—an infinitely deep and mysterious subject. The chemist in his intricate analysis deals not with elements more subtle and evasive

"Ay, men may wonder while they scanA living, thinking, feeling man." But we do not need to go to Mrs. Browning, or to "Hamlet," to be told "What a piece of work is man!" Apart altogether from the religious element in him, he is still the greatest mystery of science.

Every man is a problem to every other man—much more every spiritual man. It is hard to know a man's brain, and harder to know his feelings; but hardest of all to know his religious convictions. It is hard to know the deepest that a man has. A well-known American essayist and poet has told us that the difficulty of analyzing our neighbour's character arises from the fact that every man is in reality a *threefold* man.

When two persons are in conversation, there are really *six* persons in conversation. Thus, to put the paradox into the shape of an example, suppose that John and Tom are in conversation, there are three Johns and three Toms, who are accounted for in this way:

Three Johns:

1. The real John; known only to his Maker.
2. John's ideal John; 'ohn, *i.e.*, as he thinks himself; never the real John, and often very unlike him.
3. Tom's ideal John; *i.e.*, John as Tom thinks him; never the real John, nor John's John, but often very unlike either.

Three Toms:

1. The real Tom.
2. Tom's ideal Tom.
3. John's ideal Tom.

In this way when I talk to another it is not me that he hears talking, but his ideal of me; nor do I talk to him as he defines himself, but to my ideal of him. Now that ideal will, without almost inconceivable care and penetration on my part, be quite different also from his real self as God only knows him, so that instead of speaking to his real soul, I may possibly be speaking to his ideal of his own soul, or more likely to my ideal of it.

From this it will be seen at a glance that the power of soul analysis is a hard thing to possess oneself of. It requires intense discrimination and knowledge of human nature—much and deep study of human life and character. The man with whom you speak being made up of two ideals—his own and yours, and one real—God's, it is one of the hardest possible tasks to abandon your ideal of him and get to know the real—God's.

Then having known it so far as possible to man, there remains the greatest difficulty of all—to introduce him to himself. ou have created a new man for him, and he will not recognise him at first. He can see no resemblance to his ideal self; the new creature is not such a lovely picture as he would like to own; the lines are harshly drawn, and there is little grace and no poetry in it.

But he must be told that none of us are what we seem; and if he would deal faithfully with himself, he must try to see himself differently from what he seems. Then he must be led with much delicacy to make a little introspection of himself; and with the mirror lifted to his own soul you read off together some of the indications which are defining themselves vaguely upon its surface.

Even in social and domestic circles the difficulty of performing this apparently simple operation upon human nature is so keenly felt that scarce one friend will be found with a friendship true enough to perform it to another. And in religious matters it will be at once conceded that the complexity of the difficulties increases the problem a hundredfold. There is a danger, however—speaking next of the more directly religious aspects of the question—in exaggerating these difficulties; and, indeed, the further objection may have occurred to some minds that, by attaching so much importance to the human power we take away the one great element in salvation—its Divine freeness through the grace of God. Is not religion for the poor and illiterate?

Is not the way easy to find? Thank God it is so! So little can man do to enlighten it. But he can do something, and he ought to do more. In this more than in anything else he is his brother's keeper. Not for himself does man live. Every action of every man has an ancestry and a posterity—an ancestry and a posterity in other lives. "Each reads his fate in the other's eyes," says Emerson.

"I am a part of all that I have met," says Tennyson. And how do you explain that most wonderful phenomenon which is as surprising a contemplation to some minds as the thought of eternity itself—*the silence of God?* God keeping silence! And man doubting and sinning and repenting all alone, and groping blindfold after truth, and losing his way and working out his salvation with painful trembling and fear!

It is an unfathomable mystery; but may it not be, in small part, just for this that, on the one hand, God offers man the glory and honour of sharing His work; and on the other, that He wishes human souls to be graven with the marks of other human souls in all their free and infinite variety? God is a God of variety.

No two leaves are the same, no two sand grains, no two souls. And as the universe would be but a poor affair if every leaf were the counterpart of the oak leaf or the birch, so would the spiritual world present but a sorry spectacle if we were all duplicates of John Calvin.

Therefore has God made room for individual action in the building up of His kingdom upon earth; and therefore it is not a presumption but a duty for every man to be moulding and making the souls around him, to be perfecting and guiding his own faculties for this great work.The great danger in doing this work, next to doing it without any education for it, is to overdo it. In dealing with a case which is once put into our hands we are apt to consider it too much of a professional and personal matter. Our influence has become too conscious. We have found what a powerful thing it may become, and we seek a "reputation for influence." Thus our pride is smitten if success does not at once crown our efforts, and we attempt to second them by unlawful means.

We assume the didactic when we should simply be attractive or suggestive. We encourage the favourable and forget to notice an unfavourable symptom. We supply allopathic when prudence would suggest homoeopathic doses.

And finally, we assume too much upon ourselves, forgetting that we are but fellow-workers together with God, and by taking too officious an interest, the individual, making nothing of it, is apt to throw the responsibility of non-success upon us, and so spoil not only our whole influence with others, but his own chance of being bettered in the future by others.

There are also limits to the exercise of this power which are as yet not well defined, and which rest at present upon no religio-philosophic basis, but on mere empiricism. The whole subject, indeed, rests in the meantime only upon the merest individual empiricism; and it is a matter of profound regret that so sacred and important a subject should exist in such a dishevelled state when the scientific method, which is being applied to so many trivial matters, could be so easily applied to it.

We can conceive of some minds being deeply shocked to hear of scientific observations being taken on a human soul, and adjustments made to it, and results calculated as if it were a mere question of spectrum analysis. But the irreverence is only in the words.

We *do* wish a scientific treatment of the subject; and if there is anything to sadden and humble in the contemplation of the religious work of the day, it is the thought of the crude and slipshod treatment of one of the most sacred subjects in the religious life. We are not ignoring the power of God in conversion by not speaking of it. You say He can work with the roughest tools even on the finest of marbles. Without denying it, He would not polish diamonds on grindstones if He could get lapidaries to do it better. It won't do to talk religiously, or complacently, or *blasphemously*of trusting in Him when we are too lazy to qualify ourselves for being worth the using in His service.

Don't fear that we shall become too acute at diagnosing and prescribing for souls, and so take the matter out of God's hands.And now, in conclusion, as to the great subject of the training and exercise of the power of spiritual discernment, what is it possible for us to say?

We can indeed but guess at it. Those who have thought of it have confessed that everything yet remains to be done. Thus one of the keenest minds of New England has said, "The school of the future may be called a *Life School*, whose object is to study the strength and weakness of human nature minutely, to understand *men*, and to deal with them face to face, and heart to heart, and in regard to such a school as this, while there has been much done incidentally, the revised procedure of education yet awaits development and accomplishment."

Henry Ward Beecher, in his Yale lecture (on preaching), has given to this subject perhaps by far the most valuable popular contribution of the age. His chapter on the study of Human Nature is especially discriminating, and only the knowledge that there must now be few into whose hands that work has not fallen prevents us stealing time to make lengthened quotations.

(Let two suffice, page 85 and page 94.) Beecher, had he been less of a preacher and more of a pastor, could have been one of the greatest students of the soul. As it is, he is surpassed by few, perhaps by none in this country, only by Dr. Spencer in his own.

Spurgeon is not so much of a practical analyst as a self-introspectionist. So also were Thomas a Kempis and Blaise Pascal, and pious John Hervey and quaint Robert Bruce, and so also in a sense were Dr. Duncan and Dr. Goulburn, who has done for spirituality what Burton did for melancholy. The Puritan writers, and pre-eminent among them Baxter and

Owen, were skilled analysts of human nature, but they seem to have applied their power more in the pulpit than the pew. In this respect, too, Bunyan was quite unsurpassed, and in some of his sermons, specially his famous "last" one, the most masterly specimens of this kind of work are to be found.

Yet with all this perfection there was always something wrong about these men from the practical point of view. They knew so much about humanity that they had lost what of it they had themselves in the pursuit of it in others. Although they are always called practical hands, they are only so in a gross sense.

They were most of them wanting in that delicacy of handling which makes analysis effective instead of insulting; and many of the Puritans were quite destitute of the foremost quality which distinguishes the successful diagnosist—respect, veneration even, for the soul of another. A man may be ever so gross and vulgar, but when you come to deal with the deepest that is in him, he becomes sensitive and feminine.

Brusqueness and an impolite familiarity may do very well when dealing with his brains, but without tenderness and courtesy you can only approach his heart to shock it. The whole of etiquette is founded on respect; and by far the highest and tenderest etiquette is the etiquette of soul and soul.To know and remember the surpassing dignity of the human soul—for its own sake, for its great Godlike elements, for its immortality, above all for His sake who made it and gave Himself for it—this is the first axiom to be remembered.

Many men study men, but not to sympathize with them: the lawyer for gain, the artist for fame, the actor for applause, the novelist for profession. How well up is the actor in plot and passion and intrigue! how deftly can the novelist anatomize love and jealousy, vengeance and hate! And when there are men found to study human nature for its own sake, or for filthy lucre's sake, shall there be none to do it for man's sake—for God's sake?

There is one great reason why the ministry of so many great and holy men has been so far from being what is called a converting ministry. We read their biographies, and shrink into nothingness at the contemplation of such holiness and saintliness of life as we had never dreamed possible to man, and we marvel, and greatly, that one irreligious, unconverted man should be left in the whole countryside; but we find indeed that their parish was no better than its neighbours.

And the explanation is plain. Those men laboured under a terrible disease—it is called Theophobia—the name explains itself. A minister catches it, and his power is gone. Men are awed by it, venerate it as they venerate few things else. They will speak of it and praise it, but never imitate it. It is a grand but useless spectacle.

Those who have it become wrapped up in one subject; and though that be the highest of all, it is nevertheless a monstrosity when followed to the exclusion of everything else. The sympathies of these men are all and always Godwards. They are always vindicating God. Their whole atmosphere is of God. They have left earth before their time.

They have left human nature in the lurch; they have forgotten humanity, and humanity can no longer profit by them, it can only wonder at them. Their thoughts go always straight up to God, and are never healthy enough to be refracted upon man. Now to get to God is a high thing, but they only get at one side of Him.

They don't see over to the other side, which is inclined towards *man*. Yet to get to man by way of God, and God by way of man, is the only way to keep the entire health of the soul. We have much yet to say of this study, but the subject must end almost before it is begun. The one great thing is to study life earnestly and practically and realistically.

We must aim at the manly and sturdy type of the religious diagnosist; we must try to be, as Oliver Wendell Holmes forcibly says, "a man that knows men in the street, at their work, human nature in its shirt sleeves—who makes bargains with deacons instead of talking over texts with them, and a man who has found out that there are plenty of praying rogues and swearing saints in the world."

One thing I can assure you of. If any man develops this faculty of reading others, of reading them in order to profit by them, he will never be without practice. Men do not say much about these things, but the amount of spiritual longing in the world at the present moment is absolutely incredible. No one can ever even faintly appreciate the intense spiritual unrest which seethes everywhere around him; but one who has tried to discern, who has begun by private experiment, by looking into himself, by taking observations upon the people near him and known to him, has witnessed a spectacle sufficient to call for the loudest and most emphatic action.

Gentlemen, I have but vaguely hinted at this subject; I venture to think it a question of vital interest, giving life a mission, giving a new and burning interest even to the most commonplace surroundings, and opening up a field for lifelong study and effort.

COMMUNITY HEALTH DIAGNOSES

This column describes the work of the Nursing Diagnosis Extension and Classification (NDEC) research team, which works in a collaborative agreement with NANDA to refine and extend the diagnosis classification. This issue highlights community diagnoses. The Nursing Diagnosis Extension and Classification (NDEC) research team is completing its fifth year in a collaborative relationship with NANDA to refine and extend the diagnosis classification.

The team has seven Diagnosis Work Groups (DWGs) that conduct the concept analysis and submit work to the NDEC Rules Committee and NDEC team for critique and revision. The work of each DWG will be featured in the next seven issues. This issue highlights community diagnoses and features the work of the NDEC Community DWG, which is chaired by Carolyn M. Crowell, MN, RN, Assistant Professor, of the community nursing course at the University of Iowa College of Nursing. The definition of community used by the DWG is "a group of people living in the same locale under the same government."

Examples of community include neighborhoods, cities, census tracts, and populations at risk. The diagnosis language necessary to support the practice of community nursing differs from that of a diagnosis language for individuals and families in that it must describe aggregate phenomena with aggregate indicators. In the nursing diagnoses language, a nursing judgment about community response to actual/ potential illnesses/life processes is captured in a descriptive diagnosis label.

Indicators (defining characteristics) for community diagnoses also are different from those for individuals and families because they must be observable and verifiable in the aggregate. That is, indicators need to be observable and verifiable in community aggregates or available for extraction from community databases with aggregate data.

Compiling aggregate data is necessary to make the community diagnoses and to monitor the outcome effectiveness of community interventions. Similarly, the influence of the related factors must clearly be an influence on the aggregate.

It is clear that the development of a standardized language for community diagnoses presents unique conceptual and methodological issues. In addition, less literature is available for concept analysis than for other nursing diagnoses. Even though many of the issues remain unresolved, there is a sense of urgency in the need for refinement and development of community nursing diagnoses coming from the practice, education, and research arenas.

This urgency arises from the emerging perception of community nursing as a dominant future role for nurses.The initial work of the NDEC Community DWG has been to refine NANDA diagnoses, which was the request of NANDA leadership at the time the NANDA/ NDEC agreement was formulated. This refinement has included concept analysis on the following diagnoses: altered protection, impaired home maintenance management, risk for suffocation, risk for injury, altered health maintenance, health-seeking behavioursss (specify), risk for trauma, ineffective community coping, and potential for enhanced community coping.

Index

A

B

C

Q

R

S

T

U

V